Reflections on Therapeutic Storymaking

Reflections on Therapeutic Storymaking
The Use of Stories in Groups

Alida Gersie

Jessica Kingsley Publishers
London and Philadelphia

First published in the United Kingdom in 1997
by Jessica Kingsley Publishers
116 Pentonville Road
London N1 9JB, UK
and
400 Market Street, Suite 400
Philadelphia, PA 19106, USA

www.jkp.com

The author and the publisher gratefully acknowledge the permission to reprint:
The story 'How speech came into this world', by permission of
The International African Institute, London
The Story 'How the elephant died', by permission of
Merlin Press, London.

Library of Congress Cataloging in Publication Data
A CIP catalog record for this book is available from the Library of Congress

British Library Cataloguing in Publication Data
A CIP catalogue record for this book is available from the British Library

ISBN 978 1 85302 272 2

Contents

For Buck

Acknowledgments

The completion of this book was made possible thanks to the patience and commitment of my research assistant Jan Stirling, for which I am really grateful. Colleagues and students in the Graduate Arts Therapies Programme at the University of Hertfordshire provided a challenging and inspiring sounding board. I also want to thank Annette Brederode, Henk Hofman, Ofra Ayalon, Ann Cattanach, Jo James, Mooli Lahad and Sue Jennings for their keen interest in thinking together about stories. But without the people who joined the Therapeutic Storymaking groups this book could never have been written and, moreover, my life would have been the poorer for it. To all participants in these groups, I offer you my gratitude.

When my heart is parched and hardened,
greet me with balm of mercy.
When grace has abandoned my day and
my night, come with a burst of song.

Tagore

1. Introduction

In this book I reflect on the uses of story to bring about change – the kind of change that a troubled person, their intimate others as well as the groups of which they are part, desire. Such change needs to be experienced as betterment by most of those involved. What will constitute betterment is clarified with the person – whether we call him or her a client, a patient, a user or a member, both before and during the change-work. Whilst the work progresses it is evaluated, to ascertain not only whether the goals are being achieved, and whether any achieved change is persistent, but also whether new goals have emerged or if there might be other, more efficacious ways to achieve the goals. Though I work both with groups of people and with individuals, here I shall primarily reflect on the ways I use stories in group work with adolescents and adults with mild to severe emotional problems. I have put the discussion of group work foremost because storytelling is essentially a communal activity. Whilst the making of stories can flourish between two individuals, it thrives when three or more are gathered. None of the people who participated in the group or individual work were in the acute phase of profound mental illness. I gave priority to reflection on work with adolescents and adults because the dynamics in group work with younger children are different, though much of what is written here also applies.

The will to tell

I work with stories because we not only make up and live our stories, we also need to tell them. In the course of growing up, all of us learn, for better or for worse, how to sift, distil and communicate tales of knowledge, experience or bewilderment. We also learn to share these with others. Scents, fragments of music or the way the light plays with the chestnut tree stimulate images, ideas or recollections. They become memories that reflect the near-truth of previous experience. Deprived of the capacity to recall and the linked capacity to recognize, we are unable to read a poem, write a letter or imagine how the bulb we plant in the garden might blossom in Spring. After a brief sojourn in short-term memory, our told or untold stories move into deep storage where they dwell in embodied silence (Rubin 1989).[1] The architecture of our memory system is the subject of intense academic debate and a source of wonder to most of us. In that lush dwelling-place some memories disappear from apparent reach to go we know not where. Most stick around peacefully, some restlessly. These are the still vivid memories that hurt. Though the process by which such memories impact upon life is variously described, folk-knowledge and science confirm that we do take emotions to heart – for better and for worse (Williams and Hollan 1981). Amidst the apparent discontinuities of academic understanding of the processes of memory – recall and telling – two undisputed certainties remain. The first is that telling matters. The second is that not telling has many undesirable consequences for our health (Garnett 1996). Life experience and research findings confirm the intuitive sense that a persistent inability to tell one's stories to relevant people at relevant moments sooner or later becomes a problem (Donovan 1996). Relationships go askew, mistrust pervades interactions and confusion dominates the inner world. Awareness of the crucial importance of telling one's story is reflected in traditional tales the world over. The stories convey our knowledge that telling about issues that are of abiding human concern is, much more often than not, simply good for us.

The willingness to tell, the ability to judge the moment and the capacity to learn from telling are crucial maturational achievements. They help us both to grow up and to become more like ourselves. A generous capacity to tell and a warm capacity to listen support a comfortable fit between us and our world. Stories create sufficient coherence to facilitate talk about felt confusion or misunderstanding. The very act of telling a story confirms that planning, building and de-constructing are fundamental processes. The story creation process parallels the preparation of the soil for planting, sowing, nurturing, harvesting, further readying and lying fallow. The rhythm of the land can be heard in the rhythm of a storyteller's breath, its accelerations, sighs and steadfast continuity. In such telling, due influence is granted to the context in which both teller and listener find themselves. The moment and

---

1   For a fascinating study of Jesuit understanding of the structure of memory and the profound ways this influenced the cultural development in both the East and the West, read: Spence, J.D. (1984) *The Memory Palace of Matteo Ricci.* Harmondsworth: Penguin.

the situation matter. Economic, educational and cultural differences, with their resultant privilege and power inequities, are realities which permeate any telling situation. We are, however, greater than the sum of the influences to which we are exposed. In each telling moment we can embrace the longings, contradictions and tensions which might otherwise tear our relationships asunder.

To harvest active wisdom

Because I like and love people more than stories, but stories a great deal, I began to use stories and storytelling many years ago in my therapeutic group work practice. Something new happened: interactive abilities flourished, disturbed thoughts and feelings could be clarified with greater ease and troubling memories were often worked through in a climate of more effective compassion. The telling of old and new stories seemed to contribute to the fact that life itself was expressively felt to be at once more vibrant, more secure and more resilient. I thought that was not only neat, but also that it was interesting. I therefore systematized my interest and set about learning what the specific characteristics might be of story-work with different client groups.

I soon noticed that even though storytelling about life events or fiction-alized happenings evokes some need for post dictum interpretation, there is no absolute need for direct linkage between adult situations and childhood experiences. It is one thing to enable an individual to describe or display how events are retrospectively experienced and to reflect on how the *then* influences the *now*. It is quite another to grant events the power of original cause. I agree with Runyan (1984), who writes: 'Any given event or experience can have a variety of possible effects and meanings, depending on initial personality structure, initial environment and the causal structure of subsequently encountered environments and experiences' (p.212). Origi-nology, that is the attribution of a troubling trend in one's life to a particular experience, often creates shackling narratives which foreclose the future and condemn the past (Mack 1971). Bad things do happen to good people, clarity can be as much of an obstacle to progress as confusion, whilst homilies, stories or proverbs may contain both wisdom and nonsense. We are all prone to accept a bogus interpretation as pertinent or relevant if it fits our self-explanation. Group workers may presume, perhaps too readily, that the correctness of an interpretation will be evidenced in a member's reaction. I have come to think that all we can deduce from a participant's reaction to a story or an interpretation is merely that it was of sufficient significance to enable the group member to do something with it that mattered to him or her, not that the story or the interpretation was valid in its own right, as a precise description of something actually occurring, (Hofling 1976).

Whilst I take careful note of what I witness in the groups I facilitate, I bear in mind that whatever anyone observes is always partial. Besides this relativization I maintain several continuities. First of these is that in each group I note members' timing of contributions and their style of withdrawing from interaction as well as evident engagement with particular issues. I clarify patterns in habits of relating and listen carefully to the spoken, the near-spoken and the unsaid, whilst I check my understandings frequently. We can but feel ourselves into awareness of the otherness of another and what is whispered between and without words (Kohut 1959). Through this we ascertain whether people might be burdening themselves with too great a responsibility for what cannot be sorted or carried by one individual alone.

I think of this kind group work as education in active wisdom. The education occurs through the invited encounter with life's infinite richness and complexity, through the sustainment of tender curiosity, and through the systematic support for more comfortable ways of telling, interacting and being. This process welcomes experience in, integrates uncertainty as uncertainty and facilitates the bonding of informed not-knowing with secure knowing. In these groups people work together to ease the expression of feelings, to reflect on doubts or certainties and to reinterpret actions, statements and practices. I call this practice Therapeutic Storymaking (TSM for short). The therapeutic–educational process is characterized by storied doing and reflection because I believe, with Crew (1975) that introspection is not necessarily the appropriate, let alone the only road to truthful explanation of our thoughts, feelings and actions.

Fuzzy concepts, team work and recovery from mental unwellbeing

The experiences and ideas described in this book are not specific to any one theory. The work does not rest on any single sociological or psychological supporting theory, although it builds on awareness gained in a range of fields – such as psychology (particularly developmental and social), philosophy (moral and educational), comparative mythology and folklore studies, group work and the arts therapies. The practice is inductive; in other words, it is based more on observed phenomena and less on the exploratory confirmation or disconfirmation of proposed ideas. The people who participated in the groups experienced a range of emotional, social and economic dilemmas. Their difficulties were often linked with identified ailments which had been given broadly recognizable labels, such as schizophrenia, early onset dementia, depression, personality disorder, post traumatic stress disorder, anxiety disorder or moderate learning difficulty. In the group members' own terms their distress was described as a general sense of feeling ill at ease and out of sorts with their world. Though I recognize that many colleagues and some clients find discrete concepts of mental ill health helpful, I prefer to use the more fuzzy concept of 'people with mental health difficulties'. Not only is the membership of this group less clear cut, the concept incorporates a clear temporal factor. It acknowledges mental ill health as, in essence, episodic though, depending on intensity and duration, it may also have enduring characteristics. The fuzzy concept incorporates awareness that the long-term characteristics are not only medically but also socially defined (Harris 1995).

Many people who experience shorter or prolonged periods of mental ill health have a range of carers who are in some way or other involved in their life situation. This formal and informal network of helping relationships often consists of a social worker, nurse, GP and/or psychiatrist, volunteers from self-help organisations, neighbours, family members, friends and shop-keepers. Also pets; the importance of a cat, a dog, a goldfish or a bird to promote or sustain well-being should never be underestimated. Most of the formal contacts in this helping network do not have a clear end set to them. The therapeutic storymaking group interrupts a person's tendency to drift towards a long-term involvement within the professional or semi-professional mental health context – amongst other reasons, because the groups aim to strengthen the clients' ability to engage with greater efficacy with their informal social network. Upon completion of a TSM group, many members become more involved with educational, self-help or voluntary activities. Some members don't really change their pattern of involvement with their helping network – for them the storymaking group is primarily something to do, though the work may momentarily alleviate emotional pain. A few people use these groups as a springboard to engage in longer term individual therapy.

In mental health teams I work alongside the client and the other care workers to sustain an interdisciplinary approach. In each storymaking group we establish confirmed continuities by acknowledging the other contacts and sharing information where appropriate. Continuity with colleagues is maintained through regular debriefing, supervision and follow-up. When several health care professionals are involved in a person's journey towards betterment, everyone concerned, including the client, needs to co-operate with the others (Hilton 1995). Participants in TSM groups are neither so ill nor so young that their right to autonomy cannot be exercised. I seek their agreement to participate after I have provided enough information about the group, the setting and myself and have explained the likely thematic content of the groups and clarified the kind of dilemmas that might be worked with. This includes a discussion of the boundaries and limits of group focus and confidentiality. All clients need to be sufficiently capable to make an independent decision to be present and to collaborate more often than not with the proposed activities (Hilton 1995).

To surmount felt powerlessness through Therapeutic Storymaking

In the course of a TSM group a person's collaborative ability is evoked, nurtured and sustained by means of various activities and dynamics which I aim to clarify in this book. The chapters include reflections on the dynamics of the storytelling situation, thoughts about the experiences and attitudes most frequently brought to story-work and how these impact on practice. I explore how we might think about different kinds of narrative and how to utilize such understanding in the construction of an exercise or technique which aims to further group members' well-being. The felt powerlessness which many clients bring to the therapeutic environment not only needs situating in their actual histories and circumstances, it also needs to be engaged with. This demands the systematic promotion of the clients' tolerance for the expression of a range of emotions. I shall explore how mutuality and reciprocity might be strengthened by means of structured response tasks, which are designed to offer maximum developmental support for the ability to express and tolerate feelings. Approaching the end of a group course, a woman who was recovering from reactive depression connected with the death of her husband wrote:

> Yes, I have been frightened, like many of us are. When life is dark, it is scary. Yes, I have been lonely too. Lonely and frightened, uncomforted. I know I cannot light other people's torch. As they cannot light mine. But we can help one another to find our way by lighting each other's path. In my memory I will stay close by you all. When the shadows come, you will all be there. I will not necessarily hear you or see you, nor will you necessarily hear me or see me, but we will be there for each other. Let grief be. It all takes time. Whatever you do: make haste, but never hurry.

In order to come home to ourselves, all of us need sustenance, companionship, solitude and the sharing of experiences. Storymaking and storytelling are habits which people have used since time immemorial to vitalize both past and present, thereby to create trajectories into the future. In therapeutic storymaking the created stories are emergent realities to which I hope to do justice. I shall conclude the journey through my reflections with a brief summary of the staging posts we visited, though I acknowledge that the landscape you see when looking back is startlingly different from the one you believed you saw when the journey lay ahead. As such, the story continues.

When reading or browsing through the book please bear in mind that I have altered client-identifying data to protect the privileged intimacy of the therapeutic work. Though I have stayed as close as is possible to the actual experience and situation, especially when citing verbatim statements, I am only too aware that whenever one identifying characteristic is altered, however minute this may be, the story is changed. Propp (1984) described the kind of alterations a storyteller is prone to make when retelling a story, such as reducing something to its bare minimum, amplification or elaboration, minor or large deformations, inversions, intensification or the weakening of events and substitution. My alterations are primarily reductions and limited substitution. All accounts of therapeutic practice are retold tales with all the limits this imposes (Yalom 1991, pp.3–14). The following pages abound with terms such as group member, client, participant, facilitator. Our task in the group was different because we carried alternative responsibilities, yet we engaged together in a process of exploring truths and shared creative expressive activity. The groups played, made up stories, queried, consoled and let in life. By embracing the stuff upon which our temporary worlds are built, we articulated the stories we live on.

To grasp the dream
and make the blue sky and the white sky.
The maker of narrative sits
where the sky meets the underworld.

Uitoto

2. On Stories and Storytelling

Ever since my grandparents told me about times gone by, I have loved old stories. Their place of telling was not a dimly-lit fireside or a courtly hall, it was a stool in the garden – whilst we peeled potatoes for supper – or a chair by my bedside. The stories they composed reflected their life history. They were embellished by the rub of intervening years and tempered by the experience of war, loss and the great depression. Their stories provided me with more than an intimate experience, they created a sense of rootedness in time (Ricoeur 1984). Other people, too, allowed traditional stories or fictional tales to live by passing them on. Committed teachers told stories in schools, librarians offered children's hours during which folktales and myths from far away people nourished my eager imagination, whilst ministers tried to implant their own brand of instructive tales. My experience of storytelling in formal and informal places is not unusual (Colwell 1991). In the Western world most children first become acquainted with storytelling at home, though nowadays stories are more often told by television presenters than grandparents and only later in educational, religious or leisure settings (Rosen 1988). In these environments the listeners' willingness to hear a tale will vary according to mood, preoccupation and circumstance. Each story-teller has in addition his or her own personal reasons for wanting to transmit some specific storied knowledge. These reasons may be dubious, such as the attempt to intimidate a child with a frightening story, or potentially freeing when the teller wants to console or to instil hope.

Since time immemorial, storytellers have familiarized adults and children with vivid story images which are pertinent to the listener's character and to their specific situation (Shedlock 1951). Through the careful creation of a believable illusion, tellers weave an associative thread between the listener's world and the story characters' adventures. The story's apparently incidental relevance enables the teller to elicit and to sustain the listener's agreement to attend to the tale. Without this consent the story could not be told; it freezes on the threshold of articulation and returns to the silence of memory, ultimately to search for another listener and another telling place. Each told story therefore articulates, in encoded or explicit form, the teller-listener's respective involvement with the dilemmas of their world. It simultaneously provides containment for their concerns.

By balancing the desire to please and the wish to be liked with the need to transmit knowledge and the evocation of a tolerable level of anxiety, storytellers create the necessary tension which carries the tale's interest. The wonders of narrative vision must be combined with the non-narrative elements of performance. The voices and gestures of jealous lovers, irate children and tricky animals inhabit the storyteller in a frequently astonishing speed of succession. Peter Brook, the theatre director, observed that story-tellers not only need to memorize a tale with understanding but also need 'the intellectual capacity of a physicist, the humanity and understanding of a psychiatrist, and the flexibility of an athlete' (Brook in Haggarty 1989, pp.7–12).

Tellers of tales change a story swiftly, condense vital information in order to mark the impact of a particular event and intensify character portrayal to sustain interest in a story. The listener's attention is continuously directed and redirected to the narrative so that the tale's animating potential may be activated. The story's effect depends on this activation. It strengthens the listener's desire to search for something that can never quite be grasped: the story's meaning.

What a story says, it says only provisionally. A good story generates sufficient make-believe to produce the effects our psychological needs require at a given moment on a particular occasion. The story accommodates our actual experience and leads it on. Its function is both emotive and referential. It is a very real pseudo-statement. An example of this can be found in the Kikuyu folktale about an undecided hyena:

> Mr. Hyena is very hungry. He is very hungry indeed. He walks and walks, looking for food. Suddenly he smells food. It smells good. Very good. He wonders where the smell is coming from. Where is it coming from? He walks towards the smell, but he cannot tell where it is coming from. Does it come from here? From there? At last Mr. Hyena comes to a point where two paths meet. He stands here, and wonders where to turn. His stomach tells him he is very hungry. His nose tells him there is food. But his heart does not tell him where to go. He walks up one path, and returns. He walks up the other, hesitates and returns. He is getting worried, for surely the food might disappear before he

even gets there. He thinks: 'I must walk both paths at once'. He stretches his legs. This is what he does. At first the paths are close together. Then they draw apart, but still he tries to walk both paths. Both paths! Of course he grows tired. Of course he has to give up. He never gets that meat. He is still hungry.[1]

Most of us can recognize Mr Hyena's reluctance to commit himself to a path, to make a choice. His unfortunate resistance to commitment conveys human experience. Each story is, as Virginia Woolf noted, 'like a spider's web, attached ever so lightly perhaps, but still attached to life at all four corners' (Woolf in Tyrrell 1990, pp.115–126). This attachment matters – not only because it reflects *how* a story links with our experience or perception of life but also *how* it adds to our way of interpreting events. The story about the consequences of Mr Hyena's indecision not only increases our knowledge of human behaviour, it also enhances our skills of perceiving such behaviour.

Because stories articulate thought, they give people a chance to have a say about something without necessarily having to commit themselves to an explicit opinion. Yet in the process of storytelling a perspective must be selected as well as presented. In turn, this supports awareness of the fact that we are intentional beings who can intend or resolve to do something, can do what is intended and reflect upon outcome. Many traditional stories incorporate a clear beginning, a middle and an end. This sequential clarity enables the listener to work out their own understanding of intention, action and outcome upon cause and effect and then to make judgments, which are marked by an emergent sense of authority. In turn, this may facilitate the development of the ability to assume ever greater responsibility for one's deeds. These are by no means skills or qualities to be sniffed at – particularly in the context of an educational or therapeutic endeavour, where the development of the capacity to present a point of view, to reflect on one's position and to develop this position through meaningful action in desired directions is of paramount importance. By paying attention to what happens in the story, we can learn to differentiate between the portrayer and the portrayed. The following traditional story addresses this theme in an interesting way.

A famous new minister has been appointed to a village church. The congregation eagerly awaits his arrival. On his first Sunday the church is packed. Soon after he has climbed the pulpit the minister raises his arms, lifts his eyes to heaven and asks: 'My people, please tell me if what I am going to say to you is already known to you.' A pregnant

---

1   Retold by the author. Contemporary version in Gescan (1970, p.67).

pause falls. He repeats his question. Nobody answers. He urges once more, 'Please tell me if what I'm going to say to you is already known to you.' Some church goers uncertainly shake their heads. The minister sighs, 'Ah well, what use is an unknown subject to either you or me?' He departs from his pulpit and leaves the church. The people are stunned. They have never experienced anything like this before. After a while they get up and go home in disbelief.

The following Sunday the congregation eagerly awaits the minister's arrival. Again he climbs the pulpit, raises his arms to heaven and asks, with even greater insistence: 'Oh my people, please, please tell me if what I'm going to say to you is already known to you'. Well, during the week some important church members had met to deliberate what to do if by chance their new minister were to ask the same question as the week before. Prepared for the occasion they nod their head affirmatively. 'Ah well,' the minister responds, 'that being the case we do not need to waste one another's time'. Once more he leaves the church.

The next Sunday the church is packed. And sure enough, at the appointed time, the minister repeats the now familiar question: 'Please tell me if what I'm going to say to you is already known to you'. This time half the people nod yes, the other half nods no. A broad smile appears on his face. He rejoices, 'Well, in that case you will be able to explain to each other what I might have said. You have no need of me'. He quickly descends the pulpit, leaves the church and is never seen again.[2]

When I shared this story with a group of disillusioned teenagers in an inner city youth club, one of the girls responded: 'You're fed up with us aren't you?' The tale did certainly carry some of my feelings towards this group, which had been very demanding. However, it also described some of their feelings towards me – a woman from a different country whom they hoped would rescue them from what felt like terminal boredom and despair. The story helped us to engage in a lively exploration of what made it so complex to work together towards a resolution of the difficulties which they so abundantly experienced. One of these problems was their desire, not uncommon in teenagers, to fall in with the demands and expectations of others (Jennings and Gersie 1987). This issue was a crucial area of concern for kids who easily succumbed to group pressure which painfully affected their own and other people's well-being. The story also expressed the problems which they

2 Retold by the author. Contemporary version in Rugoff (1977).

experienced with being taken seriously. They felt that I had granted them insufficient authority really to determine what they found difficult because, at times, I tended to prefer my own interpretation of their troubles to theirs, as well as allowing them too little autonomy to decide the ways by which their difficulties could be surmounted. In other words, I treated them too much like little kids (something their behaviour certainly invited) and demanded too little age-appropriate responsibility. As a result of this exploration, we substantially changed the way we related to each other. Our mutual respect for one another's dilemmas and responsibilities had grown.

For a group of lonesome elderly people, the Pulpit tale, as it came to be known by them, triggered emotional discussions around the theme: 'When all is said and done, what knowledge or wisdom do we want to convey to the next generation?' Thus both old and young found in the story an aspect that reflected their respective situation. It offered them equally some ideas on how to work through the inter-personal complexities which had kept the members of each of these groups in a state of sullen isolation for far too long.

The story as object and subject of enquiry

As noted above, the storyteller's art relies on their ability to translate an understanding of the story recipients' concerns and preoccupations into the story. This was demonstrated by a group of scientists who worked closely together on a difficult project. They developed a story which was told and retold by different project members on occasions when they were, as one of them put it, 'most definitely in need of a good chat'. This is the tale:

> Once there was a man. He was very wealthy. In the place where he lived everyone looked to him for advice or protection. But neither of these were any good to him for he did not know about truth. So, one day he decided to sell everything he owned. Everything! Then he set out on a journey to find truth. He travelled and travelled. Years passed. He did not find truth. He became poor, old, tired, lonely and miserable, and still, he did not find truth. One day, just when he was at his wits' end, he was told that someone who knew about truth lived in a cave high up in yonder mountains. With the last bits of strength and money he could muster (and remember by now he was old and tired and lonely) he travelled there. When he saw how high up in the mountains the cave was, he nearly gave up. But he had come this far, so he decided he might as well give it a final try. He climbed that mountain. When he finally arrived at the cave, he saw sitting, just outside it, a beautiful woman in a peaceful yoga position. He was awed and felt, at last, that his journey had not been in vain. Such balanced beauty. In response

to a question about the purpose of his uninvited visit, he stammered: 'I have come in search of truth'. The woman nodded her head, as if she knew everything he was about to say after that as well as everything he had ever said on the subject. In spite of this he continued: 'I understand that you know the answer. Please tell me: what is truth?' After an appropriate period of titillating silence, the woman spoke. Her voice was vibrantly alive: 'Truth is a flower'. The man flushed with rage. This was the answer? Truth was a flower! He ran down the mountain path. Away. Away. He just heard her voice call after him: 'You mean…it is not a flower?'[3]

Story collections the world over contain tales about our human search for truth, for everlasting life, or at least an explanation. All those journeys are long and tiresome. Sometimes the journeyers succeed in their goal. They meet the One who Provides an Answer in the shape of a wizened old woman with but a single tooth, in a soldier who guards a bridge or in an ever-smiling child. Some are reported to return to reap rewards. Other travellers arrive back home empty handed. Some lie about the treasure they uncovered to find that their lie becomes a rewarding reality. A few searchers for truth perish in despair. Idries Shah points out that similar stories are used by Taoist and Sufi Masters to illustrate 'that the quest is what teaches you that only the end has meaning, not the assumption of what the end might be' (Shah 1979, p.96). This version of the story suited these scientists' engagement with a precisely circumscribed unknown. They were unaware that their story was but one version of a widely distributed folktale. Typically, their story ended with a return to yet another question. Many members of this group were far away from home, from the companionship of family and friends. The esoteric focus of their area of interest haunted some of them. They wondered whether this really was what life was about whilst elsewhere wars were fought and people starved or lived amidst criminal levels of poverty. Thus this story did what stories always do: it provided sufficient nourishment and unease to stimulate discussion of linked matters of concern.

People who know and love stories will tell anyone: tales are potent stuff – not just the material dreams are made of, but the very substance of humanness. They remind us of our capacity to be distressed by another's sorrow, of the urge to altruism, and of those events that intersect with our benignity. Stories are a history in the sense that they have existed for a long time in certain places and contain an account of facts mingled with fiction. They are a mystery when they provide metaphoric access to our inner and

---

3   Story circulating in oral tradition. This story was told to the author by Arthur Kleinman in 1994.

relational worlds (Mellon 1992). Of course, we can approach each story from a given perspective, turning our discursive kaleidoscope towards understanding the tale with the aid of a particular framework, such as a focus on bourgeois values, on emotional valedictory procedures, or to an exploration of the sociological implications of opening structures in folktales (Rubin 1995, pp.194–226). Such specific discussions yield interesting material. However, most people relate to stories in simpler ways, demanding that it be a good yarn, something to while away the time or to offer inspiration, whilst possibly quietly hoping that it might address the central, underlying story of their own life, to grant it at least a semblance of coherency and to illumine its purpose (Pellowski 1987).

In many societies the tellers of tales are, therefore, awarded substantial veneration. Lumbermen in Siberia hired storytellers to see them through the winter's long, dark night, whilst fishermen and mineworkers, ambassadors and young Susan next door, strangers who meet on the train and schoolchildren everywhere do not mind hearing just the odd story – often they crave a tale or two about noodle heads and numskulls, ghosts and talking animals, ogres and kindly sprites. Devotion and entertainment, criticism and questioning are all part of our human search for some kind of truth.

> And when the flowers had been
> threaded,
> then these were twisted
> and wound in garlands.
> Aztec

Useful doubt: learning to negotiate

Given my love of stories and awareness of the possibilities sketched above, I turned to stories and storytelling for additional inspiration and guidance in both my therapeutic and educational work. My enjoyment in connecting stories with life experience and life experience with old stories is informed by the knowledge that the long-term gains of confronting emotionally upsetting events in story form are substantial in terms of positive effect on the person's psychological and physical health (Greenberg and Stone 1992). In this process I use both old and newly-made stories for several of the reasons outlined above and, particularly, because they operate in the margin of things that need an explanation. The more a story inhabits this marginal domain, the more it can be expected not only to keep the uncanny at bay but also to reiterate social norms. As Bruner (1990) notes: 'The function of the story is to find an intentional state that mitigates or at least makes comprehensible a deviation from a canonical pattern' (p.50). The telling of such stories safeguards our capacity to live through dark nights of the soul. It enables both teller and listener to negotiate fears, to strengthen resolve and, especially, to re-develop curiosity. I once asked group members to brainstorm on various questions one might be able to ask about someone's personal story or about a traditional tale. They quickly enumerated the following ideas:

- how and when the storied events had really started
- why this story must be retold
- what kind of taste it leaves in your mouth after you have told it
- what else was happening in another place at the same time
- was the solution in the story the only one or were there others and, if so, which ones
- which other events had left their mark upon the main story character
- what kind of influence did the storied events exercise years later.

The group could easily have listed other queries about timing, location, historicity and context. They were in no doubt that storied events do not occur in isolation; they are always situated in historical moment and place. When storytelling is used in a therapeutic or educational situation, it needs to support the participants' engagement with what bewilders them in three main ways:

- by introducing stories which deal with important human issues
- by exploring the issues the story raises
- by working through these themes in ways that are individually and socially relevant.

Facilitators or teachers who use stories in their work face the reality that if a story is not interesting to the group, it cannot be explored. During the telling the listeners become distracted, whilst subsequent recall appears non-existent and discussion is laborious and boring (Berger 1989). In order for a story to 'work' it needs to activate a relevant issue and be conveyed in a good-enough manner. Such a vital issue, in this case death and birth, is movingly exemplified in the following Nupe myth.

> It is said that the Maker of All made Tortoises, People and Stones. He gave life to Tortoises and to People, but not to Stones. However, none of these, though they were created male and female, could have children. When they reached a great age and were old, they simply

became young again. This is how it was in that time. However, Tortoise wanted to have children. She went to speak to Maker of All. This One said to Tortoise that he wanted her to have life but not children. Again and again Tortoise returned, but again and again Maker of All refused her request. At last he was worn out with her insistence, and asked her if she knew that if she had children she would have to die. Tortoise answered: 'Let me see my children and die'. Then Maker of All fulfilled her desire. Once people saw that Tortoise had children, they wanted children too. Maker of All warned them, just like he had warned Tortoise. He said: 'Death will come'. But People said: 'Let us see our children and die'. In this manner death and children came together to this world. The Stones did not wish to be granted children. They do not die.[4]

Tortoise and People knowingly elect to die in order to have children. We hear the urgent dream of our species which cannot continue without this urge to procreate. Other stories which describe death's appearance in this world may convey how death was chosen in order to make the sun move, to obtain fire or to ensure life's continuity by making rain fall. Sometimes death arrives as a punishment or just as a matter of fact (Henderson and Oakes 1963). The Nupe story also addresses the pain of barrenness which many childless people feel. It reflects our reluctant struggle with purpose, death's omnipresence and inevitability. It contains both a consoling answer to the unacknowledged question 'why do we live?' and a specific way of answering this question. Direct appeal to a higher authority is used to create a satisfactory explanation for the way of the world. As such, each story appears both to close and actually to open the questioning process. The extent to which it succeeds in doing so depends on our willingness to engage with its proposed answer to a given dilemma.

Engagement with the desire to create an explanation is vital for many people who experience emotional unwellbeing, particularly because the explanatory frame which they have generated to explain the cause of their malaise is frequently in and of itself a contributory factor to their troubles. During the initial stages of a therapeutic or educational group it may be useful to cast some doubt on the apparent certainty of an implied cause and effect relationship. I sometimes initiate such discussions by inviting group members to make up 'that's why' stories about phenomena in the natural world. Catherine, a member of a short-term group for adults with moderate mental health problems, wrote a 'that's why' story that was entitled 'Why the Beaver has a flat tail':

4   Retold by the author. Contemporary version in Beier (1970, pp.58–9).

Beaver was always busy scurrying around the river, searching out nice juicy logs and twigs to build his home with. One day he saw a particularly useful log sticking out of the river bed. So he began to gnaw at it, but it would not give way. No matter how hard he tried he couldn't move it. He then decided to grip it in his teeth and give it a sharp tug. He did this and the next thing found him desperately swimming away from a hail of huge boulders. Fast as he swam, he was just unlucky and one large boulder hit his back and trapped his bushy tail. As he struggled he felt a sharp sensation. He turned round and saw a terrible sight. His truly bushy tail was no longer. In its place was this short flat one. He rested a long time. Then he moved it up and down and found to his surprise that it was very useful for swimming. So in the end his unfortunate accident turned out to be a piece of good luck.

This story signalled substantial change for Catherine, who had until then preferred to think of life as inevitable and non-reinterpretable. The very introduction of concepts such as 'good fortune or misfortune' into her tale indicated development (Klecan-Aker 1993). The ability to come to grips with the concept of chance *per se* signals a vital developmental step. Unbeknown to her, the Beaver story linked with an old Chinese tale:

In a certain village there lived a man who had one son. His wife had long since died. The two of them were neither poor nor rich. They survived on what the mountains yielded and their hands created. It sufficed. One day the son caught a wild horse. He was able to bring it home. The neighbours were awed. They thronged into the small dwelling. Congratulations hailed from their mouths. But the old man said: 'How can you be so sure this is a blessing?'

The son tried to tame the horse. One day he was thrown to the ground so violently that he broke his leg. Overflowing with concern the neighbours visited the old man to cheer him up. But he was as cheerful as ever, saying: 'How can you be so sure this is not a blessing?' The very next day the emperor's army passed through the village. Every young man who was remotely fit was taken away. But not his son. His leg swaddled in rags, sweat pouring down his face, he was left behind. And once more the old man grumbled to his neighbours: 'How can you be sure this is a blessing.'[5]

---

5   Retold by the author. This story circulates in oral tradition. I have heard it told in the Netherlands, Britain and USA.

The emergence of useful doubt about an existing way of interpreting important life events can feel as if a ray of light has entered a previously dark room. Such a re-view places events and relationships in a new perspective. This newness in itself reinforces a recognition of the inevitability of change. Many stories present the listeners with descriptions of events and implicit beliefs or norms. Such events are often at an angle to the listeners' own, experienced reality. A well chosen story provides a fruitful, tangential difference. When a person's felt craving for purposeful telling about life is lost beneath the onslaught of torrential feelings, the restoration of a helpful internal relationship with the capacity to perceive difference matters. It enables distressed people to tell stories about their longings and experiences, which are implied in the following statements:

- ○ It is wrong not to be loved
- ○ It is wrong to be unhappy
- ○ It is right to live
- ○ It is wrong to kill
- ○ It is right to acknowledge people you know.

These are the words of a group of tough youngsters, all of whom had been in serious trouble with the law. The life-stories which informed these statements needed to be given new form and voice, so that their hopes and beliefs might find more efficacious expression. The very engagement with discursive, storied communication enables both teller and listener to negoti-ate the implicit or explicit perspectives in the story concerned *as well as* uncertainties or disagreements about the values proclaimed. Because story-telling is a device to communicate knowledge and wisdom, it generates talk – both about the story itself and about the subject to which the story refers. Such story-talk often begins within the protective frame of an analogy. Though listeners sense the presence of a known referent behind the storied words, during talk about the story this referent *may*, but does not necessarily *have* to be acknowledged in order for meaningful communication to occur. This potential for clear obliqueness is advantageous in any situation when direct confrontation or revelation is either too dangerous or too intrusive. An example of a story that carries such multiple, veiled references to political, social and personal relationships is found in the following Russian folktale:

> A long time ago Bear, Wolf and Fox met. All three were very hungry. After bewailing their fate at some length, they decided to live together as brothers. Thus resolved they warmly embraced, vowed to be faithful to one another and set out to hunt. They ventured deep into the woods

and traveled a long, long way. At last they spotted a young wounded deer. Quick as a flash the creature was killed. They agreed once again that they would indeed share the food with each other. Bear invited Wolf to begin the division. Wolf proposed: 'The head must of course go to you Bear, for you are our Lord and Master. The trunk will be for me as I'm middle sized, whilst Fox you must receive the legs as you are swift of foot.' Wolf had hardly finished speaking when Bear walloped him in the face so hard that even the trees trembled. With simmering rage he growled: 'Master Fox, please, you divide...' Sweetly voiced Fox answered: 'Ah Master Bear, the division is obvious. The deer is yours by right. The head cannot be but yours as you are our Lord and Master. The body has to be yours as you care for us like a father. And of course the legs are yours as you always step forward to benefit us with your strength.' With contemptful contentment Bear sighed: 'Mistress Fox you are very clever indeed'. To which Fox replied, 'Master Bear, you flatter me. I saw how you taught Wolf'.[6]

Versions of this story's theme exist the world over. This widespread distribution does not need to surprise us. Problems with the division of scarce food supplies are only too painfully common and unequal power relations between people abound. The story highlights these. Stories are created, remembered and retold in a socio-political context. They describe the social dynamics of co-operation and opposition, of betrayal, faithfulness, indifference, compassion or fairness. When I have worked with the above mentioned tale in school or work settings, the animals' ill-fated alliance rapidly brought out memories of being bullied. It has also stimulated reflection on the disastrous consequences of starvation on decision-making processes, let alone on health, whilst much was said about greed.

Though not necessarily explicitly didactic, each story provides the listeners with a basis for confronting a perspective on a specific life theme and for trying out particular ideas in relation to this perspective. This exploration can help people to become more aware of the characteristics of a situation to which the story characters react and of how these reactions effect situations (Bauman 1986). The exploration of these dynamics supports not only the listener's memory of events within the story but also their memory of events related to the story. In this manner stories can teach about life and affect experience. The presentation of experience in story form enhances a person's sense of more truly inhabiting their life history (Butler 1964).

---

6 Retold by the author. Contemporary version in Zheleznova (1969, pp.172–3).

When elephants fight
the grass gets trampled.
Somali

Practice vignette: brief intervention in long-term settings

The people with whom I work are sometimes strangers to each other. More frequently, they share a great deal of time together in the peculiar ways bestowed by hospitals, hostels, school or work settings and family homes. Such group members will be in touch with one another long after I will have gone my very own way. For them the storymaking group is but a punctuation mark in their extended time-span of mutual involvement. In such groups, intimacy and its complexities are often a matter of serious concern. Professional help is mostly only sought when the group no longer functions effectively. In other words, relationships have gone sour; habits of problem solving are ineffective and exhausted. The attempt to close the stable door is made after the horse has bolted. In these groups I use story-work, amongst other things, because it easily introduces a discussion of how things are right now whilst it brings to the fore longings of how things might be – longings which are so closely linked with the group's beliefs about how things ought to be. These are the kind of 'oughts' which have often caused the group to run into difficulties in the very first place – if only because a firm commitment to correct position undermines the capacity for flexible negotiation and tolerance.

I remember a small staff team (six members) who requested help with tension in their group. They attributed the tension to irresolvable personality conflicts. However, as none of the staff intended to leave their job in the near future, they realized that they had better learn to make the best of their situation and find more fruitful ways to co-operate. During one particular session I introduced the story of Bear, Wolf and Fox and the way they deal with the division of food. Each staff member in turn played Bear, Wolf and Fox. Not only did they have fun performing the various roles – which were frequently switched whilst the tale was elaborated – and they had not had fun together for some time, they also used the story as a vehicle to convey one of the dramas of their staff team: namely their difficulty with sharing attention. Though there are numerous ways in which this team's difficulties could be interpreted or understood, it mattered that the story made it possible, by means of a protective metaphor, for them to express fears of being the one who would be left out. Once they had regained some expressive mastery over previously dreaded emotions of envy, isolation and greed, they learned to address these issues as a team (MacKinnon 1984).

They acquired new habits of relating professionally to each other, not only through understanding but also through doing. The story generated much needed access to viable patterns of social negotiation (Bruner 1990).

Group work around stories and storytelling can also be used to help participants to explore the fact that we neither can nor need to know everyone's business, even though we need to know certain realities in order to maintain a good quality of relationship. This constant balancing of closeness and distance is an important theme in families, residential homes, prisons and long-stay hospitals. In institutional settings the thin line between concern and gossip is frequently crossed, to the detriment of all involved. When this happens, some people withdraw too much whilst others become the unauthorized conveyers of personal detail. Both ways of coping with somewhat enforced intimacy provide a sticky foundation for the maintenance of community coherence. When bitterness and mutual suspicion have become deeply entrenched in an institutional setting, I have sometimes used the story of Li chi, The Serpent Slayer, to enhance the process of bringing about community change.

> In this old Chinese story a village is overwhelmed by fear of a great serpent who lives on a nearby mountain. This serpent not only ravages their flocks, it devours whatever crosses his path. The villagers despair. In their dreams they discover what to do. Once a year on a day during the eighth month a thirteen-year-old maiden will have to be delivered to the serpent's cave. Thus each year a girl is chosen from amongst the poorest families and taken to the hills. In this way nine maidens die. When the tenth year comes an unexpected event happens. Li chi, the youngest daughter of Ti lum, volunteers to go to the mountain on the condition that she will be given a sword, some food, a piece of flint and a snake hunting dog. Her parents desperately try to dissuade her, but their pleas are to no avail. On the appointed day the villagers let her go. She carries her chosen gifts and is accompanied only by her dog. Li chi's feet carry her to where she knows she has to go. She sits down awhile in that place of anticipated darkness. Then she gathers wood, makes a fire and cooks the food. Soon the serpent's shadow flashes across the sky. Li chi and her dog fight with that serpent and kill it. It wasn't that difficult. Then Li chi ventures into the serpent's cave. She knows what she is looking for. She gropes into the heart of darkness and searches with all the determination a thirteen year old can muster, for the skulls of the nine girls who went to this cave before her. At last she returns to the light of that fierce day. She carries as many bones as her small body can hold and slowly begins the journey back home. In her arms the skeletons of the girls that died. It is a slow

journey. When the villagers see young Li chi return from the serpent's mountain they know not what to say or do. She simply requests a proper burial for the girls who were also her friends. This is done. Some storytellers say years later Li chi left that village and that nothing else is known about her. Others recount how the king of Yu heard of her deeds and asked her to become his bride. (Gersie and King 1990, pp.89–90)

I clearly remember one group's response to this story: the users and staff of this particular day centre for elderly people wanted to work together for six sessions in order to improve their centre's atmosphere, which had gone sour after a staff conflict had resulted in the dismissal of the centre's director. Several day centre users had liked this director very much indeed. This added to the complexities the staff and users experienced. The first two TSM sessions were devoted to rebuilding some confidence in the group process, amongst others through the facilitation of more open expression of mistrust or suspicion and of the equally felt need for mutual support. During the third session I briefly told Li chi's tale. I then asked each group member to write a text for a possible memorial monument in Li chi's honour. We subsequently shared the memorial texts. Gerald was a kind, dignified man who used the centre's facilities twice a week. His voice cracked a little as he read his words. He said: 'She did a good thing but who now remembers her? Despair travellers or tell her tale.' The implications of his words were not lost to the group. The reference to Shelley's poem about Ozymandias was picked up by some. But the link to the sudden departure of the centre's female director, whose name the users felt could really not be mentioned, was heard by everyone. A few people also made a connection between the text and Gerald's sorrow about his daughter's death from cancer some months earlier. One or two people who sat close to him reached out and briefly touched his arm. Every single memorial poem was similarly relevant both to the individual, the group and the institution. The brief response poems, which had been written in just a few minutes, offered a great deal of material for further work.[7] The storied dynamics of Li chi's village in a state of terror became a vital part in the group's journey through its own confusion. The powerlessness the users felt about the staff conflict, the staff's futile attempts to protect the users against knowing too much about the troubles and the director's departure without as much as a good-bye were easily linked with the exploration of how the villagers in this story coped when the serpent of mistrust and suspicion threatened their survival.

---

7   For a classic introductory text on the uses of poetry in therapy read Lerner (1978)

Gossip, refrain tales and the renewal of trust

When life is troubled, as it was for the users of the day centre for elderly people, it is tempting to tell and retell the way events are understood. Refrain tales emerge whenever the events that are talked about are not really worked through. After a while, these tales incorporate the freely floating gossip of everyday life in a vain attempt to lift the oft-told story out of its compelling groove. However, rumours and gossip do not lead to fundamental change, they simply add to core convictions of something being wrong. Neither does such tale-telling lead to the person's integration into an already fragile web of community. On the contrary, greater isolation often ensues for the tale-teller. Refrain tales are also boring. Before long, few people still bother to find out what the repetitious telling might actually be about. Slowly and gradually the individuals concerned are left to their own devices. The coherency necessary for institutional functioning is even further undermined. This increases the community's vulnerability to conflict. A down-turning spiral of organizational turmoil is set into motion.

Many residential, therapeutic or health organizations rely, by dint of unit size, habit or constraint, predominantly on oral communication. In such environments disclosure about deeply-felt issues can easily become either rare or explosive, whilst the organizational climate is often, by its very nature, socially and inter-personally restrictive (Lowe and Herranen 1978). In these mini worlds, refrain tales abound whilst little ever seems to change. In such environments, ill-considered talk may lead residents or employees to feel that though they are surrounded by people, they live or work in a social wasteland. They do not feel supported by the resources of a healing community. When such feelings dominate, the client only too readily assumes that there will be no-one to count on when help is needed. In turn, this leads to a high degree of anxiety and a related high uptake of professional service provider's hours. A troubling trend towards further emotional exhaustion in already difficult circumstances is generated. The community's very survival becomes threatened by yet another destructive act or bitter statement. The few remaining bonds are repeatedly strained because people who die, improve or deteriorate are removed from the setting. The experience of people coming and going further supports the defence against making emotional ties. Yet these ties are needed in order to ensure the well-being of the treatment community to which both staff and patient willy nilly belong. In such circumstances, learning to talk and to relate differently is vitally important.

In these settings, staff and facility users alike need to clarify and work through simmering conflicts. This can, amongst other things be achieved by enabling people initially to think together through story-based analogies and to reflect on behaviour exemplified in the stories in less confrontative and yet more personal ways. Such story-work can be used to create access to communicative practices that demonstrate commitment to the community's well-being. It also fosters ways of being together that provide everyone with some joy. By offering new practice in reciprocity, the community of users can learn to address its concerns in a different, more productive manner. When a group's interactive reaction spectrum has consisted of withdrawal, the covering of important comments in ambivalent terms, or in cantankerous bluntness, participation in structured storytelling activities can help, particularly because storymaking enables people to have a say, supports responsiveness over reactivity and provides a format for the integration of both long-held grievances and unvoiced appreciation. Old and newly constructed fictional stories permit a large degree of depersonalization and universalization by, as Abrahams (1983) noted, 'Couching the description of how specific people are acting in terms of how people have always acted'. This can be deeply comforting for people who live in artificially close proximity – such as hostels, workplaces or prisons – where the revelation of intimate feelings often requires a strategic degree of indirectness and where a community of performance in which contested voices are woven into a tapestry of shared expression is established only with the greatest difficulty.

≈●≈●≈●

When all was unwrought simplicity,
then without having been created,
things came into being.
Han period – China

Storytelling and the negotiation of difference

Conflict resides at the heart of virtually every folktale (Durrell and Sachs 1990). This often takes the form of antagonism between story characters. At other times, though more rarely so, the tension that moves a story towards resolution focuses on intra-psychic dilemmas. Both conflict and conflict resolution depend on the character's capacity to take up a position, to defend a want, a desire or a need. The way a position is taken, how it is defended and how a character relates to the other party's point of view enhances or defuses the conflict situation (Goforth and Spillmann 1994). The omnipresence of a trouble in stories contributes to their usefulness in therapy or education if only because difficulties in the management of conflict are at the core of the problems a client brings to these settings (Rosen 1993). Especially when a story fails to offer any prospect for negotiation, it invites ideas about what went wrong or what could have been done differently. This is exemplified in the following traditional tale:

> Still dressed in their wedding finery, a newly married couple arrive in their new home. It is a dark and stormy night. Just as they are about to snuggle into bed, they hear the sound of a door flapping in the wind. They realize that in their hurry to carry the wedding gifts safely indoors, they must have forgotten to shut the door. The groom says to the bride: 'The door has been left open, hasn't it?' When she asks him to close it, he replies in anger: 'Me? Why should I? Can't you go and do it yourself?' She refuses. They haggle, urge and accuse one another for a while, but to no avail. Neither of them wants to go downstairs and close the front door. However, as this is their first wedding night, they decide that they must find a solution to their problem. They agree to stay in the room, go to bed and to keep silent. The first one to speak will have to go downstairs to close the front door. They believe that their wager of silence will only last a little while. One of them surely will say something to end this hassle. But they grossly underestimate the other's stubbornness. They lie there next to each other, eyes closed, determined not to speak. They bring to their battle of wills all the defiance and commitment they can muster.
>
> Well, as it is a dark and stormy night, the flapping door has been noticed by thieves who are doing their rounds. Under the cover of night they creep into the house and take whatever wedding gifts they can lay their hands on. As the couple are still awake, trying their very best not to be the loser in their wager of silence, they even hear the thieves wander around the house. But still, they manage not to speak. In this way they spend their first wedding night, neither succumbing to the other's will.
>
> When daylight comes disquieted neighbours notice that the front door of the newly wedded couple's house is wide open. They talk about what to do. At last they decide that they must go into the house. Stunned at the havoc the thieves have wrought, they knock at last on the bedroom door. There is no reply. Terrified at the thought of what might have happened to the couple, they open the door. To their horror they see the newly weds sitting upright in bed. They look proudly defiant and still refuse to speak. Whatever the neighbours do,

they can't get them to talk. In exasperation one of them shakes the man by the shoulder and shouts 'Talk, talk'. The young woman cries: 'Please, don't hurt him. Don't hurt him.' Triumphantly the husband croons: 'I won! I won. You have to shut the door.'[8]

I have worked with this story in many different situations. It often evokes a sad, pensive response and kindles memories of weddings, rows, and uncomfortable feelings about the distribution of tasks in relationships. Group members are often eager to demonstrate how the couple in the story might have been able to resolve their predicament differently, so that they would not have had to embark on their blind struggle for control without resolution.

When a person is stuck in a problematic situation it is initially easier to elicit suggestions for alternative ways to resolve the issue by means of exploration of a storied example, not because the alternative approaches are necessarily applicable to the person's situation but because they provide a framework of alternatives as well as a habit of considering alternatives. Once this habit is firmly established, it can be applied to the generation of a reinterpretation of the person's problematic situation. Group work with stories inspires the following areas of exploration:

- what interested/puzzled the listener(s) about the story
- how was this puzzlement expressed and worked with
- what kind of explanations did the listener(s) create for the bewildering aspects of the story
- which alternatives were considered
- which interpretative choices were ultimately made.

Watzlawick observes that when we have a problem, it is rarely the problem that constitutes the experienced difficulty (Watzlawick 1976). More often than not the relationship with the problem needs improvement. When the relationship with the problem is shifted, it takes on different characteristics. A good story allows the listener to place problematic occurrences within a wider horizon of possibilities. It nurtures the capacity to perceive possibilities where none are believed to exist and supports the development of an individual narrative voice because every story brings people's perceptions or feelings within the reach of shared deliberation. This applies to traditional tales, newly created fictional stories or memory-tales. The story is a sign. What it means for us, makes it a signifier. Zipes (1979) notes that this signification is of primary importance. He suggests that a story's value depends on how it is produced and received in a social relationship. The way in which a story is told and the dynamics of the teller-listener relationship

---

8   Retold by the author. Contemporary version in Shah (1979).

may contribute to greater autonomy for the listener or lead to submission and dependency. The exploration that often follows storytelling exposes the listener to the reality that stories trigger different memories and lead to rather different understandings of what happened in the tale. Because a story links with occurrences in the audience's life in many unpredictable ways, it stimulates the listener to remember and to share their own stories. One tale calls forth another.

To develop thickened judgment

Groups thrive on the constructive exploration of difference. The greatest possible tolerable variety is the material out of which well-functioning groups are fashioned. Each storytelling audience contains some people who are happy to listen to the story but whom it does not touch, several who liked it but who, during discussion, realize that they interpret it very differently from others and a majority who felt that the story was not only just right for them but who understand its theme in similar ways. They agree on its dominant meaning. Rather than closing down discussion, these differences of interpretation and perception generate an opportunity for group members to learn more about each other's way of being in the world. During the discussion of a story's possible meanings, a separation is established between the story's characters and the acts which they perform. The dancer is distinguished from the dance. This characteristic of distinguishment allows stories to function as instruments in the process of social negotiation. A man reflecting on his experience as a student in a male hall of residence wrote:

> In my day we had bull sessions. It occurs to me now that the stories were an important part of male bonding. We called them war stories. We realized that these war stories were not objective accounts of events. They were the sort of accounts that men who shared a war might later tell. We were young. None of us had seen war. But we told accounts of experiences which emphasized the thrills. It wasn't the story that mattered, it was the rhythm of life. It articulated communality. We called it bullshitting.

Most stories are fictional constructions which are intimately attached to:

- the intrapsychic world of teller and listener
- their interpersonal world
- the dynamics of mutual influence between these worlds and the individuals' larger historical and socio-economic context.

The storytelling occasion is, therefore, not just lightly connected to life, it is thickly grounded. During storytelling, one's self-perspective is momentarily submerged in the absorption in the story. The teller–listener pair is granted the opportunity to un-self by paying close attention to something outside of themselves. The story supports the exploration of the commitments which bind or divide them, especially because it represents such themes through analogy. By means of these various processes storytelling enables us to develop, what Altieri calls, a thickened judgment (Altieri in Tyrrell 1990, p.124).

People who live, work, play or study together need to cope with differences of opinion, with pairing and the various complexities of emotional ties. They also need to experience intimacy and a sense of wholeness. Rather than closing down potentially explosive discussion or the sharing of intimate experiences, storytelling can be used to open these up. Structured group work based on storytelling is more than an invitation to debate and argumentation. It is a training in reflecting with one another on important life themes.

Unreliable words, strong feelings and untold stories

Because we cannot but formulate stories about experience in the back of our mind, we are the containers of numerous tales. Though some of these stories are told and retold, the vast majority remain unvoiced. They rest seemingly unnoticed in memory's vast palace, to be lifted to the fore if, perchance, we were asked if we could remember how our feet had felt that morning or whether anything special happened on the way home. Most of the time we do not talk much about the special way we squeeze the toothpaste from its tube or what we thought when we looked at the kind of patterns the windscreen wipers create on the car window, gathering raindrops by the thousand. What we note remains, as John Cage (1968) so succinctly phrased it, 'mostly noise' (p.3).

Consciousness enables us to construct a story out of every event which befalls us and each activity we undertake. At the start of a new group I sometimes invite participants to reflect on something they noticed earlier that day that they had not yet mentioned to anyone. Following initial bewilderment and the voicing of fear that no story will emerge, group members realize the sheer abundance of untold observations, thoughts and feelings. In one TSM group such untold but noticed experiences included:

- standing still by a fountain and noticing the rainbow in the water
- a man behind a window. He laughed. About what?

- flowers on a coffin travelling by in a hearse
- a man who took up too much space on the seats in the train
- the toy bear next to a daughter's head in her bed
- an unpleasant phone call.

The miscellany of recollections consists of stories waiting to be told, discarded or distilled into a flavour of the day. In early groups I like to encourage group members to lift one or two such memories momentarily to the fore, if only because attention to the little events needs to precede attention to major life events. This builds not only a capacity for resilience, it allows for the testing and growth of trust. This process of gradual development is vitally important, especially when a person's trust in life has been severely wounded. In this exercise a group member first introduces him or herself by name and then describes their impression-vignette in a few sentences, with an accompanying movement. The group repeats the story-teller's name as well as their gesture. This is Jane's story:

> This morning, when I was about to step into the car to go to work, I heard a bird sing. It was sitting on a branch of the tree in our front garden. It gave me such pleasure to have a bird that sings in our garden.

Her accompanying movement consisted of a gentle sideways turn of her upper body. Her face lit up with pleasure. She scooped her left hand behind her left ear and raised her head as if reaching tenderly for the bird's song. The group responded in unison: 'Jane' and repeated her delighted, listening gesture. This added to her pleasure at recalling the memory. The group's movement permitted me to see each individual member's movement capacities, to weigh levels of engagement and to learn about their responses to particular stories. This simple exercise also helps group members to become aware that storytelling is both a way of telling about life and a way of creating access to other telling. In the process of mirroring Jane's movement, each group member could not help but recall their own memories of bird song, of leaving home in the morning, of gardens and of sound. Some of these memories may have been joyfully charged. Others may have trailed deep melancholy in their sway. When we describe how we water the plants in the morning, that we walked past our office because the front door had been newly painted, or how we struggled to moor a small sailing boat whilst on holiday, the experience is organized in story-form. Through stories we convey: 'This is my world'. At each moment of our conscious life we are in the midst of telling and listening, asserting and asking, confirming and disconfirming stories (Mair 1989). The countless events of every day and the thread which connects these and the jarring episodes which leave us pained or bewildered constitute the miscellany out of which we construct our story of life. Over time we emphasize some aspects, others are minimized. A few trail by our side, tugging at our consciousness, as if to say: 'What about me'. When we notice the multitude of stories that dwell near the surface of articulation, we may be struck by how much we could tell if only we had the chance. There are many reasons why we may not speak much about our experiences. Absence, uninterest or a scowling put-down by important others may have frozen our stories on the threshold of articulation.

The gap between experience and the account of experience

The silence engendered by the inability or unwillingness to tell about life can have a disturbing edge (see Long 1969). In my mind's eye I recall many loudly silent storytellers – such as the skinny child on the school playground, shivering stiffly in a coat of thoughts too big for its small body; the teenager, arms defiantly crossed, seeking support from yet another stone wall; the woman alone in the cafe, smoking breathlessly. I have touched upon their presence on park benches, in doctor's waiting rooms, in the underground, at parties and, above all, in class- and therapy rooms. When we behave like 'a silent talker', we do not yet allow shared acknowledgment of our experience of the world (Wells 1987, p.196). The ability to give voice to multitudinous perceptions is halted by the heart's commitment to some form of anonymity. In the inner world of people in this predicament, silence feels, and may well be, safer than speech.

Spoken language keeps the company of truth and of falsehood, of sincerity and dissemblance. Stories may be used in the service of greater authenticity, to create misperception, or both. Because stories convey unstable truths, they demand that both teller and listener wrestle with their content to establish a shared truth (Cole 1995). Each story represents external and internal realities. It is a tool to reach greater understanding, a bridge between worlds, but not the journey across it.

The human capacity to speak and to name things, whether these are experiences, places, objects, animals or people, governs our lives in many ways. Language helps us to create and to assimilate our image of the surrounding world (Grinberg and Grinberg 1984). Since time immemorial people have devised stories about the way speech came into being. In many such stories speech and language dwell not only at the centre of social life but at the roots of life in general. The Dogon people's insight into this process is conveyed in the following traditional story:

Water and words came together at the birth of the world. Numo placed fibres of water and words on the earth's body skirt. Thus he clothed the earth, the mother, and gave her Speech, a simple but beautiful language. Speech itself is good for its function is to bring order and agreement. Nevertheless from the start Speech also let loose disorder. This was because Jackal, the deluded and deceitful son of Numo, desired to have Speech too. He tried to get the fibres which contained the water and words by placing his hands on the mother's body skirt. The mother, the earth, resisted this action, but in the end she had to admit defeat. Jackal was thereby endowed with the gift of Speech. From that time on he was able to reveal what ever the gods designed.[9]

This myth exemplifies that speech is an agency of both order and disorder (Abrahams 1983, p.21). It is the means by which we express our power and give our blessings. Through words we deceive, argue, construct knowledge and preserve memory. By means of words we pursue beauty and accuracy. They enable us to emancipate vocalized sound from the realm of emotional utterance into the interpersonal world of denotative attribution. Through the use of language we proceed from momentary experience to enduring conceptions, from sense impression to formulation. Cassirer (1946) describes this as the ability 'to transform the rhapsody of perceptions, by which the world is actually presented to us, into a system, a coherent epitome of laws' (p.27). Whilst stories bridge the gap between experience and the account of that experience, storytelling allows the experience to enter the social domain.

The capacity to story our life enables us to make sense of even the most painful life-events. The willingness to tell is vital to our well-being. This awareness is encapsulated in the following Irish story:

Brian O Braonachain of Barr an Ghaith manfully refused ever to tell a story. Saying he couldn't and he wouldn't. One day, he goes out into the fields to cut rods for the baskets he makes. A thick fog strikes the field where he is working away hastily, for he is in the very den where the fairies live. Had not his wife scolded him for being the laziest and dullest man she'd ever known, he would never have been there. But that fog is so deep, he cannot get out of the field. He cannot find his way out. Then he sees a light. At last, a light. He hurries towards it. There's a house with a man and woman. They beckon him: 'Come in...'. He goes inside. The old people make him welcome, offer him food, sit him by the fire. When he has finished eating, they ask the one, the very one, question Brian dreads most. They say hopefully:

---

9   Abbreviated and retold from Griaule, M (1965), *Conversations with Ogotomêlli*, Oxford: Oxford University Press, p.21 (first published by the International African Institute).

'Now Brian, please tell us a story.' Brian says he can't, for the life of him, he cannot tell a story. He will do anything to please them, but he cannot and will not tell a story. Well, the old people are much surprised, but, being kindly, they ask him to go out and fetch them some water from the well. As soon as he bends over the well, he feels himself lifted up. High, high into the sky. In the place where he falls down, he spots another little house with a light in it. This is a wake-house.

Again he is made a warm welcome and again the people ask Brian to perform several tasks. He plays the fiddle for dancing, says the Mass of the Dead, and shortens the legs of a rather tall man who has to carry the coffin with three short people. In a moment's breath Brian O Braonachain of Barr an Ghaith, the rod cutter and basket weaver, has fiddled, prayed and severed legs. When at last he is thrown back through the sky to the old people's dwelling, they receive him warmly, feed him, put him by the fire and invite him again to tell them a story. This time Brian is only too glad to oblige. He tells them about the smallest detail, doesn't mind repeating a thing or two, and eagerly answers the questions the curious old people ask. When all is told, the old people are well pleased.

A bright sun shines when Brian wakes up by the side of the glen where first he got lost. Had he not been somewhere? A great storyteller was made.[10]

Gergen and Gergen (1983) coined the term 'self-narration' to describe the process by which we tell stories about ourselves to ourselves. They suggest that we create self-narrative in order to make connections between various life events, thereby to generate a sense of meaningful sequentiality. Marianne, a participant in a storymaking group for people who had experienced complex bereavements, observed:

'When I first arrived in this city I was deeply impressed by how many people were walking on the street talking to themselves. I just realized that maybe what they are trying to do is to tell themselves their story.'

The experience of his night in the fields certainly jolted Brian O Braonachain of Barr an Ghaith into narrative ability, as his story to the old couple demonstrated. However, Marianne's, and our own, well-being demands more than the ability to self-narrate, we also need to tell others. The facility to construct an explanatory framework in story form links our understanding of our world with our daily way of being. The narrative process clarifies

---

10 Retold by the author. This story is often told by storytellers in Britain and abroad.

thoughts and feelings and anticipates future deeds (Baumeister and Newman 1994). Storytelling conveys such understandings of a real or imaginary past, of current or future events to others. In this process the storyteller surrenders spoken words to the multiple possibilities of meaning entailed in a gesture, a tonal variation or a wink. They need to trust and to check that conventional scripts and knowledge about cause, effect and their world of reference continue to enable the listener to make sense of their story. These predicators of meaning help the listener to scramble a story together from even very piecemeal information (Bower and Morrow 1990). More often than not these suffice.

When a pained inner story veils the experienced world

However, the capacity to derive meaning from even the most scrambled or incomplete information fails bitterly when a person is shocked, tired, in pain or frightened. In the throngs of emotional unwellbeing, the capacity to make sense of unstoried information is sharply reduced. Many people can recall a visit to a doctor to hear the outcome of a particularly important test: how they had been determined to remember everything they would be told and how, at the first inkling that the news was not good, the mind went into a tangle. It suddenly was hard to make sense of what was said, even though everything that was heard was perfectly understandable (Yates and Nasby 1993). The ability to make sense of language failed. The words seemed different from the story that was presumed to be spoken. Had the doctor told the information in story format instead of offering sequenced informa-tion without a story-line, we would probably have been able to discern with greater clarity what was said and to have recalled it with greater accuracy. When we are upset, shocked or in pain, we become preoccupied with our inner world. This inner story is insufficiently checked to see that it actually matches the outer circumstances (Wigren 1994). This process was aptly illustrated by Heather, a client, whose son Peter had died in a car accident some years previously. She described the following event:

> Earlier that morning her doorbell had rung. She had opened the door expecting to see a neighbour. Instead, Muriel, her sister-in-law who lived in another town, stood on the doorstep. Without a pause, Heather had sighed: 'Oh, my god, what has happened.' Momentarily not understanding Heather's response, Muriel had simply explained that she was in the area and had wanted to drop by. Then she realized that her unannounced visit echoed the other unexpected arrival, some years earlier, when she had brought the tragic news of Peter's death. On

that occasion too she had arrived without notification. Heather's response made it unambivalent that she was reliving the past and, equally, that she expected similar bad news now. They felt the potent grip of the past on their present. The two women had fallen into each other's arms and wept.

Heather's old scenario had superimposed itself on her current situation. When present and past were de-identified, she wept bitterly. She realized that she needed to work through yet another previously unrecognized trigger of her grief: sudden visits. Her recent preference for 'announced' visitors met with deepened self-understanding.

Though the circumstances of someone's life may be painful, the capacity to relate a story remains (see Bruner 1986; Gardner 1971; Gersie 1991; White and Epston 1990). The willingness to absorb or to convey a story, and thereby to comprehend vital aspects of what is taking place around them, is rarely lost (Bygrave 1994). Moreover, participation in storytelling activities can significantly strengthen a troubled person's ability to make sense of their world (Dimino *et al.* 1990).

In the wake of the Los Angeles earthquake, a woman, one of a group of dazed residents who stood outside their collapsed apartment building, said, when a reporter asked her what they were talking about: 'We're telling each other the stories of what's happened. We're telling each other the stories. It's just: we don't have the words. There are no words big enough to describe what's happened. But tell we must. It's just terrible. I myself was...' Then she embarked on her tale of the night that shook the city in the spring of 1994. Through telling and making stories we perceptually organize the life we live (Sawyer 1942). When storytelling and storymaking run into difficulties, more than a feeling of belonging is lost – the person's awareness of their place in the world dims (Moloney 1995).

Prolonged silence is constructed on the ashes of betrayal, fear or shame, hatred and hopelessness. It rests on the assumption that telling is dangerous and that the possible story will be unacceptable to a more powerful other. The unwillingness or the inability to tell generates a structure of muteness which, if it persists, ultimately leads to a contraction of humanity (Freire 1972, p.78). When the conditions of a person's daily life are dehumanizing – due to persistent poverty, violence or great lonesomeness – an eerie silence falls. At first this silence is filled with the clamour of protest. However, when the situation continues unalleviated, and the risk of merely expressing the wish for a new situation remains great, meaningful words grow to dwell beyond the reach of expression. Only the eyes continue to speak the story of the endured experience in a precisely encoded glance.

When talking does not get people anywhere, when tears are exhausted and rage is paralyzed, they cease to exercise authority over the events of their life. Devoid of authorship, deprived of agency and filled with a pervasive sense of helplessness, the person refrains from speaking their mind. Paralyzed by the inability to act in accordance with desire and needs, the individual or the group ceases to think about their efficacy in their world. The way things are, however bad this may be, is taken for granted. Thoughts about their reality, and the consideration of possible actions to change that reality, are not understood as problems to be explored. On the contrary, both the situation and the way of life are accepted as inevitability, necessary givens in a world out of which there is no escape, and beyond which no possibilities can be perceived (Coles 1989). In such circumstances it takes courage to learn to trust the inherently painful process of expressing subjective experiences and to articulate perceptions of one's situation, particularly because the memory of earlier efforts to put difficulties into words, and the fact that these had failed to result in constructive change, is also poignantly present.

The narrow margin of acceptable conversation

Many people who join a therapy group have experienced the suffering caused by speaking too little too late about important life events. They bring to this work an incomplete story about a troubling experience which causes a persistent pain. Many explain their reluctance to tell about their trouble in the detail it deserves with well rehearsed arguments in favour of highly selective life-reportage. Each of these protestations about the value of selective reportage bears sad witness to low expectations as regards the possibility of being listened to with sympathetic understanding. Some embraced the habit of superficial telling after feeling shocked by the response a particular story received from someone they loved. Prolonged exposure to indifference might also have led to important issues being left undisclosed or to the embrace of a quasi jocund pretence that all was okay, when it blatantly was not. Whatever the explanations, the outcome was similar: what mattered emotionally was hidden behind surface tales. Allison embodied this predicament. We met in a youth club where I worked. During one of our regular 'chats' I pondered out loud that, amidst all the stories, she seemed to keep her thoughts about her life pretty much to herself. She responded: 'Why should I tell your kind of people what's really happening. It will only get me into trouble. Or it gets my mum into trouble. People like you take kids away from home.' She then talked about an apparently clumsy intervention by the social services department years earlier, when she and her siblings had suddenly been taken into local authority care. The social worker's visit had

taken place immediately after Allison had talked at school about problems
at home. The intervention and its aftermath had convinced her that she
should never again say too much to any would-be helpers, such as teachers,
youth workers or probation officers. As we grew to trust each other I was
allowed to engage with her sincere conviction that it would have been
altogether better for everyone concerned had she, at the time, kept quiet
about the violence in the family following her father's redundancy. It took
time and the experience of a different kind of helping relationship to enable
her to review the memories of those years. In this process of reviewing she
learned to speak to her heart's content with greater trust and, above all, with
less fear.

   We often try to set memories of loss, shame, betrayal or disappointment
adrift, beyond the reach of the desire to speak about them, and believe
ourselves to be safer that way. Thomas, a middle-aged man who was on the
brink of some major life changes which frightened him, once wrote some
statements on the theme of 'silence':

> No-one can jump down your throat if you keep your mouth closed.
>
> You have freedom of thought as long as you keep it to yourself.
>
> You can be silent when you know you are right.
>
> One ounce of keeping your mouth closed may be worth a pound of
> explanation.

As he had primarily thought of his taciturn nature in a self-dismissive manner,
he was initially delighted to discover some thoughts which appeared to
commend his ability to maintain silence. However, the more he reflected on
what he had written, the more he felt that he actually longed to share his
concerns and wishes. Not speaking about what really mattered had become
a constraining habit. His capacity to give voice to more private thoughts had
shrivelled. He used mere headlines to describe core events. Though stories
about important occurrences were still constructed in the silence of his mind,
his self-stories had become detached from ideas made available to others.
This generated large communicative gaps which contained those aspects of
his experience that were of interpersonal concern. His inner mental model
was related to the world it represented and perceptual information rendered
into self-talk, but the means by which these inner narratives were allowed to
flow freely towards others were disrupted. The silence which ensued because
his stories were untold made both him and his untried listeners very alone.

   Luckily, the longing to share unspoken stories rarely goes entirely out of
reach. It survives, however tentatively, in the harbour of our inner realm.

Here the untold tales pursue their unvocalized, yet enacted, discourse. But the loss of a sense of recounted life authorship does not feel good. When the heart is consistently prevented from informing the tongue, trouble follows sooner rather than later. Such trouble often manifests itself in depressive or aggressive behaviour. It results in depression when a person withdraws from discursive interaction which is actually desired or in aggression when potential stories are repressed beneath the noisy claims of violence, the abuse of alcohol and drugs or chronic overwork. The rage contained in depression and the sorrowful core of substance abuse hides a distressed person's confusion about the value of revealing their life's more intimate tales. Until this confusion about talk and self-exposure is eased, the world will continue to feel very wrong.

Narrow margins of acceptable conversation create big, lonesome gaps between people who calculate whether or not to share their heart's concerns. Ever more professional listeners are hired to listen to tales of personal or interpersonal turmoil. The reluctance to make a claim on time or the sense that because others have problems too they might not want to listen, move the sharing of the toil, trouble and delight from the dining room to the consulting room. In the first instance, group work around stories aims to restore the participant's willingness to tell about life in the contrived environment of a therapeutic or educational situation; it ultimately aims to facilitate the use of a reawakened storytelling capacity in those situations that matter to the participant.

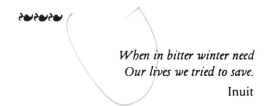

> When in bitter winter need
> Our lives we tried to save.
>
> Inuit

On latch stories and tumble tales

Many forms of therapy are based on the assumption that, when granted an opportunity and a context, we have something pertinent to say about our experiences to ourselves and to others (whether through words, imagery, sound or movement) (Nisbett and Ross 1980). I think of the work of therapy as primarily a storytelling process. In the therapeutic space, the client can try out new ways of telling, efficacious ways of responding to telling and more productive ways of going about life. In this process I use specific forms of story creation, storytelling and story responding to help a client to bring about betterment in their situation. In therapy, a client's capacity to distinguish between experiences, and the thoughts or feelings they have about those experiences, needs to be revivified. This revivification facilitates the exploration of the borderland between reactivity and responsibility (Heuscher 1974, p.114). Responsibility, at the very least, for having told these stories and for having put them together in this particular way. The responsibility for the telling, *per se*, matters, especially when a person is not yet ready to consider issues of co-responsibility for either the story's construction or for its emergence. Through facilitated storytelling, the client learns to re-construe their perspective on what happened. He or she is also helped to enter into a more fruitful relationship with the events reflected in their stories. This involves clarification of their understanding of the storied events in terms of what they believe to be morally valued, appropriate and uncertain. These are particularly vital arenas of exploration when pain has turned the rich inner terrain into some barren jungle of hopeless thought for far too long, for such pain obliterates a person's connection with the meaningful context that gives direction to their efforts (Scarry 1985).

Long-term forgetfulness of intentionality has extremely serious consequences. It renders a person not merely inactive, it gives birth to irresponsibility. Heuscher (1974) makes an important distinction between reactivity and responsibility. Responsibility, in his terms, refers to the inner experience of choice between various alternatives and the capacity to exercise choice. Reactivity describes those behaviours about which we feel we had no choice. Whereas the capacity to respond implies a degree of detachment and judgment, the capacity to react is linked with instinctive, spontaneous immediacy. Though we are nothing without it, reactivity is far from everything. Once participants in storymaking re-accept the narrator's position and attempt to make their life comprehensible in new terms, they become, though not necessarily without reluctance, aware of the changing tides of their perspective. This enables them to consider: 'If I think this now, and I thought that yesterday, then how does this affect my ideas and how do my ideas affect my way of being in the world?' This kind of reflection results from interactive narration. The very act of storytelling demands the continuous re-positioning of the storyteller in relation to him or herself, to the listeners and to the told story.

I can still hear the voice of a middle-aged woman, whom I shall call Sheila. The psychiatrist's letter which accompanied her referral described her as 'a typical revolving door patient' who had been severely depressed for many years. She had returned to the psychiatric hospital at regular intervals for further treatment. During our first meeting, Sheila said: 'Why should anyone want to listen to my stories? Why should they? I'm just an ordinary person.

I've done nothing special. Nothing bad and nothing good. I got up in the morning, had my breakfast, spent the day and went to sleep. That's all I ever did, you see. I haven't told anyone stories for years.' When at last our eyes met, she allowed me to see how adrift she was. I felt that she was bursting at her inner seams with the need to tell, if only because she too longed for a confirmed existence (Williams 1995). One simple glance and the abundance of her inner world – which overflowed with anecdotes and hopeful and bitter tales – was, in principle, acknowledged. The rest was merely a matter of time. In that brief exchange of exploring looks we became somewhat less distant strangers. I queried: 'But it's by no means all you ever thought or felt?' Unfolding a most tender smile, she sighed; 'If I told you what I thought about what I've seen, we'd be sitting here for years...!'

Like Sheila, many of us tell a well-tried, yet limited, repertoire of life stories – if only because they are familiar. However, when someone listens attentively to what we say and to how we say what we say, tales may be drawn out of us which we have not told before. Such stories may have lingered for many years on the edge of awareness, yet failed to make the crucial transition to articulation. I remember an old Buddhist monk who spoke about the pain he had felt many years earlier when he had seen a young couple fondly embracing beneath a tree in a park. Upon his return to the monastery he had not spoken about his experience. His silence had been rooted in numerous explanations, not the least of which was his love for a woman who had made kindred religious vows. He had feared that speaking about the young couple would have meant speaking about the woman: one tale calling forth another. Thus the latch-story, as I like to call such an untold tale, remained unspoken, simply because he supposed, not unreasonably, that once shared with a truly listening person, the story would unleash an unstoppable current of other tales.

The stories that are unlocked when a latch-story is told burst forth not only because of the felt relief at finally being able to speak one's truth, but also because a sympathetic listener welcomes the story into existence. A careful listener registers the changes in the teller's voice and posture, the choice of words or the way sentences are constructed, the enthusiasm (or lack of it) with which an event is recounted and the sequence and acceleration of events as well as a story's aftertaste. Initially these notations provide little more than miscellaneous information; however, after several stories have been told, the ways of telling accumulate into a pattern. This awareness of habit and style leads to an enriched understanding of what the storyteller means to convey through their telling. This is their meta-story. Rennie (1994) suggests that regardless of whether a teller intends to contact feelings associated with their story, once the storytelling has been initiated it will develop its own momentum, intentionality and consequences. In surprise, such a teller might say: 'I didn't know I was going to tell you *that*. The story just slipped out of me.' In therapeutic group work each storytelling activity must optimally strengthen a teller's capacity to tell such storied events safely and to integrate the experience of having at long last told the story into their overall life narrative.

Robert Coles (1989), a psychiatrist, remarked that people who need to see a doctor, minister, counsellor or therapist bring them their stories in the hope that they will tell the stories well enough so that the truth of their lives may be understood. Therapy is concerned with the alleviation of suffering. It aims to bring about healing as quickly, efficiently and efficaciously as possible. If we accept the notion that storymaking is a fundamental way of making our interpretation of events and ideas available to others, then the establishment of the best possible procedures for the co-creation of relevant narrative, and for making optimal use of interpersonal resources, is of the utmost importance in all forms of therapeutic practice. This requires the early generation of a client's faith in the possibility that a sufficiently meaningful, and, therefore, 'good enough', life story can be helped to emerge (Laube and Trefz 1993) – a story that will have its roots in the same actual life experience but which, through re-telling and re-exploration, embraces new emphases, resulting in greater meaning, energy and ease.

In my work with troubled people, many of whom are initially very reluctant to accept authorship for their deeds, let alone responsibility for their process of healing, I have noticed that some degree of relief from emotional and/or physical pain was found whenever I was able to help the person initially to tell about their experience within the protective analogy of a story. Such a story might either be a traditional tale, a newly created fictional story or a memory tale. I found that some important processes of healing were activated merely through enhancing a troubled person's ability to construct numerous stories at will (see Pennebaker 1993).

Come and let us sing together,
Let us now begin our converse.
Finnish-Ugarithic

A brief description of Therapeutic Storymaking

Therapeutic storymaking (TSM) is a form of creative-expressive group work which focuses on the restoration of people's ability to tell stories and the parallel development of their willingness to interact meaningfully with other people's stories in order to alleviate emotional pain. In the therapeutic group work situation, the participants learn to tell stories and to listen to and respond to each other as carefully and attentively as is humanly possible. A client who had recently joined a group said: 'My own stories are bad enough. I'm not sure I want to tackle the rest.' When someone has been ill or troubled for a long time, social purpose and bonds are often badly affected. This makes it even more urgent to aim to re-tie the myriad connections that exist between us. Storytelling activities raise awareness of how deeply involved we are with images, meanings and social bonds. They do so in a manner which is manageable for a distressed person. Whatever we do and wherever we are, our action is always situated (Bruner 1990, p.19). In the process of telling stories, group members not only articulate experience, they learn to demand space, have their say and ensure that they are heard whilst they develop a habit of exploring judgments. Meanwhile, each storyteller has to come to grips with the fact that more often than not they search to express something that can never really be grasped, simply because words aren't big enough.

Gergen and Gergen (1983) postulate that when we change our story in important ways, we concurrently and inevitably change both our way of going about things and the meanings available to us. In TSM this aim is pursued through structured storytelling and storymaking activities. In the course of a brief number of sessions (average 8–12 sessions of 2 hours duration) group members are introduced to some pertinent traditional stories. They also learn to create and to tell new meaningful stories at will. The interaction with each story is structured around visual, movement, sound or writing exercises. These include various creative-expressive audience feedback response-tasks. These latter techniques provide group members with written or visual feedback from others about a specific aspect of their story. In other words, each storyteller invites the listeners to address, through a painted, written or enacted response, a particular issue in their story. At the observable level, group members are seen to meet in a circle, to participate in introductory exercises, to make and tell stories by means of further exercises and to respond to other people's stories through so-called response-tasks. These latter tasks are specifically designed for the particular person, their situation and their story. When these are a painting or a written response, the responses are later given to the storyteller. Upon receiving their 'gifts', the storyteller looks at what has been made especially for him or her. Then they explore the impact of the 'gifts' on their understanding of their story and their life's events.

During a TSM session various time-limited, creative-expressive tasks are offered in easy, rhythmic sequentiality. These tasks are clearly defined and individually relevant in terms of a group member's personal history, their developmental needs and the stated aims for their participation in a group. I have found that 'what' a group member is asked to do in activity-based group work, must be interesting, surprising, satisfying and stimulate thought. The storymaking work is structured to be both challenging and relatively easy to perform – this matters particularly for groups with a low boredom or competition threshold. Group interaction patterns are likewise conducted by means of unfamiliar, yet comfortably different, exercises. Interpersonal feedback about the storytelling and response-making is given in such a manner that it can be thought about, shared and integrated. The facilitator's creativity is expressed in the formulation of these tasks, their therapeutic skill in the timing of use, the holding of the therapeutic purpose and the working towards the establishment of manifest change.

Through these explicit procedures, which include exercises to strengthen a person's listening, making, telling, responding, receiving and reflecting abilities, TSM group members are helped to develop a more self-reflective, informed relationship with their stories and, thereby, with both their life-events and other people. They participate in a process of self-interpretation through storymaking which focuses on meaning clarification. This involves the elaboration of purpose, the recognition of efficacy and control, the examination of justifications and values and the recognition of self-worth (Baumeister and Newman 1994). Whilst much of this occurs through the use of verbal language, movement, visual and sound-based exercises are also used to underpin this process. These various activities support group members' experience with the never-ending process of attempting to translate desired change into actual change.

However, the right stories and exercise-patterns introduced at the right time do not alone suffice to bring about healing change. In TSM, as in other forms of group work, healing change emerges from a group culture which generates respect, sympathy and reassurance, from the exploration of exercises and their linkage with emotionally laden issues and from the systematic use of relationships in which change can be engendered. Amongst these relationships, the one between group facilitator and participants is of paramount importance. In TSM the facilitator steadily encourages distributed leadership, promotes self-esteem, bolsters the courage to query and to interact, safeguards norms, supports the expression and exploration of feelings and explains emotional or behavioural responses to ordinary and extra-ordinary situations (Heron 1977). They serve the group to enhance each group member's optimum mastery of problematic areas. A space is provided where participants can be with other people to tell and make up stories, to laugh, to weep, to express bitterness or irritation and to change their mind; to begin to trust an atmosphere where it is possible to give and to receive feedback in all manner of ways. Though the creation of such a space relies on solid knowledge of technique and theory, it is created with the heart and inspired by humanized understanding (Pines 1989).

The capacity to develop through learning is closely related to curiosity, defined for now as a desire to find an explication, an interpretation as well as an explanation, for something that is of interest. The ability to be curious and inquisitive matters. Our life depends on it (Piaget 1952, p132). Therapeutic storymaking supports this vital process of constructive exploration in three ways:

- by arousing interest in events and people that might otherwise be taken for granted
- by providing satisfaction of the desire for explication and feedback, whilst forestalling that this closes the exploratory process
- by offering practice in countless ways to initiate, use and develop interpersonal relationships by means of engagement in storytelling activities.

These three curiosity-supporting functions are fundamental to the uses of story in therapy. They guide the selection, the specific application and the evaluation of efficacy of any stories or storymaking and storytelling modes used.

3. What Kind of Stories?

When I tell a new person that I work both as a teacher and a therapist, and enjoy using stories in my practice, I often get the response: 'Oh, that sounds really interesting...' The words will be uttered in a distant, dreamy kind of way. Nowadays this doesn't surprise me, but when it first happened I couldn't help but feel that these words were meant to prepare me for an imminent conversational closing move. However, more often than not, something else occurred. The person who had just asked me what I did would continue with: 'But what kind of stories? Like Snow White or Peter Pan?' Then, ignoring the usual give-and-take of discourse between newly acquainted people and as if the very mention of Snow White and Peter Pan activated some distant realm, my interlocutor's personal reflections would come tumbling out. The very word 'story' triggered a long-since unvisited store of early memories and longings. Suddenly I would be granted entry into the private world of favourite stories, the circumstances of telling or reading, of secret whisperings, buttered scones and tea, grandparents' visits or tree-huts.

A distant, dreamy way

During one of these conversations, a man, who works as an international government adviser, pondered: 'I actually tell a lot of stories whilst I play golf. That's mostly what we do when we play.' With surprise in his voice, he continued: 'Yes, that's mostly what we do. Whilst walking from one hole to the next with a heavy bag on our shoulders, we tell each other stories. I guess you could say that we're a group of wandering storytellers. I like that: a wandering group of storytellers.' When asked what made this so clearly important, he replied without much hesitation: 'To have the space to share experiences. That's what you do when you tell stories. Don't you agree?'

When later I reflected on the change that had come over this man as he talked about storytelling (from a brisk sullenness to bright friendliness), I set his thoughts and memories next to those of other people of all ages, poverty or affluence, creeds, race and gender, and was struck by the similarities in the reasons they gave to explain the importance of making experience into a story and then telling about it:

'It makes you feel you are someone who has got something to say.'

'Stories bring experiences back to life whilst you share them.'

'It is not just an exchange of information. You get a shared response like laughter, or distress. It articulates communion.'

'It shows you possibilities you didn't consider'.

'I guess they also exercise social control.'

In his attempt to convey to me the magic as well as the logic of some kind of 'storytelling golf', the man cited above created not only a bridge between our two rather different worlds but he also generated a new explanatory narrative that justified his actions to himself and his important others as well as his social others (Sloan and Solano 1984). Most of the time we attempt to do just that. In the right environment, both traditional and personal stories facilitate reflective dialogue. Through discussion and elaboration they contribute to the integration of complex life experiences into the ordinary fabric of human community. In the attempt to achieve imaginative verisimilitude, the storyteller skilfully manipulates the felt tension between fictional and empirical reality. This quality of story-emergence allows for the concurrence of events in the putative real world with those recounted in the tale. Especially when we feel poor in a poor place, we need to create or hear stories about perilous journeys to distant mountains or about victim heroes and heroines who invent riddles which only the most clever can solve. Above all, however, we need to share such stories.

In my group work with stories, I use three identifiable types of narrative to enable both the exploration of the realities represented in a story and the clarification of the story-teller's relationship with the storied situation or experience. These narrative forms are separated for the purpose of discussion, even though they are more like a chorus of mutually-entailed resonances. They include stories from the oral tradition, newly made fictional tales which borrow images and storied pathways for their heroes and heroines from traditional tales, and personal stories in the form of tales from memory. The narratives have in common that they are created or told because they contain vital information and because they pull, in some way or other, at a homesickness for a land of our own dreaming. That is why the development of an informed relationship with these storied images matters. The lure of mere passive dreaming is ever present in the realm of story-work. The three ways of storying belong together in what might best be called an ecological way – like the rain, the soil and the tree. Each narrative domain reflects remnants of the other stories' impact, their history and fruitfulness (Jacobs 1971).

Traditional stories

Traditional stories have for centuries been part of a people's oral tradition. They have been passed from one person to another by word of mouth through a process in which faithfulness to the received version mattered more than originality. The English word 'folktale' is highly inclusive. It covers all kinds of traditional narrative and applies to forms as diverse as sacred myths of creation, western European fairy tales, the elaborate frame-stories of the *Arabian Nights*, or Greek and Roman myths about Orpheus or Demeter. Folklorists have come to use terms such as Legends, Animal Tales, That's why stories, Myths and Fairy tales with some degree of definiteness (Kirk 1970, pp.1–4). However, the boundaries between these forms of story are loose, and the academic debate about the respective territories is alive and well.

Legends have their roots in historical accounts, though over time the exploits of the heroes and heroines have often become flatteringly exaggerated. They link with a special place – such as an unusual building or an old tree or centre on an object, for example an ancient piece of cloth, a stone or a tool. The story conveys a fragile, yet enduring memory of events a long, long time ago.

Myths describe the emergence, intentions, concerns and field of actions of the Gods or of a God. They narrate how the universe at large, or the earth in particular, came to be. They clarify our understanding of life's purpose and predict the pattern of its future unfolding. Humankind's most intimate search to make some kind of sense out of our brief sojourn in this vast universe is reflected in myths which explain our struggle with death, suffering, meaning, destiny, sacrifice and afterlife. Time and again the answers found by a people have been recorded in their myths, and been granted absolute, sacred status. This tendency to render myths absolute continues to this day. It has all manner of undesirable consequences: wars, lack of forgiveness and shunning are but some of these. How to develop a human relationship with the sacred, which is built upon respect, compassion and tolerance, is an enduring challenge for all myth-makers.

Fairy tales are the young cousins of myth. Most began their long life in the oral tradition. Some were first written as a short story, and later entered the airborne world of storytelling. These stories grant us entry into realms where animals, fairy queens, ogres, fairy godmothers, ghosts, gnomes and people live side by side. In this land, Newton's laws do not apply. Mysterious feats are continuously performed. Though some people believe that fairy tales almost always have a blessed ending, this is by no means the case. Many a fairy-tale character is cruelly killed or endures years of hardship, only to perish in despair.

Animal tales explain how animals have come to behave in the way they do. They contain precise observations of an animal's behaviour and environment. Such stories honour a creature's strength, whereabouts, dangers and useful-ness. They also clarify our own place in the natural world and position people next to animals instead of above them. Human wit is set against animal wit, human strength next to animal strength. Another category of tale, the so-called **'That's why' stories,** is closely related to animal tales. They provide causal explanations for natural phenomena which were interesting or bewildering at the time the story was created. The stories render the inexplicable less peculiar by proffering explanations.

These categories of story can be gathered together under the umbrella title of **'traditional tales'**. They have in common that they are retold more or less as remembered. The story-re-teller is occasionally required to adhere to strict instructions regarding the conditions under which a story might be retold. Such conditions often relate to precision of wording, intonation, presentation and performance conditions, such as time of year, day and place (Marriott 1963, pp.v–xv). However, the majority of traditional stories may be freely told. The stories contain memories, information and understanding of a highly specific nature. They are a history and emotional map of sorts. Whereas in the early stage of a story's creation an attempt may have been made to represent an event or some information as accurately as possible, over time the story represents its original source more obliquely. The storytelling event repolishes a tale with different concerns and priorities.

I understand myths and folktales as forms of psycho-philosophical knowledge which preserve in encoded, symbolic form a people's awareness, knowledge and guidance about fundamental aspects and preoccupations of their lives. The stories implicitly present ways of dealing with everyday concerns. I select particular tales for use in group work by considering their completeness, complexity, coherence and relevance in relation to the specific problems of the group at hand. Each story transmits a historical legacy and confirms the existence of times, customs or even peoples that no longer exist. This matters to group members who often feel forgotten and excluded from the historicity of their own time.

Approaches to the study of myth and folktale

Various theoretical schools argue for a particular approach to the study of myths or folktales, each of which differently defines the domain of myth and folktales and offers alternative propositions of why a myth or folktale was constructed in a particular way, of where it originated, how it developed, what its function was in the society which valued its meanings and how it related to other stories of its kind. The nineteenth century saw a flurry of interest in myths, stories and folktales. The activities of the brothers Grimm are the best known amongst these. They were, however, not exceptional in their investigative and collecting activities. Many other scholars realized that old myths and folktales were a valuable heritage and phenomenon (Georges 1968, pp.12–14). Explanations about why this material mattered abounded. Though many nineteenth century approaches to the study of myth and folktale have long since been discredited, they continue to exercise influence on various theoreticians of story and are therefore worth noting. During the nineteenth century the newly discovered relationships between languages led to a strong philological approach to the study of connections between myths from different peoples. Brinton (1868), a proponent of this school, wrote: 'The inquiry will be put whether the aboriginal languages of America employ the same tropes to express such ideas as deity, spirit and soul, as our own and kindred tongues.' He believed that the object of this inquiry was majestic, namely to 'draw evidence of the unity of our species far weightier than any unity of anatomy, evidence of the oneness of emotion and thought' (p.5). Lang (1885), his most vociferous critic, responded to this position: 'The objections to this method are so numerous that it is difficult to state them. …The method is called "orthodox", but among those who practice it, there is none of the beautiful unanimity of orthodoxy' (pp.2–3). Their differences remain unresolved and inspire the debate about uni-focal versus poly-focal human evolution to this day.

Meanwhile, the astro-mythological school (sometimes also called the zoological mythological school) developed its own theory. Proponents of this view suggest that traditional stories can best be understood if seen as translations of astronomical observations and as metaphors for both the weather and the dawn–day–sunset–night sequence, in which each morning gives birth to a new solar hero who is destined to perish (night) and yet will triumph (the new day). In response to the debate about evolution theory, concerns were also raised about the derivation of folktales from multiple centres (independent origination or polygenesis) or from one single centre and thence to have departed on their long distributive journey (diffusion). Lang was also an articulate proponent of the polygenesis option. His work, which aimed to open folklore and mythology studies to a wide range of theoretical explorations, was once more stifled into a uniform theoretical frame by Tylor and Frazer who argued in favour of a logical and parallel sequence of stages of development of thought amongst so-called primitive peoples (Gaster 1959).

Not until this century did Malinovski (1922) somewhat ease the hold of structure-bound approaches on the interpretation of myths and fairy tales. He articulated the view that myths should be considered as charters for customs, institutions or beliefs, which they validate. His study of the mythic world of the Trobiand Islanders effectively established that myths are extremely important elements of culture, and that therefore such cultural components must be studied and understood in order to formulate an approximate understanding of how the myth might function for the people whose story it is. Though Malinovski's work was given a warm reception, the plethora of explanations which rely on explanations interior to the myth has continued with the voices of Freud, Jung, Levi-Strauss, Campbell, Eliade and Neumann. In their work, the search for 'ur-forms' (the pure form from which all others derive) has not been abandoned, nor has the longing for some kind of invariant picture of the human psyche or the hope to find in myths archaic revelations of timeless existential themes (Cunningham 1973). The project which aimed to establish with St Paul that 'God has made of one blood all nations of the earth, that they should seek the Lord, if haply they might feel after him and find him, though he is not far from everyone of us', remains alive and well (Brinton 1976).

Opposition against this approach to the study of myth and folktales was primarily formulated by Boas (1940) and Thompson (1977). Thompson draws attention to the fact that it is characteristic of scholars who seek to find some general principle of myth that they are more interested in motifs than in complete tales, and that this has led to the most diverse and mutually exclusive explanations (p.383). His emphasis on the need to collect both motifs and whole tales has resulted in the detailed study of more complex tales, particularly by folklore scholars. This so-called historical–geographical method for analyzing folktales includes the assembling of all known variants of a tale or myth and their careful description in order to identify both the story's most stable structure and specific traits. The systematic study of the frequency of individual trait occurrence, the density or otherwise of a story's distribution and the identification of striking qualities enables a map to be drawn up which traces the character, history and geography of an entire complex tale with its variants. However, this method does not take account of the environmental or cultural factors which also influence a story's content. The teacher or group worker who wants to use stories in their practice not only faces the task of finding their own position amidst this plethora of interpretative possibilities but, in addition, needs to clarify how such a story might be optimally used in their situation. Theories about stories are one thing; theories about the application of stories to a therapeutic or educational setting are a linked, but different, matter of concern.

Traditional stories and group work

As recently as thirty years ago there was no established therapeutic or educational practice which made systematic use of traditional stories and virtually no theory to suggest how it might be done. Psychoanalytic study of myth was restricted to interpretations of underlying psychological configurations (Bettelheim 1975). Anthropological study focused on meanings and social and cognitive functions of myths in their cultural context. Philosophically-oriented study of comparative mythology was restricted to graduate university courses. While a few scholars of folklore/comparative religion – such as Thompson, Eliade, Luthi, Burland and Campbell – indicated that stories and myths were ways of informing one's life, they did not suggest how this could be translated into behaviour, let alone a group work method (Campbell 1959; Eliade 1957; Luthi 1975). I hypothesized that there are connections between what individuals believe can be narrated, their capacity to narrate, and their experiences of narrating – that is, how individuals recount stories, and what they emphasize or omit, shapes what they claim of their reality. I therefore developed a group work method in which the facilitator and the participants explore together how these dynamics of influence operate, and call this Therapeutic Storymaking (TSM). Recently the school of narrative psychology has also posited that people organize life experience as a story (Bruner 1986). They define such stories as particular kinds of narrative constructions, which are told to self and others throughout life and are influenced by a person's current understandings and perceived life-constraints (Freeman 1993; Linde 1993). However, narrative psychology conceives of these stories in the mode of monologue and text, thus it excludes the listener in the therapeutic situation from involvement in the evocation of narrative. TSM emphasizes the story as an emergent dialogue and performance. It utilizes the listener's engagement in a speaker's narrative construction and facilitates constructive re-narration by means of creative-expressive dialogue-based processes (response tasks).

The groupworker who wants to work with traditional stories needs to be aware that theoretical discussions focus on myth as:

○ a proclamation of the holy

○ 'gestaltete Welterkenntnis' (which, in English, might best be described as 'knowledge of the world and about the world, embedded in forms which are greater than the combined value of their symbolic component parts might suggest)

○ a functional aspect of religion, not as purely theoretical speculation but in the broadest sense as the vital basis for all human action.

Considerations such as these have had substantial consequences for the uses of story in therapeutic situations (Schuurman 1963). Participants who join a therapeutic storymaking group often have some desire to learn about stories or storytelling. They also want to clarify themes such as the presence of pain, purpose and meaning in their life. Moreover, they often have deeply ambivalent feelings about religious education and church life yet want to learn for themselves 'how sacred songs are made'.[1] The re-evocation of a sense of wonder is fundamental to groupwork with stories. Not only do participants not approach storywork with the attitude that the 'literary value of a great deal of primitive literature, whether myths or tales, is *nil*' (Kroeber 1959, p.7) but literary value is not at stake. Close beneath their interest in stories and storytelling lies the longing to know more about the compound relation between body/mind and word/world as encapsulated in traditional stories and as relevant to themselves (Maclagan 1977). They embody the eternal search to become more fully human by gaining access to storied realms which illumine their human existence (Dunne 1973). Many clients echo Chomsky's (1971) belief that 'it would be tragic if those who are fortunate enough to live in the advanced societies of the West were to forget or to abandon the hope that our world can be transformed to a world in which the creative spirit is alive, in which life is an adventure full of hope and joy, based rather upon the impulse to construct than upon the desire to retain what we possess or to seize what is possessed by others.' (p.83). They seek a transformation of kinds through a deepened understanding of complex life themes. The

---

1 Halifax (1979, p.30) quotes an old woman diviner whom Knud Rasmussen, the great explorer and anthropologist, met during his journeys amongst the Alaskan Inuit. One of Rasmussen's notes quotes this woman from the island of Little Diomede as saying: 'For our forefathers believed that the songs were born in stillness while all endeavoured to think of nothing but beautiful things. Then they take shape in the minds of men and rise up like bubbles from the depths of the sea, bubbles seeking air in order to burst. This is how sacred songs are made.'

echo of the question 'What then is the light of mankind?', which King Janaka asked of Yajnavalkya in one of the Upanishads, lies never far from the surface of such groups (Burland 1974, p.250). How to address such needs adequately in the group becomes a shared search.

> *What use is there in your assembling*
> *together in the great hall*
> *only to go to sleep?*
> Zen Buddhism – Japan

The uses of traditional stories: simple telling

Stories which are passed by word of mouth from one person to the next rely for their survival on four constraints: comparative brevity, perspicuity, relevance and truthfulness (Calvino 1992). These constraints are particularly important in the therapeutic context, where a participant's ability to describe something concisely or to embellish life's stories at will has frequently been lost to a torrential onslaught of contradictory feelings which submerge the felt craving for purposeful telling about life and its various events. The restoration of the ability to tell a story within the possibilities offered by these constraints may help a troubled person to recover some stable emotional ground. When a person's life story is stuck in repetition or is still too painful to be told, traditional stories can provide a platform for emotional exploration, or simply some necessary encouragement or consolation – particularly because no retelling is ever the same (Bruner 1993).

The most straightforward use of a traditional story in therapy or education involves simple retelling. The following Nootka myth is a good example of the kind of story that might be introduced to a group. Several therapists told me that they shared this story with distressed clients who felt scornful of their reluctance to face their difficulties.

> Someone stands by the sea, overlooking the wide water. A person stands and looks at the sea. There are rocks on the coast and trees. Trees which are twisted and stripped of bark. Rocks which are twisted, as if in pain. Turning, turning away from the sea. The trees and the rocks are screwed into agonized shapes, because they tried to flee from where they could not move. They had seen Sisiutl, the gruesome monster from the sea. Sisiutl has two heads, one at each end of his body. Heads which fill us with the greatest fear we shall ever know.

Whosoever sees Sisiutl, knows but one blind urge. To run. To run as fast as feet will carry, as far as the land will reach. For the Monster who dwells deep in the sea is terrifying to behold, and clasps our heart in frozen, haunting terror.

This is how it is.

You stand on the beach and see Sisiutl. You want to run. And yet, you know that if you run, you shall be like the trees and the rocks. Turning, twisting, spinning, lost. Forever wandering. Forever terrified. Meanwhile the waves will carry Sisiutl toward you. The mouths cast cutting panic into your soul. All thoughts cease. You want to tear yourself away. The heads come closer, and you know that if you run, you shall run forever. The wind too holds its breath. The air you gasp is filled with Sisiutl's foul stench. No rescue anywhere. Nowhere to go. No way of going. And the devouring mouths come closer. Whatever you do, stay firm. Do not run away. If you know words of protection, say them, and above all else, stay firm.

The next wave, and Sisiutl's heads shall close in upon you. This you know. They reach towards you. Closer and closer. Both mouths open. One more move, and they shall fasten upon you, fasten upon you forever. And in spite of this, you stand firm.

The last wave. Both heads turn towards you. Then this happens. Just before the twin mouths touch you, each head suddenly sees the other, because you are there. Because they both want to be near you, Sisiutl sees his other face, and whosoever sees the other half of Self, sees Truth.

Sisiutl, the gruesome monster of the sea, spends eternity in search of Truth, seeking those who dare stand firm. Who let him look into his own eyes, into his own other face.

Then Sisiutl will bless you with his truth. Truth which will be yours forever. And the vision people will visit you often, reminding you of the place where truth may be found. You are no longer alone.'[2]

On the rare occasions that I myself have shared this story with a client a poignant silence has followed my telling – as if the story clarified my client's suicidal longings, their exhaustion, anger, fear and their blind hope for change without quite knowing how to go about achieving this, other than to stop running away. I have told the story as a simple gift for my client's state of giving up on giving up. Such storytelling and such silence is pregnant with meaning and possibility. During any period of major emotional up-

---

2 Retold by the author. The principal source of the tale is Cameron (1984).

heaval or profound exhaustion the body is exposed to high levels of hyper-excitation, which cause the person to feel isolated. This felt lonesomeness often results in a blurring of the apparent boundaries between factual circumstances and felt realities. Prolonged exposure to intense intra-psychic activity can result in a de-differentiation in the matrices of thought and feeling. People then crumble more than just a little, they sense that they are about to collapse – as indeed they might if no re-structuring or rest-creating intervention takes place. The temporary partial loss of a sense of identity due to emotional overload, which demands rest and recuperation, is not easily accepted – particularly because, in such a state, we feel uncertain in the presence of others (May 1969). After all, 'our place in the action' has become unclear. If all goes well, the slide into isolation and uncertainty is halted. Then, instead of running, the person becomes able to tolerate their burning rage, despair or fear. In such a 'period of staying with the feelings' they are granted the opportunity to become truly alone in the presence of others and to realize more fully 'life and what was made of it'.

When a person has become strong against the pull of exhaustion or emotional disintegration, they may walk again towards their people, hold out a hand and say something like: 'Hello' (Miller 1988, p.242). That may not sound like a great deal. However, it makes all the difference for, in such renewed encounters with the other, people become felt presences. They are no longer appearing and disappearing instantaneously, as they are likely to have been doing until then. Some therapeutic theoreticians would say that the client has strengthened object constancy (Lacan 1979, pp.230–262). The return from a temporary experience of '*reculer sans sauter*' is frequently marked by a jumping forwards, inspired by fresh awareness of the life that follows, precisely because it involves the adoption of a scheme or a system of thought which made sense of the distress. Once this occurs, a new innocence of the eye and a stronger ability to enter into a fruitful relationship with another person have been developed.

The story of Sisiutl is told primarily in such a tender, raw atmosphere. Those present know the reality of the fear and sense of dread, and the profundity of the hope for a blessing. Told at the right moment, it becomes a sacred gift; at the wrong moment it may be an insult or even risk further emotional injury. How to judge that the moment is 'right' is a knack and a knowledge which can be taught only to a limited extent. The capacity for good 'telling timing' derives from intimate, processed knowledge about the experience of the actual moment, a clear sense of the location of this moment in the greater pattern of the client's and one's own life and an informed understanding of what the persistent calling of the story, on the edge of awareness where it requests articulation, might be about. After such attentive inner processing, a therapist-storyteller needs to decide whether to tell the tale, merely to refer to it or to use the tremble of the storied metaphor in the mind's eye as simply another level of information about the dynamics present in the encounter between themselves and their client.

Practice vignette: to find a story for John

This process is illustrated in the following case-example from individual brief story work I undertook with a troubled and isolated twelve-year-old boy.

During my first diagnostic session with John we explored a range of issues, including 'a bad memory in his life'. He described how some years earlier he had suddenly been invited to go to a friend's house after a long period of silence because they had fallen out. He had hopefully cycled there. When he arrived in his friend's street he had been set upon by his former friend and a gang of other boys. The phone call had been a scornful trap. Not quite succumbing to the pain evoked by his memory, he queried: 'That was a terrible thing to have done?' We reflected on his uncertainty and, shortly after, concluded our first session. The assessment would continue the next week. After the session, his description of the scene with his friends resonated with me. I pondered what kind of stories, associations and personal resonances his memory evoked for me. The first story that came to mind was a classic tale of betrayal, the ancient Norwegian myth of Loki and Baldur. Briefly, in this myth Baldur is killed by a mistletoe arrow which the blind Hod unknowingly throws. Loki had tricked Hod into throwing the deadly arrow for the sole reason that he wanted Baldur to die, whilst not wanting to cast the arrow himself. The story caused me to wonder what murderous or omnipotent fantasies were transferentially being generated. The finiteness of Baldur's death did, however, make the use of this story in therapeutic work with John at this stage inappropriate. My focus stayed with tales of trickery. The Massai story of 'How the elephant died' jumped to the fore during my inner consultation of my repertoire of remembered stories.

In this tale, Hare, a notorious trickster-character, wants to cross a river. When looking around for a suitable carrier, he notices an elephant with a large bag of honey on his back, which he is taking to some relatives. Hare adores honey and soon he convinces Elephant to carry him across the water. Comfortably seated on Elephant's back, Hare begins to eat the honey. Whenever Elephant asks what he feels dropping onto his back, Hare replies: 'Those are but the tears of a poor creature weeping'. He eats even the very last drop of honey. On the other side of the river Hare and Elephant part.

When some time later Elephant discovers what trick Hare has played on him, he begins a furious pursuit. The story continues:

> Whilst Hare was running along he spotted a group of Baboons. He pleaded for help. Ponderously the Baboons inquired what caused him to run with such great fear. Hare cried that he was being chased by an enormous creature. The Baboons comforted Hare and offered to protect him. He no longer needed to be frightened. They gave Hare shelter in their home whilst they kept guard outside. A little later Elephant also came that way. He asked the Baboons if they had seen Hare. They turned his question over this way and that. Finally they demanded to know what price he was willing to offer if they told him Hare's whereabouts. Elephant said he would give them whatever they asked for. They wanted a cup full of his blood. First he looked to see that the cup was a small one, then Elephant consented. The Baboons made a hole in his neck and Elephant's blood gushed forth. Time passed. The Baboons were still filling the cup, Elephant asked wearily: 'Is the cup not full yet?' They showed it to him. It was only half full. The Baboons had made a hole in the bottom of the cup and whenever they showed it to Elephant he saw that it was not full yet. The Baboons made fun of him. They said that he lacked courage. Could he not even fill such a little cup with his own blood? They bled him and bled him. The cup was never filled. Elephant sank to the ground. There he died. Hare was no longer frightened. He left his hiding place. (Gersie 1992, pp.130–132)

I was clearly still focused on themes of deception, violence and death. This impressed upon me the extent of John's rage and sorrow. I also wondered whether anyone in his family circle had died and, if so, how recently. I reflected that the management of feelings about death and destruction was, in all likelihood, a major issue for him and I wanted to clarify with John the extent of his awareness of feelings around these issues. I also needed to ascertain with greater accuracy how much expressive access he had to emotional range and what use he made of internalized relationships. I also needed to explore further how attainable his ego-ideals were in order to help him to modify his ways of dealing with the ordinary frustrations and disappointments that inevitably arise in life.[3]

---

3   Though John was not a latency age child, his self-indication that some aspect of him was stuck in this period started me thinking along 'latency intervention' lines. For a good discussion of therapy goals in the early stages of such practice, see Ackerly (1967).

In my repertoire of stories I found several tales which connected with John's feelings about his misjudgment of the situation with his friend. After all, not one human condition, problem or hope is not also meaningfully addressed in a folktale or myth (Heuscher 1974, p.374). The important question, therefore, was not would there be a pertinent story but how to decide pertinence (Barker 1985). I had to be as certain as possible that the experience contained within such a story was likely to contribute to the constructive reworking of John's life-limiting self-narrative which turned around the theme 'nobody can be trusted really'. This certainty would offer me good enough guidance as to how to use the emotional imagery of a story in order to promote his desired change.

As I further explored the images evoked by the tales which I had considered but rejected, and tried to understand better why they did not feel right, I recalled John's voice when he had said: 'That was a terrible thing to have done?' At the time he spoke these words, they had confirmed my earlier impression that he was capable of self-empathy. This had been reassuring for I knew that once we are empathic with ourselves, our capacity for self-reflection can be enhanced. Had he not uttered those crucial words or expressed self-concern in similar ways, it is unlikely that I would have recommended him as a suitable candidate for a brief therapy. I would have advised both a longer assessment period and, probably, a different modality of longer-term therapy. Once damaged, our self-empathic capacity can be restored through receiving good enough informed empathy from another person, particularly a therapist, who in addition offers us his or her explanation of how we are understood (Goldberg 1988). Indeed, this possibility for emphatic repair is one of the basic assumptions of most forms of psychotherapy. Maybe the look on my face in response to his story had helped, maybe other imperceptible body movements, or my later reflections, or maybe none of these, had contributed to John's questioning statement: 'That was a terrible thing to have done?' His intended narrative had conveyed: 'This event happened to me and there were horrible consequences'. His unintended, what Makari and Shapiro (1993) call 'shadow narrative', presented him as not only a helpless victim of the attack but also as helpless as regards his long-lasting response to it. As such, it could be said that his painful story was also his private prejudice about the victim he had become: a victim who acted furiously but who was quite out of touch with the full measure of his rage. However, during our encounter John had been able to step sufficiently outside of his situation hesitantly to query: 'That was a terrible thing to have done?'

I recalled Festinger's (1957) observation that change occurs when an inconsistency can be introduced into any one juncture. I applied this to my thinking about John's situation and concluded that, once we feel sufficiently supported in our chosen version of an event and its consequences, we may allow ourselves to question whether or not these consequences (which are getting us into trouble) must continue unaltered, let alone unchallenged. I realized that the very process of considering a possible reconstrual of the order of reality, as experienced and retold so far, casts useful doubt on the assumed inevitabilities of life.

According to cybernetic theory, which Bateson (1972) elaborated, events in systems (in this case John's interpretation of the betrayal-event) feed back on themselves, making it impossible to distinguish between cause and effect. This closed feedback loop creates our consequences, the endless going round and round in circles, which makes it difficult to break out of a painful pattern once it is well established. It hurts to know that change does not come easily – not only because the possibility, let alone the actuality of such change, is frightening but also because we get caught in traps of our own making. John's loop could at this stage be described as: 'Friends are friendly. Friendliness means betrayal. Betrayal hurts. Therefore friendship hurts. Consequently friends have to be avoided because, when they are friendly, they mean betrayal.'

Building on Bateson's theories, Watzlawick, Weakland and Fisch (1974) suggest that in order to effect substantive change, we need to bypass our known and unknown resistances, without even realizing we are doing so: to play ourselves, with the help of carefully constructed metaphors, into the creation of new rules and assumptions about our problems. When we succeed in doing this, the perfect fit between our self-narrative and its explanation will be somewhat loosened up. Developmental leaps by means of suitable metaphors create a degree of bewilderment. This bewilderment can exercise a constructive influence as long as the person is able to stay with their confusion. However, when the confusion generated by the bewilderment is too great, it activates a further desire to establish a new order with a concurrent explanatory structure. There is, therefore, but a brief space of 'suspended knowing' during which different ways of behaving and relating can be practised and the seeds of transformation be sown. This phenomenon also explains why the conscious use of time and space as structural boundaries facilitates 'longer lasting' play states in already confused clients.

Bearing the above in mind, I considered some possible priorities. The first task would be strengthening John's commitment to development; to enhance his sense of purposefulness, both as an end in itself and as a way of becoming embedded (metaphorically and at some point in the future literally) in the wider social network of intimate relationships, his reference groups and beyond. It was an absolute given that whatever we might be able to accomplish together had to be relevant to his emerging sense of identity. We needed to explore some terrain beyond the expected 'but that's how I'm supposed to be' structures of his experience of self; to play with other possible ways of expression. This would mean helping him to appropriate new meaningful forms of expressivity and to increase his awareness of the extent to which he had internalized the dominant values of the 'boys who didn't like him', along with the associated negative judgements about his own likes and dislikes. These considerations led me to think that I might, during our next session, introduce him to the Burmese folktale *The Three Eggs* (Gersie and King 1990). In this story, a woodcutter gradually develops a close relationship with a tree he first saw in a dream. One day he finds three golden eggs in a nest high up in the tree. Due to various misadventures, the eggs are lost. Through a mixture of action and luck, they are restored. Amidst the turmoil of gladness, disappointment and recovery, the woodcutter's relationship with his tree remains one of constant trust and comfort. This felt the right story for this boy, who, upon entering my room, had appreciated a vase of flowers on my window-sill and said: 'I like green things that grow'. Working with the image, metaphor, archetype, self-symbol (whatever you wish to call it) or, even better, the reality, experience of a tree might therefore not be a bad option. Duryea and Potts (1993) note that traditional stories reflect values and therefore permit the exploration of values. Each story imaginatively maps possible ways of moving a situation forward without demanding commitment to action. It provides a measure of implicit support for the idea that fruitful change is possible. Above all, old stories contain the vital message that change not only requires effort but also involves actual cost.

The prophet Isaiah once exhorted that a person shall be as a hiding place from the wind, a covert from the tempest, rivers of water in a dry place and the shadow of a great rock in a weary land (32:2). In my experience, the desire to offer such comfort and companionship to others is bred deep into people's bones. In spite of many participants' emotional pain, they long to be someone whom others can trust, who can be relied upon in a time of trouble, who can sustain commitments and provide comfort when needed. A painful internal feedback loop of anxiety, rage and shame has led to decreased activity and responsiveness and generated a mounting disbelief that action will ever lead to results. Life's uncontrollability is presupposed in a manner which parallels the response Arthur Koestler described, when, aged five, he was taken to a doctor to have an unexpected tonsillectomy. He writes: 'It was as if I had fallen through a manhole, into a dark underground world of archaic brutality. Thenceforth I never lost my awareness of the existence of that second universe into which one might be transported, without warning, from one moment to the other. The world had become ambiguous.' (1952, pp.32–3). Though only a young boy, John had grown to anticipate the future without hope. He felt it was but a sombre lane, without exits and without easement. His pessimistic outlook on life is well encapsulated in a German folktale. The story describes how God came to fix the life span of both animals and people:

> At that time God wanted to give both ass, dog and monkey thirty years. Finding life hard and unrewarding each of them protested. They wanted God to take many years away from them. Reluctantly God obliged. When at last God came round to give a life span to human beings, they too were offered thirty years and they too protested. They wanted more, not less time, saying thirty years just wasn't enough to build a house, or to plant fruit bearing trees. Surprisingly God told them that he did not have any spare years, and that he could only fulfil their wish for a longer life if he gave them the years the animals had just refused. Therefore following the first merry thirty years we now have the years of the ass, heavily burdened and with endless harsh kicks as thanks for faithful service, those of the dog, scowling and barking in a dark corner, and those of the monkey: weak headed and the jest of children.[4]

This painful perspective on life, and particularly on the process of aging, casts a shadow of hopeless expectation which affects each activity and each relationship (Tinker 1992). However, even when fantasies about more benign possibilities have long since been surrendered to a prevailing sense of uselessness, the client is still left with the one choice which always remains – namely, to decide again in a new situation whether to try to be known to fellow humans as one believes one is at that moment, or to seek instead to remain an enigma, an uncertain quantity (Jourard 1964, p.27).

John trusted me sufficiently to risk telling his vital memory. During subsequent sessions, story-work based on traditional stories strengthened his fragile longing to become known – especially because the stories provided ample space for ambiguity. Stories create such hiding and disclosing spaces. In this work I explicitly acknowledge that even though words may not be quite big enough to convey the depth and complexity of our experiences, we also have to make do with them. I encourage my clients to take an active interest in any patterns of coping displayed in a story and to find words for

---

4   Retold by the author. Contemporary source in Tandin Chabot (1974).

what they perceive. Such patterns might include typical behavioural responses, such as where the character runs away when faced with a potential conflict or the character refuses to make a reasonable effort. Alternatively, repeated use is made of certain imaginary solutions, for example at the critical moment a magical helper appears who resolves the situation without any difficulties. The clients thereby develop a habit of articulating perceptions and a capacity for reflection as an ongoing tool for change. Berne (1970) noted that 'in the long run the client must undertake the task of living in a world in which there is no Santa Claus'. Healing change relies on the internalization of some kind of permanent change-ability. Each of us faces the existential dilemmas of freedom of choice, necessity and absurdity. In therapeutic situations this reality requires open and early acknowledgement. Disappointment, the emotion which arises from the acknowledgement of these dilemmas, is a fundamental feeling. When people are emotionally troubled, such disappointment must be worked through and become divorced from anger at the impossibility of ever reaching so much as a completely certain, unambiguous mutual understanding between people (Schrodinger 1983, p.83), thereby to achieve the awareness that our life's retellings are never more, but also never less, than a reconstruction and an interpretation of the story of one's life based on the best evidence available (Bromley 1977, p.163).

The traditional story as prompt

In my work I rarely tell a traditional story without accompanying preparation and processing procedures. This includes warm-up exercises, sensory awareness-raising techniques, and techniques to elaborate certain aspects of a story. I translate a story's general developmental pattern into a series of creative expressive exercises which parallel the story's development. Some such exercises are individually based, others involve work in pairs, small groups or with the whole groups. The exercises enable participants to superimpose their individual predicaments and life-characteristics onto the story-ground. The traditional tale provides the outline and the dynamics for the exploration of the personal material; it offers both a framework and a prompt. The prompt might be the beginning, the end, or be a particular aspect of the story. When I use the story as prompt, I often interrupt the story at a charged moment where several developments are possible. Alternatively, I begin the story at a point in the story-line where an important event has clearly preceded the presented situation. The group member is then guided to create a linked story with an explanatory bent. This newly made story is vitally connected with the stimulus story. It borrows situation, character and complexity (Gambrell and Chasen 1991).

Though TSM overlaps with other story-prompting methods when traditional stories are used to stimulate 'new' stories, it also differs from this way of working in important ways. A participant's story elaboration is informed by warm-up tasks in which they have participated before the story is told. These warm-ups fit both the specific story and the purpose of the elaboration task. Though these warm-up exercises seem innocuous, are often fun, and generate energy, reassurance and useful bewilderment, they consist of precise sequences of 'experience, possibility and memory' enhancement exercises which are subtly linked to the story and specifically designed to meet the particular needs and history of the group or individuals in the group. In most sessions the whole or part of a traditional story is told after these exercises have been performed. Therefore participants will not be able to connect the exercises with a story's theme. They simply participate (or not, as is sometimes, though rarely, the case) in various action-techniques. The group members' involvement in the warm-ups, the listening to the story and the anticipatory readiness to elaborate the story in accordance with a proposed pattern mean that the group member is, when requested, primed to write. They are able to respond quickly because the material has already been made to tingle close to the surface of awareness. Furthermore, the resistance to the material or to the facilitator has already been engaged and, where possible, worked through in the warm-up phase (Emunah 1994).

At the point of story-elaboration, the group member utilizes an element from a warm-up input. Not only does such an appeal to an earlier activity create a momentary helpful internal disorientation between habit and newly acquired learning, it also makes it a little more difficult for the same old story to emerge. This further encourages the group member to discover different solutions to old predicaments. When the group member succeeds in doing so, which is often the case, this provides further supportive evidence that it is actually possible to change both story and habitual approaches to difficulties. I will illustrate this not by discussing a specific case, but by offering a more generalized description of such a sequence of exercises and some reflections upon these.

Practice vignette: warming up to the maiden with the wooden bowl

Many years ago I worked with a group of girls, all of whom had attempted suicide. As part of a warm-up sequence around the theme 'the ability to cope', I suggested various group games which involved play with numbers. I then invited the girls to brainstorm on activities a six-year-old child might like to do. The group continued with a discussion of the kind of complex emotional situations a child might face and recorded the titles of such situations on a wall-chart. This was followed by some miming activities, including:

○ group sculpts of strong emotions, such as fear, anger, joy, envy and sorrow
○ play with a favourite toy like a toddler
○ saying goodbye to someone who matters like a young person
○ learning a new skill like a twelve-year-old
○ eating food like a nine-year-old.

Subsequently, I asked group members to record on a piece of paper three numbers below seventeen and to keep these numbers with them. I then told the first part of the story of the Maiden with the Wooden Bowl.

> A long time ago there lived an old couple with their young daughter, a lovely, graceful child. After her husband died, his widow grew concerned about her daughter's future. She spoke to her child, 'My beloved daughter, the world can be a cruel place. You are too fair to live alone so I am placing this bowl on your head. You must wear it always. The bowl will protect you against those who would do you harm.' Soon after, the old woman died. The maiden, with the bowl on her head, went to work in the rice fields to earn her keep. Those who saw her laughed at the strange sight of a maiden with a wooden bowl on her head but the young girl paid little attention. When young men tried to pull the bowl of her head, it would not move. After a while they stopped trying, contenting themselves with calling her names. (Gersie and King 1990, pp.233–234)

Having heard the story, I invited each girl to treat the numbers they had recorded as an actual age in the Maiden's life, then to imagine and to describe an event that had happened to her at each respective age, the outcome of which had been such that she was able to cope with her parents' death and with the ridicule she experienced. The chosen events during her childhood had retrospectively to make sense of her ability to deal effectively with the difficulties she presently experienced. Each girl was able to think up such situations, briefly to write about them and subsequently to engage in meaningful discussion of what constitutes coping ability and how this can go wrong.

In TSM each exercise and each story needs to have a logic as well as a purpose. Play with a favourite toy, the learning of a new skill and the eating of food evoke different inner landscapes and memories. Each of these suggested activities was primarily undertaken by one individual only. It would have made a fundamental difference to the group had I structured the miming exercises as follows:

- a group of toddlers building a sand castle together on a sunny day on the beach
- two adolescent friends learning to use a new personal computer
- a girl eating a sandwich with a pussy cat on her lap whilst a friend sits nearby reading a book.

The precise wording and structure of each task provides TSM participants with new experiences, different memory-network activation and different opportunities to explore their relationships with the other group members and with the facilitator. During this session I used these particular activities because they resonated with issues and activities previously described by participants, met their emotional needs and stretched their current phase of individual and group development (Boal 1992). The work with activities of an infant, adolescent and latency-age child purposefully reminded the girls of the differences between developmental stages. I used my tone of voice, position in the room and selective participation in the miming of the activities, as well as appreciative utterances or friendly comments about the work, with spontaneous awareness. These facets of facilitator behaviour and style rely on secure knowledge of why group members are asked to mime play with a favourite toy or to present a teenager acquiring a new skill, to participate in a ball game or to dramatize saying goodbye to a loved person. Each of these is a different activity with taps into alternative, yet related, emotional and experiential domains. Therefore, each activity and its place in the sequence of activities must have its own justification for being included in the repertoire.

Participation in such action-oriented and memory-prompting warm-up tasks and the developing relationship with the facilitator who enables the group members to develop through participation in structured play and storytelling, primes the group member for listening to the story, for writing or drawing activities and for the integration of material evoked by the story. Like the warm-up exercises, the story-elaboration and integration tasks are specifically designed optimally to support and to reinforce any necessary learning for a particular group member.

❧❧❧

The place does not feel
to me
As the place used to
feel to me
On account of it.
Bushman

Creating new stories by means of brief answers to structured questions

As part of story-creation procedures I occasionally enable a group member to write a newly invented story by means of a question and answer technique. In this exercise, a participant records short answers to a carefully structured and worded sequence of questions which has been pre-formulated. The questions are appropriate to the therapeutic task of the group. The answers, which may be written or drawn, provide the group member with a story outline, which is elaborated either through writing out the story in full (generally, the story length is between half a page or two sides of A4) or through direct telling. The questions follow important story grammar elements such as location, main character, problem or dilemma, the need to do something about the problem, helpers or opponents, solution attempts, twists, reactions, resolution, outcome and learning. I purposefully qualify aspects of each question in order to generate particular kinds of tales. This question–answer procedure is also used after a set of warm-up activities which have a priming, developmental purpose whilst the sharing of these stories is likewise embedded in response-task story elaboration activities.

Practice vignette: A birthday cake for Peter

I will illustrate how such story-creation is embedded in a session by describing some aspects of a session which was part of a one-week project (five morning sessions) in a residential home for frail older people. Some days before the group commenced I attended a residents' meeting to clarify my professional background, to discuss the therapeutic storymaking project and to explore any concerns or queries. As a result of this meeting, six people asked to join the group – one man and five women.

At the beginning of the group the five female group members introduced themselves by saying how many children and grandchildren they had. Peter, the only man, said quietly that he had been an only child, that his wife had died some years previously and that they were childless. One of the women, Maureen, responded: 'That must have been terrible for your wife, the two of you not having children'. He whispered, barely audible, 'For me too'. This was ignored, though his eyes caught mine. He registered that I had heard him.

At this stage the group would have found it easier to continue to address the theme of having a family out there rather than to explore whether they could be a family of kinds to one another here. When I shared this thought with the group, Mary worded the dilemma succinctly: 'If I tell you people things that I want to tell my children, I'll feel that they are even further away. I hardly know them at all really, but if I tell you about what is going on I think I'll feel even worse.' Shaking her head, she added, 'Strange really'.

The group was about to take protective refuge in the idea that intimacy in the group would inevitably generate conflicts of loyalty with their family – a family of origin to whom they also wanted to be faithful. This loyalty would also prevent them from having to deal with life here and now in this home. When I shared this reflection, their fright eased. Mary added that she actually wanted the others to know how lonely she had felt since her husband had died and how guilty, too, about her longing for male company. Though there were without doubt several issues, such as competition for a male, or trying to be the group's spokesperson, Mary also needed to have her actual desire heard. The group talked briefly about our society's somewhat dismissive attitudes concerning intimacy and older people (Moody 1992). They collectively seemed to breath a sigh of relief at no longer having to remain silent or alternatively to talk just about ill health, death or the children (Ungerson 1987). 'Those are legitimate subjects of concern for elderly people, but touch isn't', Susan put it. They briefly addressed their felt need for intimacy. This was a somewhat urgent issue, particularly because this was a new group.

During the early stages of therapeutic storymaking, group members cannot yet believe that the stranger across the table may also have felt blown by the wind like the spume of a wave. When assumptions about the strange otherness of others dominate a group's atmosphere, the participants urgently need to discover their shared concerns. In this process they have to ease up on thoughts about assumed isolation and develop a clearer understanding of the awe-inspiring averageness of human life. They also need to become more aware of the vital difference between an imagined response to an imagined situation, and actual responses to experienced life events. It is after all impossible to know how we would have reacted to a particular situation had we ourselves been previously exposed to kindred pressures, endowed with similar gifts, or been forced to live through parallel misfortunes. We can only be mindful of the Samik poet's words, when he says: 'How would anyone who has eaten his fill and is well, be able to understand the madness of hunger? We only know that we all want so much to live!' (Rothenburg 1972, p.396).

The group continued the process of getting to know each other by means of various brief creative-expressive exercises. I introduced the idea of finger painting. At first this evoked lots of comments about 'kids' stuff' and mess. But the resistance was quickly overcome. The colours were simply too inviting. Soon each person freely used the paints to create images around the theme of 'Beginning a Journey'. After hands had been cleaned, they jotted down word-associations around the same theme. Each person then described in one sentence a memorable journey. A gesture which conveyed an aspect of their journey completed the sentence. The gestures were then copied by the group. As several group members had real difficulties with physical movement, all gestures were done seated in a circle, with hand, arms, shoulders, face and neck used as primary vehicles for expression. In this manner the group shared a visit to the zoo, a journey to the seaside, a trip to Spain, going to work for the first time, going to hospital and the car journey to the residential home.

I then asked group members to record short answers in response to a series of questions:

o   In which landscape will this story take place?

o   What kind of dwelling can you see in this landscape?

o   Who or what, which animal(s), creature(s) or person(s) lives or live in this dwelling place?

o   What does this character (or do these characters) really want right now?

o   How can this be achieved?

o   What is the final outcome?

The questions provided the bare bones of a story outline. Each participant was invited to write a brief story on the basis of their answers to the questions. Peter's story involved a lizard-like animal called Sprog, who travelled aimlessly in the wide, wide world. Sprog did not know what he wanted, and nothing much was achieved. The outcome was an aimlessly wandering, lonesome Sprog. I therefore asked Peter if he had even the slightest idea of what Sprog really wanted, apart from travelling aimlessly. He smiled wistfully. Speaking quickly, as if worried that if he spoke slowly he would silence himself, he said: 'Friends, a birthday, candles'. I recorded his words as he spoke, intending to invite him later to use these components to elaborate his

Sprog story. A similar process of storytelling, followed by a deepened exploration of what the character wanted, was then pursued with the other group members. Using his additional story-components, Peter subsequently extended his story. He wrote: 'Sprog meets friends: dog, reindeer and rabbit. But he wants a birthday cake. When is his birthday? When was he born? He cannot remember how to find his mum and dad. He didn't know where they were. Touch him. Touch him. ...They touch him. Then today will be your birthday Sprog, the 12th of February. Let's make a cake.'

When Peter read this extended tale the other group members became very quiet. They heard that his voice broke and saw, with some trepidation, that the emotion evoked by his story brought him close to tears. The extended story spoke clearly of Peter's growing confusion and associated self-loss, of his untouched body, his need for emotional and physical succour, of his unclear ideas about death or afterlife and, finally, of his momentary fragile willingness to accept his existence on this very day (Sabat and Harre 1992). Although the group did not take place on his actual birthday, it was the 12th of February – a day in which something different might be made to happen that could lift its everydayness into a new-born freshness.

Peter's entrance into a somewhat more shared existence was welcomed by this group of people, who lived in a rather dull residential home. They appeared to recognize the tension that exists between mourning the numerous losses that old age entails, the celebration of each day as it comes and the longing not to have to deal with the unresolved issues which many in their midst still carried with them: the unforgivens of their life. My interpretations could easily have focused on such losses or on Peter's wish to become the centre of attention, the birthday boy. He was after all the only male participant. It would have been too easy to presume that his story merely expressed the group's nuclear conflict around birth, death and competition. As this was our first session, I noted the presence of the themes but directed my structural interventions towards building group cohesion (Vinogradov and Yalom 1989, pp.43–55). I therefore invited the participants to create a group finger painting of Sprog's birthday cake. This was done with great vigour. Similar collaborative group paintings around a group member's theme were then made for every other story. The process of collaborating on the paintings elicited much talk, physical contact and sheer joy at discovering unexpected images and possibilities. Above all, it made people interact in different, new ways.

During storymaking I place great emphasis on the interactional and interpersonal here and now meanings of group members' overt behaviour and on their conscious wishes or expectations. I assume that, irrespective of actual age, each individual acts with varying degrees of conscious awareness of what they perceive others see them doing. I believe that interaction and clear feedback are needed in order for this awareness to be both developed and maintained (Klein and Astrachan 1971). The elderly people's trouble centred around the internalization of the unexamined assumption that, due to their advanced age, their emotional and intellectual horizons needed to contract. They were set aside from life's hurly-burly within the walls of their residential home. They felt marginalized and wanted to oblige by focusing on those issues which the young believed older people should pursue. They were only too aware that judgements of rationality and of appropriateness involve conceptions of normality that have normative force. They felt that the classification of an emotion as preferred or unpreferred often disguises disagreements about what is wholesome or right (see Oksenberg Rorty 1988, p.355). They understood their task to be: how not to be a nuisance and how to die gracefully. However, in spite of their unwell bodies and sullen surface behaviour, these were also lusty, passionate, curious people who wanted to surmount these unexamined confines of what old age was supposed to be about.

I quietly encouraged the exploration of their assumptions about old age. I aimed to help the group to implement the goals it had set for itself – namely to achieve a workable intimacy in their residential home, to work through some issues in people's individual lives which bothered them, and to learn to share both their feelings about their present situation and miscellaneous feelings as regards their future. The meaning we were able to create out of our work with each other was, of course, a social product. It emerged from the various interactional activities and from what each person brought to this group. Both covert group dynamics and overt interpersonal dynamics influenced the group's interactions and its direction. It can never not be so. Attention had to be given to the following processes:

- Emergent group wish or disturbing motive: in this case, the wish for sensual pleasure, intimate friendships, a partner.

- Problems (difficulty, risk, fear) regarding the attainment of these wishes: such as concerns about loyalty, competitiveness, the need for approval.

- The attempts used to create solutions to this predicament, i.e. in this group: withdrawal, gossip and narrowing of the conversational focus on family, previous relationships, ill-health and death.

I aimed to develop the group's awareness of itself by offering interpretations which could be worked with, and which were simultaneously experienced as something new. I also aimed to help the group to operate with somewhat greater ease on a pre-conscious level (Stock and Lieberman 1962).

The technique of generating 'question/answer stories' demands cautious application. The evoked story bears witness to the dynamics of the participants' inner world, reflects situational aspects of the group in question, and is linked with events and circumstances in the world at large. It offers food for thought. In addition, the question–answer technique teaches participants how to use stories as a vehicle for expression, a tool for communication and a method for emotional development. These three aspects inform the choices made about which exercise to use when and in which manner, which interpretation to offer and which story material to propose.

> *The pleasure of running water,*
> *The hill we climb.*
> India

Memory tales

Personal recollections reflect our tendency to think about life events in story form. They include anecdotes, perceptions and the long-term thread of a life narrative. Some such stories pertain to intimate occasions and others describe social or political events. These lived experience stories are provisional models which help us to figure out both the issue reported in the story and what it demonstrates. The telling and retelling of a life experience more or less as it is remembered enables us to share experiences and to gain insight into possible meanings and implications (Paul 1993). Each story facilitates the construal of meaning (Moloney 1995). The recounting of several memories permits the emergence of themes or constitutive patterns.

In my storymaking work I am particularly interested in the story a participant tells him- or herself about their trouble, and most especially in those aspects of their story that describe how the difficulties have been dealt with. During early group sessions I want to learn about aspects of the participants' lives which are important to them. In work of brief duration it is particularly important that a client's main problem and strength are established early on with relative certainty, so that the work may address the area where it is most wanted. During such an exploration of his particular ways of dealing with trouble, Kevin, a man in his mid-forties, said:

'My dark thoughts always keep me company. But when life gets really bad I use a few good memories to see me through. I couldn't bear it if it was the other way around.'

It is wise to remember that not every untold memory pertains to betrayals, secrets or unhappy life events. I have learned in the course of my work that virtually every participant uses some memories of a few, however transient, benign interactions, to keep them going during the hard times. An example of such a memory was provided by Marianne, a profoundly unhappy woman in her late fifties, who had joined the same group. During a session in which the group worked around the theme 'The Kindness of Strangers', she wrote:

> I was once hopelessly lost in Rome trying to make my way back to the home where I worked as an unhappy au-pair. I was in my teens, about seventeen. No money for the bus, no map and not much language. I pretended to look into a shop window. I tried not to cry. Then I heard a voice next to me. A woman said in English: 'Are you lost?' She helped me find my way to the right bus and gave me money for the fare. She was really kind to me.

After reading her memory-story to the group, she added, 'I've never told anyone about this before now. Never. It's been an important memory. Yet all those years I never mentioned it... I wonder why.' Her self-question could be answered in numerous ways. In my practice, it mattered to ascertain with her whether telling this story *now* in this group made a difference and, if so, what kind of difference. She said: 'Yes, it makes me realize that I do not want to keep saying that nothing good ever happened to me. I do not want to keep saying that.' She added quite tearfully: 'Somehow I would like to say "thank you" to her. But that's silly.' At this point I invited her to formulate a group response-task. She wanted the group to do something around the theme 'expressing gratitude to strangers'. I placed a sizeable sheet of drawing paper in the middle of the table. Group members then painted or wrote images and words on this sheet around her theme. When it was finished, Marianne called it: 'Thanks'. It constituted the beginning of a re-formulation of her life's narrative.

The shaping of our life's trajectory is influenced by the events we encounter, and the stories we create, and is guided by the tellings we are willing to share. In group work which enables people systematically to explore their told stories, it is important not to aggravate memories of earlier overwhelming situations through the relentless recitation of traumatic life stories. I believe that access to redress needs to be created through the careful processing of what is heard and told – this involves optimal enhancement of group members' ways of accessing and expressing responses to other people's life description – to enable members to notice the impact of another person's life-story upon themselves and to translate this noticing into purposeful interpersonal responsiveness.

A commitment to emotional range

Though we cannot truly know another's subjective experience, because as Kohut (1959) notes, 'our thoughts, wishes, feelings and fantasies cannot be seen, smelled, heard or touched', we can feel ourselves into an intimate awareness of the otherness of the other – and clarify our experience of transient identifications, shared unconscious fantasies and pseudo-understandings (p.459). In therapeutic groupwork the client gradually learns to untangle this mishmash. This demands a scrupulous continuity of focused attention to noticeable, interactive and intrapsychic processes, plus diligent recall of associated memories, fantasies and theoretical considerations – the willingness to hear what is whispered between and without words. In TSM, these levels of directed awareness are supported by creative expressive group procedures, which are designed specifically to strengthen the participants' commitment to create and process stories, and to clarify ideas, memories and feelings linked with the stories. I have found that such procedural tasks nurture a person's desire to communicate. They strengthen their ability to interact with others about all manner of complex issues which otherwise might have been avoided (Solano and Koester 1989). In the above mentioned example of group work with older people, the processing took the form of a theme-specific group painting. In suggesting this task I not only reminded the group that in these groups disclosure of personal material is meant to happen, but also that it needs to happen at a pace and in a space that feels comfortable, safe and supported. The response-tasks teach group members ways of listening to a storyteller's language 'as slightly foreign, a dialect no-one else speaks, in which numerous histories animate the all-too-familiar words in that speaker's mind'.

Marianne's self-chosen silence about some good occurrences had survived a well vocalized torrent of troubling events. Her silence had not only sustained some fragile internal hope, it had also supported her external image of great woundedness. Once the picture of her life had become publicly mottled with some light points, her capacity to tolerate ambivalence and ambiguity gradually increased – thereby she strengthened the much needed leverage point for self-reflectivity. Her telling of her storied memory in this group provided just such an opportunity. In this same group, Jack, a professional man who struggled with substantial self-alienation, also recalled a moment in his life when being alone had felt not too terrible. Upping the score of remembered goodness well beyond the level of my constructively pessimistic request for a 'memory of feeling somewhat contented', he wrote:

> It was a dusky evening, and I was drinking a glass of wine on a terrace. I felt very much caught up in being alone among many others, when across the chatter came a clear violin tone from a street musician. Suddenly the noise of many voices hushed and the one clear voice of the violin banished my line of thought as clearly as it banished the conversation. I was carried by sheer delight in the music and so was everyone around me. It was not a polite silence, it was a mass entranced silence.

He read his words cautiously, as if he anticipated that others would not identify with his memory. When another group member spontaneously shared her experience of listening to music, his face seemed to light up with secret pleasure, but his gaze was cast away from the group. I invited him to make some actual eye contact with the other group members. What he noticed in their eyes brought a most tender, warm smile to his face.

As the TSM group progresses, each participant's chief complaint will be brought into precise focus. Before the stories which underpin this can be shared, a strong enough base needs to have been established in the group. Such strength is, amongst other things evidenced by the participant's ability appropriately to soothe self and others. Renewed access to the willingness to share and talk about the little stories of everyday life goes a long way to establish this.

Traditional, fantasy and memory stories often deal with trouble of one kind or another. This characteristic enhances their fruitfulness when they are knowingly applied in a therapeutic or educational situation. Story-based therapeutic group work involves the careful assessment of participants' needs, the gradual elicitation and recitation of the story of their difficulty and the creation of new, more adaptive narratives about what will constitute betterment from their point of view. Stories readily facilitate the expression and working through of complex emotions, particularly when this is combined with the purposeful development of listening skills through the use of structured response-tasks. Together, these often accelerate the client's emotional growth.

For a short while it is lent us,
the glory of that
by which everything lives.

Nahuatl

4. Genuine Empowerment

In spite of a basic love of stories, most people who join a therapeutic storymaking group abhor the thought that it includes visual image-making and writing activities. Every act of painting or writing is, after all, value laden and symbolic. It has social as well as individual meanings. Given that schooled image-creation ability or literacy may be limited, feelings about exposure to such practices abound. A person's response to image-making or writing exercises must therefore be understood in their historical context (Landreth 1993). In most participants' educational and social world the appropriate use of words or visual images represents the authority of a different class. Their 'school history' is often troubled. They expect neither success nor praise. Unable successfully to negotiate entry into a shared linguistic realm, many emotionally troubled people rely on idiosyncratic or echo-saturated word usage.

When an ineffective communicative habit pattern has been adopted, the individual needs to learn new ways of communicating in order to bypass the socially constraining effect of their current way of relating. This learning can be facilitated through the person's participation in specific creative-expressive exercises, which provide scope for inter-personal feedback. Such exercises need to promote the re-appropriation of communicative habits which support sociality and reciprocity. As noted above, marginalized communities – such as people with learning difficulties, frail older people, or people with mental health problems – have often internalized the values of dominant literacy and image-making practices, along with the associated judgements about their own capabilities (Barton and Ivanic 1991). Where this is the case, the internalized failure trap – which suggests that nothing good will come of any activity anyway – not only needs to be noted, it is better circumvented.

Practice vignette: Dorrie and the inescapable imprecision of language

In a TSM group for elderly people in a residential home, Dorrie, a physically frail, and initially very angry woman wrote, after some sessions, the following good-bye poem for a fellow group member who was unexpectedly moving to another home. It said:

> When I think of you I'll miss your face;
>
> But your voice with me will be.
>
> Beyond this day I send my hope.
>
> The time we shared is here to last,
>
> It's true I feel a little sad,
>
> yet we must part,
>
> farewell.[1]

When Dorrie gave her poem to the woman concerned, she said: 'It's not much of a poem really'. Catching her self-deprecating words, she looked around the group and added: 'I know about poetry. This one isn't any good. But it says what I mean.' The way she spoke bore witness to the progress she had made. During the early stages of this group Dorrie had increased the risk of being misunderstood by speaking so quickly that it was virtually impossible to understand what she said. Her speech style demanded other people's maximum interpretative effort. When her rapid cascade of words was taken seriously, her flow of words tended to calm down. It emerged that Dorrie had been a bright girl who had enjoyed school. We learned that during adolescence her awareness of the inescapable imprecision of language had combined with confusion about strong sexual feelings in a strict, orthodox religious home. Her parents had been intolerant of most forms of sensual, let alone sexual expression. The pain this generated had drawn her into writing poetry. Her poems were discovered and torn up as 'dirty trash'. Not long after, she embraced the rapid cascade way of speaking, keeping intimacy at bay through language-torrents (Austin 1962).

Dorrie knew only too well that words as well as stories have a double character. The very act of speech permits both intimacy and dissemblance, truthfulness and gossip. The power of words resides in their potential for utterance and in their potential to remain as unspoken thought, not even to be unveiled by indirection. The redirection of her communicative strategy, which had long since outlived its usefulness, became a major part of Dorrie's

---

1   I am indebted to Ditty Dokter, who designed a good-bye poem-writing exercise in which key words, such as 'I feel', 'sad', 'face', were given for inclusion in the poem. In this group we brainstormed words related to transitions and farewell before group members wrote their individual poems. I asked members to draw a small outline on a piece of A4 paper, to decorate this outline with some colouring pens and then to write their poem inside this frame.

therapeutic task. She not only had to regain faith in the benign possibilities of relationship but also in relational continuity (Townsend 1986). She touched upon the re-emergence of this awareness in the brief poem cited above. In the course of her process of re-appropriating language as intentional communication, she was deeply comforted by Eli Wiesel's words when he says: 'The more I talked, the deeper I sank into my own ignorance. I was touching madness, I was going to lose the use of my tongue, become a child again, speechless, innocent. I began to pray' (1974, p.131). It was moving to be allowed to accompany her during the gradual emergence of an effective communicative style which enabled her to make and to maintain warm relationships with others. Story-making and writing poetry were vital to this process (Morrison 1986).

During her prolonged state of social isolation, Dorrie had remained preoccupied with four essential questions. These concerned the existence of self, the existence of a world outside the self, the ceasing (or not) of the self with bodily death and the ceasing of the world with bodily death. She had needed the kind of relationships in which it would be possible freely to reflect on life's complexities and its meaning. The poem reflected her progress, both whom she had become and who she was, chisel and block. It was a gift of extraordinary transparency in which she had employed direct formulation, direct addressing and direct authorship (Gofman 1978). These gains bore witness to Dorrie's emerging faith in the possibilities of affective bonds.

Language-based ambiguities and internal contradictions are inevitable. In every act of communication inconsistencies must be tolerated and where possible resolved, multiplicities and differences acknowledged (Mensen 1993). Her poem reflected her current feelings and anticipated her future. As far as Dorrie was concerned, however, the poem was above all a gift for another person: someone whom she had grown to trust a little. This trust had evolved from the prevailing climate in the group, from the quality of the developing relationships between group members, and from my systematic attempt to help her to adopt an internal perspective where the merging of objects and ideas was not so intense that she could not emancipate herself from it (Waelder 1965, pp.59–60). The warm-up exercises, the stories she wrote and the response-tasks contributed to her steady improvement because they provided her with the experience of instinctual pleasure, the celebration of mastery and evidence of her growing capacity to use a detached position from which to observe and to introspect through the naming of feelings. Abrahams (1983) observes that to be human is to control words and to pursue eloquence (p.22). To tell stories is to enter into the constant recreation of the world, of community and of mankind. Whereas Eli Wiesel's writings put

Dorrie in touch with the need for connection with a greater life, the following story helped to clarify her vulnerability to the opinions of others.

> Once upon a time there was a man, his son and a camel. They were on a journey. As they walked along, they heard a bystander say: 'How foolish, they've got a camel and they walk.' Heeding these words the man climbed the camel's back, whilst the son lightly led on foot. Soon the man heard a passer-by comment: 'That man has no pity. Look at that boy.' The man immediately descended from the camel's back offering his son the comfort of the ride. Hardly were they on their way when a woman scolded the son: 'Have you no shame, letting the old man walk.' So the son reached down to help his father onto the camel's back. They had not gone very far when a passer-by urged them to take better care of the poor camel, who carried such a heavy load. 'Have you no heart?' a man yelled. They saw only one solution. They carried the camel.[2]

The story adequately encapsulated this group's mistrust of advice and implied solutions. When people are emotionally unwell, like Dorrie had been for much of her life, they can feel very preoccupied with the fine line between misunderstandings, the invalidation of perceptions and the encouragement of a different outlook on life (Efran and Schenker 1993). Valid as such concerns may be, the persistent struggle with getting language and relationships 'just right' may also be a fierce attempt to prevent '*Ergriffenheit*', that state of joyous absorption in the otherness of people, animals or natural phenomena when the boundaries between self and other are temporarily loosened – not because they are loose, but because they have become less relevant.

When I first met this group of older people they struck me as more than a little isolated and joyless. During the weeks we worked together they came more home to themselves and to each other. They re-found an inner position of wonder in the emergent sense this term also implies. Numerous warm-up exercises and traditional stories supported their developing appreciation of the actuality of experience *per se*. Both Dorrie and the other group members thus became the living embodiment of Schrodinger's (1983) observation that even when there is resistance to transformation, transformation is bound to take place, with all the necessity of a natural law.

---

2 Retold by the author. Oft told story circulating in oral tradition.

Groups, stories and social empowerment

In turn-of-the-century Boston, Joseph Pratt organized groups for people with tuberculosis. He did so because of the advantageous features of group work, which permits large numbers of clients to be treated with efficient use of time, space, personnel and other resources (Konopka 1963). Other treatments were unavailable because these people were poor and could not afford individual talking therapy. Limited economic resources meant that group treatment was the most practical modality available. Throughout the literature on group therapy, reference is made to its cost-effectiveness and expediency. Many years ago Julian Wohl (1983) wrote that the effort to find treatments other than individual talking therapy for people with emotional difficulties was not simply inspired by the thought that it was rational to do so. Alternative treatment patterns were sought that did not demand as much talking from the clients because people who were economically poor were also judged to be poor talkers. He observed:

> Approaches were attempted that put less responsibility upon the patients because they were believed unable to accept it. This framework came to be part of the assumptive world view of the largely middle-class, white American mental health establishment, and much of the literature embodies this demeaning view of the patients. (pp.343–355)

Regardless of these roots in economic expediency, group work offers participants unique opportunities for healing. However, when benefits as regards efficient use of resources are noted more than responsiveness to client need, and when in much of the literature little reference is made to themes of race, poverty, prejudice or unequal distribution of economic resources, it is important to reflect on the possibility that the group practice might take place within the framework of an unconscious politics of constraint (Marzillier 1993). Such politics allow for the early recognition of an undesirable other, namely the one who challenges the *status quo*. The question then arises as to which set of circumstances and value-judgements the client is required to adjust to (Hugman 1991). This is particularly so when clients' righteous outrage about appalling housing conditions or about the humiliation and loneliness experienced during long-term unemployment is refracted through group-psychotherapeutic theories dominated by methodological individualism into an understanding of ourselves as the locus of our own foolhardiness and the agent of our own distress – as Thomas Szasz so succinctly puts it (1956).

The fact that stories about poverty, hunger and violence are told to this day bears stark witness to the continuing, sad pertinence of these themes. These storied events describe, but do not interpret the link between disempowerment and the abuses of powers by others who are differently positioned in society. As in the tale of Bear, Wolf and Fox, the suffering inflicted by powerful people or creatures is rarely condemned in stories; it is merely represented. There is an apparent resistance of orally transmitted tales to the declaration of a moral or ethical stance. The story's transparency invites the listener to formulate their personal judgement. Human experience is readily organized in storied ways. We cannot hear a story without imparting a structure of significances upon it (Fromm 1951). These significances derive from values, experiences, hopes and fears. Though the way a story is told may expose its most obvious ideological assumptions, we do not necessarily become conscious of its more tendentious implications. Therefore a story's ultimate value will depend on how the teller and the listeners relate its content to their own actions or intentions. Zipes (1979) proposes that unless a story's latent meanings are explored, a story's effect may well be to limit rather than to enhance behavioural options (p.177). He invites us to wonder how many girls were effectively discouraged from going into the forest in red or multi-coloured capes, or how many boys decided not to protest violence at home in case they would not be believed. Though it matters to remember that Poseidon seduced, some say raped, Medusa in Athena's temple, or that Athena placed the Gorgon's mask on Medusa's face, it may be more fruitful to explore how poor Medusa might have felt when she saw herself, much later in the story, reflected in Perseus' shield, just before she was slain (De Lauretis 1982, p.134); to ponder how Snow White made sense of her life in the dwarf's home; or to query whether Jack ever suffered nightmares about the beanstalk.

Most old stories evoke multiple questions about a character's intentions and their implications for human behaviour. However, a story's potential to evoke such questions requires activation – particularly when a person's capacity for silent receptivity has outweighed their ability to participate in vociferous discussion for too long. In a therapeutic or educational context it is therefore not advisable to reduce the multiple possible understandings of a story's social dynamics, or of its description of historical human actions, to one highly privileged approach which emphasizes, for example, the interpretation of the projections of an individual's imagination over all other understandings (Cooper 1983). This reduces the story teller and the listeners to a level of privacy which disclaims the influence of their social spheres. In my experience, any story told, apart from being (one hopes) a great yarn, is also a fictional construction which is intimately attached to both the intrapsychic and the interpersonal world of teller and listener.

The impact of suffering

Stenhouse (1973) draws attention to the fact that if intelligent behaviour is to evolve from instinctive behaviour, a number of developmental moves must be completed (p.67). The first of these concerns the power not to respond to situations in the usual way. This means becoming able to delay a consummatory act in a strong stimulus situation which otherwise generates a virtually instinctive sequence of deeds and thoughts and emotions. This ability to delay a stimulus response is fundamental to the emergence of adaptive variation. The inhibition of motor activity when we are awake and engaged in thinking is a process that is preliminary to action. It allows us to scan possibilities, to link concepts and to review possible strategies. We postpone possible action for the sake of contemplation upon action. Apart from this capacity of the elective postponement of action, the evolution of intelligence also requires the development of a central memory store. In this memory store there must be a functional relationship between the items that are located within it. Without such a functional relationship the memories would just float about without enabling the owner of the memories to compare, contrast or evaluate experiences. Some capacity to abstract or to generalize also needs to be developed. This latter capacity is closely linked to the presence of the first two, whilst all three depend upon each other for the emergence of intelligence.

In a situation of profound emotional pain, this kind of intelligent well-being is severely threatened. Impulses dominate behaviour, memories are wildly adrift in the inner world, and the capacity to make sense of it all is surrendered to a helpless feeling of confused disorder. In this torrential inner world experience, storytelling can help to rekindle the kind of balanced curiosity that enables someone to make the effort to understand something by searching for information; to grasp differences of opinion, and to try various ideas out for size *before* deciding whether to co-operate or to oppose alternative ideas or approaches. This kind of exploration supports the emergence of the kind of balanced well-being that underpins recovery from mental ill-health. In a TSM group for lonesome elderly people, we listed, after a few sessions, the kind of things you might ask a story character and, by inference, one another. These were some of questions:

- What was yesterday like for you?
- What might happen next?

- What's your most recent dream?
- Tell me about your family.
- What are you going to do about the situation (in the story)?
- What does the event (in the story) remind you of?
- Tell me how you are feeling now.

In the grips of emotional pain, group members need to gain access to felt mutuality and reciprocity, to different story themes, to the courage to test the reality of their relationship with others, to ease up on their harsh inner conscience and to internalize a range of good enough relationships (Smith 1980). Above all else, they need to practise a form of narrative grammar that invites looking forward to the next event whilst fixing attention on the present moment. The very act of having joined a therapeutic group demonstrates their desire to bring about at least a degree of change. Combined, these may help the person to ward off a sense of overwhelming despair or helplessness, gradually to learn how to contain and/or to discharge painful emotions effectively and to become less vulnerable to psychic flooding. In this process they will need to have their feelings recognized for, although their disturbance has been shown in a wide range of behavioural indicators, it has often been surprisingly unclear to a distressed person that their behaviour has been read in accordance with the signalled intent. The therapeutic group work needs to offer conditions that not only facilitate a felt breakthrough of pained inner process into verbalization, overt mood and behaviour but also generate a feed-back structure that will enable the distressed person to sense that their trouble has been received, registered and contained.

Practice vignette: Roy, the dead gull and voiced concern

The troubling complexities aroused by finding oneself not quite as alone as was imagined in a group that is working well are demonstrated in Roy's storytelling. He was a deeply confused man, a religious priest in trouble with his marriage, his children, his job and his life-philosophy (see Haring-Hidore et al. 1985). He wrote the following tale:

> Bare Scottish beach. Wrecked boat. A gull with a damaged wing. It is hungry. If it does not get food it will starve. It has an urgent longing for food. Many hours pass. It finds no food. It does not find food. Facing the despair of hunger it goes to sleep in the sheltered part of the boat. It dies.

When a fellow participant voiced concern at the bleakness of this tale, Roy protested saying: 'It's how it is.' Pleadingly, he added: 'Life's bad.' His words suggested that he needed time and space gradually to transform his deeply pained rhapsody of thoughts into some more benignly coherent perspective on life; this had to involve feeling safe enough authentically to express feelings (Cassirer 1946). When Roy first joined this group his contributions had been few and far between. They were like pieces of a jigsaw, each of which had its own image but where the larger picture does not yet unveil itself. The story about the dying gull, as well as his response to the concern, exemplified his progress from severely curtailed emotional utterance into the clearly communicable denotation of something he knew: lonesomeness, hunger and dying within. Roy had lived with this storied self-experience for many years. It seemed that the concern now voiced by others about the level of his pain could not yet be worked with. It appeared to challenge too many self-protective assumptions and evoked too many memories. The immediacy of the response to his story nearly made him hurry back to the protective shelter of bewildered emotional withdrawal – nearly, but not quite.

His involvement with the group had already become such that he was at least a little curious about the concern evoked by his tale; he also did want the group members to perform a response-task he had formulated, namely to imagine that someone found the dead bird and to create a picture of this someone. Another participant had formulated a similar request the previous week in relation to her tale. Roy had liked (envied?) her response to what she had received then. However, given his emotional troubles, I pondered that his self-chosen use of this particular group-task in response to his story probably stretched his capacity for tolerating newness to its very limits. I therefore created some space by first inviting the group to reflect on how we cope with another person's expression of bleak misery, following statements such as:

> 'I don't want to know',
>
> 'I try to make light of it', and
>
> 'I don't think I really take it in'.

Roy turned to me saying: 'I wish I hadn't written it now'. Hearing his words at many levels, I said: 'It's hard to hear other people's feelings, when it feels like criticism, isn't it? And is that what it used to feel like?' I took care to reflect with the group on previous occasions when voiced interpersonal feedback had been interpreted by the recipients in a persecutory manner. Whilst the group reflected on this theme, Roy crumpled the piece of paper on which he had written his story in his hand and held it tight. He uncrumpled it as the group pondered the dynamics of attack on a good enough or, as one participant said, a spot-on response. I encouraged the group to reflect on the wish to make things better for Roy and for the gull, or for that matter any other group member, to rescue them from despair. They shared their deep longing for a life where horror, and particularly the horror of separation, does not happen and on the lonesomeness that ensues when the fact that it does happen cannot be acknowledged. Whilst the group's capacity to tolerate the expression of complex feelings slowly increased, Roy quietly began to flatten and to caress his piece of paper, as if to soften the impact of his early angry attack on its existence. He made some eye-contact with the participant who had first voiced concern. They shared a sadly-glad consoling smile. A degree of intrapsychic tolerance and its accompanying interpersonal space had been negotiated. Then the group engaged with Roy's story in the manner he had requested.

I offer the brief examples of Dorrie's and Roy's work to suggest that expression in a creative medium confronts us with the experience that we are not only using it (the medium) but that it uses us. In every act of speaking, making or writing, a continuous feedback process is established between accessible skills, available tools, desired process and current, as well as past experience (Berry 1973). Our creative product, such as a story or a painting, emerges from this encounter between the subjective pole of the inner world and the realizable possibilities in the world beyond ourselves – worlds with which we cannot not interact. The stories, images and dramas created in a group context are emergent products of the interactive dynamics between the participants and their respective, as well as their shared, worlds. Synthesizing is a creative process which involves seeing new patterns within a body of evidence, viewing an issue from a variety of perspectives and learning to integrate new evidence (Johnson and Johnson 1993). When a person becomes capable of doing so again, they do not stand aloof from those who think differently than they do. On the contrary, they wrestle with these issues, sharpen skills of debate and deepen their understanding. Such ego-strengthening activities can calm a bewildering inner world and clarify what is troubling about a person's current patterns of relating to others. This function of the synthesizing process should not be underestimated. In any group situation the wise facilitator encourages inter-personal curiosity, frank inquiry, a keen desire to solve problems and an atmosphere of open minded mutual interest. In order to achieve such a climate, a group first and foremost needs to learn to agree and to disagree, to feel passionately about something and, above all, to feel safe with saying: 'This is how I think about this and this is what I feel or need'. In TSM this development is, amongst other things, facilitated through the purposeful use of both stories, storytelling and various accompanying exercises. It is demonstrated in the way the facilitator engages with contentious, challenging themes.

❧❧❧❧

Waves falling
High waves falling
Against the rocks.
Australian Aboriginal

On pain, stories and relearning to imagine

In every group I am granted the opportunity to trace with the participants their implicit beliefs about the support that certain modes of life deserve or merit (Rogers 1974). I hope thereby to enable each of us to become more aware of our developing perspective upon the life that is worth living, whilst supporting our willingness openly to reflect upon these perspectives through action as well as through the contemplation of action. The 'how' of life is consequently greatly privileged over the construction of answers to the question 'why'. As such storymaking is best described as a pragmatic, social groupwork method in which issues related to the praxis of living are granted priority. With the primary focus established, each group explores memory- or self-generated fantasy stories as regards

- ○ logical soundness (however biased this concept may be)
- ○ comprehensiveness in terms of accounting for puzzling aspects of the events reported in the story
- ○ consistency in terms of the full range of available evidence
- ○ their consistency with the group's (including myself) general knowledge about human functioning
- ○ credibility in relation to other explanatory hypotheses.

The very use of concepts related to the reliability of evidence or explanatory relevance and force in relation to life events often results in challenging discussions with participants who sometimes say that they have been treated only too often as people without grasp, comprehension or compassion. Through such 'storied doing', a person's ideas of how being alive affects them, their circumstances and their important others may be systematically explored (see Radin 1957, pp.275–89).

Genuine empowerment rests on the ability to recognize and to define one's needs in connection with those of others and, above all, on translating needs and imagined possibilities into action. Anthony Storr (1989) points out that the human mind seems so constructed that a new balance or restoration within the subjective, imaginative world is felt as if it were a change for the better in the external world and vice versa (p.124). He proposes that this is the secret of creative adaptation. However, when people are emotionally unwell this fine balance is disrupted. The links between what is needed, imagined and acted upon become unclear. Purposeful determination is weakened. Pain about unsatisfied longings or incomplete acts tragically damages the motivation. The capacity to effect change and to be active in the world, as well as the ability to imagine an alternative to a felt predicament, become curtailed. This curtailment may entice a person to substitute a particular difficulty with action for the exercise of action-inhibited fantasy. When we fail to mourn an imagined possibility that appeared to be within reach but is not, it becomes a fantasy which is quietly or passionately sustained. Sometimes its continuing presence in the inner world is innocuous; a simple dream waiting for the right moment to be fulfilled. Occasionally an unrealizable fantasy infects other imaginings with an alluring call towards passivity, because 'nothing will come of it anyway'. Imagined options which might have been turned into realities are dragged into its demotivating sphere of influence. A paralysis of will and a laming of desire are the cruel sacrifice demanded by unlamented dreams. We enter a timeless world. The energy to realize options, which is the gift of our imagination, becomes stuck.

Though the laws of science do not distinguish between the forward and backward directions of time, human beings do. We have established a small corner of order in the universe where we try to gain hold of a personal awareness of time. Here we set ourselves bravely against the scientific facts of time, that point towards the increase of disorder over order and the collapse of the universe, which will follow its expanding phase. In flowing time we anticipate events and are ready to meet the world, its probable occurrences and realistic possibilities. The development of the capacity to anticipate has undoubtedly bestowed evolutionary advantages on the human species by enabling us to be ready to plan, to fight, to flee, or to search. Its accompanying sense of urgency has, however, some distinct disadvantages, for urgency is a fore-grounding experience and pushes behind itself the equally important evolutionary necessity of being able to stand still, to muse, and to rest (Holt 1987, pp.89–90). Tranquillity and urgency are uncomfortable bed-fellows. When they work together they make for a great team. When they desire to exclude the other from the operational forefront of our life, we face trouble. We need the one as much as the other. Illness ensues, sooner or later, when their joined presence has become unacceptable to the owner-occupier, the person who runs the show. Time-Urgency or Hurry Sickness is often experienced as anxiety, 'nerves', stress, or hypertension. The treatment includes tranquillizers and anti-depressants. Sometimes low-cost prescriptions such as training in physical activity, play, drama or dance, biofeedback, relaxation, meditative techniques, and auto-hypnosis are given (Locke and Hornig-Rohan 1983). This latter category of treatment options might also be called time-therapy because it enables a person to move from the intense experience of time's inexorable flow into a clearly felt sense of having 'all the time in the world'. Such time is altogether less urgent, less hectic and, above all, less anxiety provoking. Both inactivity and hyperactivity beget illness. Our general wellbeing is not very negotiable; it demands that hurry, activity and rest become good friends.

This inner befriending is no easy task. In the throes of emotional or physical illness, the experience of time contracts. The awareness of time throbs with the aching pulse of unrelieved pain. Time feels not only slow – it is as if there was never a world before this pain, and there shall never be a world beyond it (Achterberg and Frank 1978). This is movingly illustrated in Michael's story. Due to a childhood injury to his back, he suffered chronic back pain. During the third session of a TSM group he wrote the following story:

> Kaga has lived long. He is very tired, lonely and bored. Today is very hot and sunny, yesterday was too and the day before, so will tomorrow be. He wanders around aimlessly, trying to find food, water and more than that, he wants to meet someone, he needs to talk. He finds no one. He has to talk to himself. He is bored with his own answers and realizes that he must continue to live life alone, as he has already done for so many years. He hates the idea and determines that he is going to live with others. He runs until he finds a village and decides to live there. The people ignore him. They do not greet him, nor do they spurn him. This is worse than being on his own, so he plays tricks to try to get attention. In the end the people are so cross with him that they banish him to the desert. He remembers that this is how it all happened those 500 years ago when he was last born.

Michael's injury had left him feeling isolated, separated and definitely not whole. His sense of connection with people or objects around him was fragile. The management of his pain depleted his capacity for attention (Morley 1993). Considerations about mortality, birth, death, longevity, illness and health appeared irrelevant to him; he only wanted his pain to stop. Though he needed other people to listen to him, his capacity for mutuality was minimally developed. Whilst his thirst for attention longed for satiation, he also needed to learn to take his place amongst others, to give and to get. He had become locked up in a claustrophobic, pain-saturated inner world. With his felt sense of time constricted, the pain was magnified. He appeared, and felt, spaced out, lost and confused.

A timeless space

When life is this bad, the awareness of being able to move out of this inner state by means of imaginary journeys may spontaneously present itself to the sufferer as a healing solution. A nurse, doctor, friend, relative, therapist or casual visitor can also invite the one who hurts momentarily to explore an imaginary world, to wander in an internal, fantasy realm where mind and body become separate. Sheila, a woman who experiences chronic, severe pain, said to me:

> I take all the pain killers I'm allowed to take. But they only help a little. After that I can only try to forget about the pain. When that doesn't work, because the pain is too great, I go off with the fairies, dear. If people knew what I do in my mind they would think me peculiar. But I'm not. I just go to fantasy land. It helps, you see, it really helps.

Unbeknown to her, she used auto-hypnosis and constructive imagination to bring about those changes in brain physiology that alter pain perception. Her journeys in fantasy land set in motion complex biochemical events, which include beneficial changes in hormonal levels in the blood and variations in heart-rate and blood pressure as well as changes in levels of muscle tension and blood flow to certain regions of her body. In the course of her pain-relief experiments, Sheila changed at will her usual sense of time perception for one in which time ceases to flow. Even though the events in her imaginary situations were sequentially changing, and could be separately perceived or commented on, they were experienced as placed outside flowing time.

In her attempts to cope with the intense, physical pain, she had chanced across a potent therapeutic agent which she believed to be a little weird but which she nonetheless pursued with vigour. Her fantasy images evolved as time-asymmetric events. She dwelled outside this time-frame, looking on. In this inner space, time ceased to matter (Siegel 1990). It became an irrelevance. Though the imaginary occurrences were significant, their positioning in time was of little or no actual concern. This supported her subjective experience of both analgesia and time expansion. In the process of learning to manage her pain, she found out that not all images were effective. Some definitely worked better than others. Describing her process of self-witnessed experimentation, she added: 'It took me a while to work out which ones work best. I have one where I sit on a rock by the sea. I make sure I can feel the wind on my face and listen to the birds.' She added: 'I won't tell you about some of the others. They might not work any more. I discovered that too. I lost some that way.' The images that help to relieve pain are intimate, personal and pain-specific. Some people thrive on sitting by a river, seeing things flow by; others visualize their pain as a red hot needle point which gradually changes colour, is drained of burning energy and re-absorbed as a cooling whiteness whilst yet others meander through forests, stand on mountain peaks or rest by a fireside. Some listen to sounds, a few imagine an enveloping, sweetly-scented paradisical breeze. These visual, tactile, oral and olfactory images commonly invoke a specific psycho-physical response mode with regard to time perception. Breathing changes and the person is freed for a while from any awareness of trying to arrive or aiming to become. The time experience is at once actual and chimeric.

Such journeys into fantasy are both more and less than flight from so-called felt reality. They are a conscious attempt to manipulate the experience of reality and to facilitate healing. They aim to initiate a mind-body event that might bring about at least a reduction in pain experience and, at best, actual easement of symptoms or even recovery. It is a mental exercise in creating time-awareness beyond the human perception of the flow of time in order to enter, as Einstein put it, physicist's time. This faculty and facility is, as Dossey (1982) suggests, no less part of our sensory capacities than touch, hearing and sight (p.166). How we return from such journeys and what we do with them ultimately determines whether they become lasting, healing solutions or a problem in their own right.

Luria (1987) warns that imaginal activity which is no longer directed towards the reality of action becomes a substitute for action by making action seem pointless (p.52-3). When this happens, life is transformed into a waking nightmare. All that is done becomes merely temporary, something to do until what is expected in fantasy will come to pass without the exercise of either influence or control. Many people who experience profound emotional illness live in an inner state of provisional existence without imaginable end, because the end cannot be envisioned.[3] The future feels out of reach. This

---

3   The links between extensive use of wish fulfilling fantasy and rumination (as opposed to reflection) without such fantasy being translated into purposeful actions is demonstrably linked to growing anxiety and depression. Prolonged pining and clinging to hope for the trouble just to go away increases despair (see Upton and Thompson 1992).

involves an existential loss of structure. Both long-term unemployment, social isolation or chronic illness can lead to existence 'outside of time'. Frankl (1963) points out that people who can cling to no end point or time in the future are in danger of allowing themselves to collapse inwardly (p.97).

In such a plight, episodes of security and satisfaction are short-lived. There is little sensual pleasure and encounters with people who offer explicit appreciation and acceptance are rare, whilst satisfying experiences of excitement or adventure in relation to the natural environment or play with peers or pets can be counted on the fingers of one hand. In such circumstances the retrieval of the capacity to prepare for the future through benign and constructive uses of the imagination is of the utmost importance (Grainger 1990).

Sutton-Smith (1979), a world expert on children's play, uses the term 'vivification' to describe the role that day-dreaming or fantasizing might play in our lives. Such dreams not only provide us with moments to savour, they also lend intense colour and potential experience to our daily existence. Singer (1981) suggests that: 'We must of course build into our day-dreaming a self checking system that keeps us from driving off the road or bumping into objects as we walk down the street. But surely we can fit a considerable amount of playful day-dreaming into a sequence of activities and by so doing can make life richer and more effective' (pp.255–6). He identifies several functions to day-dreams. These are: calming and soothing yourself; strengthening yourself during troubled times; dealing with loneliness; using day-dreams to understand behaviour better; exploring memories to ponder on alternatives in the future; to develop skills at work; and to increase creativity and originality. Fantasies which are inspired by such strength of purpose and such clarity of longing do indeed perform an extremely useful function to enhance our well-being.

Fatalistic pessimism

However, such positively and joyously toned day-dreams are frequently replaced by rather painful and self-hurting day-dreams when people feel depressed. The negatively-toned fantasies pull forever at the certain kind of homesickness that makes the person long forever for a land of their own dreaming. In this land people do not necessarily encounter blessings, opportunities, achievement and recognition. On the contrary, the stories and images which emerge in those inner worlds are painful, lonesome and full of sadness. In TSM I encounter such depressive affect in stories the group member makes up about characters or situations. These pained, helpless images include, for example:

- a totally silent, frozen mother
- rabbits whose young are killed by hunters
- a lonesome old man whose wife has recently died
- a girl who is lost in a strange, terrifying city, whilst everyone refuses help
- a man who lives in an icy landscape, abandoned even by dogs
- a woman alone on a barren island shortly after her children have died
- a woman who lives alone in a village, no food, only increasing despair.

These are the kind of characters and story themes commonly produced by children or adults who are in the grips of profound, emotional pain (Cattanach 1992). Their inner process is given expressive form in three readily recognizable ways:

- Spontaneous stories are dominated by themes of maltreatment. This includes fierce criticism, blame, loss, abandonment, torture, death and wounding as well as a relentless thwarting of any effort to bring about change or betterment.
- Verbal expression of feelings and thoughts linked with these painful situations is readily accessed. The clients' expressions focus on a profound sense of guilt, on being unwanted, unloved, helpless and hopeless.
- The group member shows little energy, has a low mood and complains of being unable to sleep and of having little appetite. Movements are heavy and slow.

The embrace of 'felt helplessness' results in ever diminishing activity, hostility and preoccupation with painful thoughts (Lynch 1977). In this state of mind each activity is anticipated like a version of the famous race between Donkey and Toad:

> Convinced of his invincibility, Donkey agreed to race Toad. Toad had planned his assault on Donkey's superiority for a long, long time. When the race-track is set out and the conditions of the race have been agreed, they begin to run. To his fear and astonishment, Donkey notices that whenever he looks to this side, Toad is always there. However fast he runs, he can never seem to get ahead of Toad. He

tries harder and harder. But Toad never falls back. He has tricked
Donkey by placing his countless children alongside the road. They
run the race in ceaseless relay. Each time Donkey cries out so as to say:
'I'm here. I'm ahead. I'm winning', a little Toad cries out too, so as to
say: 'You haven't won. I'm keeping up! You're losing!' Donkey becomes
more and more tired and so very angry. Until he gets so sad in his
mind that he just gives up.[4]

Donkey's sad, non-comprehending anger at having lost a road race to a Toad
and Toad's ambiguous victory due to trickery and deceit becomes a cauldron
of troubled energy. Were both Donkey and Toad to persist in their demonstrated behaviour and responses, both they and their buddies will run into
difficulty. Ever more limited action options clash with a desire and a need to
act differently. Not only do they need behaviour clarification, they need
repertoire expansion. Both Donkey's and Toad's self-limiting assumptions
about their capabilities need to be translated into more supportive inner talk.
When people live through Toad's or Donkey's plight, they often experience
intense fatalistic pessimism, as well as a longing for imagined plenty – a blind
desire for so much more than can ever be granted. In the throes of profound
need and greed, the client's ways of coping with the inevitable frustration
and disappointment of human interaction is limited. In this state, substantial
inner disturbance is activated by the very attempt to create a friendly,
supportive and, above all, gratifying atmosphere in a group. This disturbance
is frequently expressed through mass evacuation of confusion or hostility.
The fear of love tries to create affirming evidence that, ultimately, love will
not be possible, simply because destructiveness cannot be contained. Winnicott (1980) emphasizes that emotional well-being depends on the permission we need as children to be allowed to attempt to destroy the object of
our primitive love (p.105). The successful containment of this attack and
therefore the object's survival permits the integration of the destructive
impulse. Helping a group or an individual to make sense of these processes
is, at some stage, high on the agenda of effective short-term or long-term
group work. A discussion of some possible dynamics of these processes can
be inspired by the following story:

At the beginning there was a large circle of milk-like dew. Then
Doondari came into being. He created rock. Rock brought forth iron,
whilst iron created fire. Fire gave birth to water, which in turn gave
birth to air. When the world was thus made, Doondari acted for the
second time. He gathered stone, iron, fire, water, and air, the five basic

---

4   Retold by the author. Aesop's fables have been retold by numerous authors and storytellers.

principles. He used them to make people. But people were proud of their being. Doondari created blindness and people became lost in their blindness. When blindness became proud of its being, Doondari created sleep. Sleep struggled with blindness and blindness lost. However, sleep too surrendered to pride. Therefore Doondari created worry and worry was victorious over sleep. When the time came that worry was too full of itself Doondari created death. Death mastered worry. When death became too convinced of its own importance Doondari intervened for the third time. He became Gueno, the One who is evermore, and Gueno overcame death.[5]

The story suggests an inevitable link between worry, pride, sleeplessness and death. During the mourning of aspirations, we need to surrender an image of a possible self; to let go of an ambition, a longing and a self-perception. This surrender is often felt as a diminishment, a dying without inner resurrection, a curtailment without emergence into a new abundance. In story-based group work the facilitator and the group members jointly aim to promote the capacity to mourn the options that are foreclosed whenever we make a choice, to celebrate the ones we do choose and to translate what is believed possible into reality (Jennings and Minde 1993, pp.169–86). As noted before, the imagination is exercised whenever we envisage possibilities, work them out in detail, formulate their viability and turn possibilities into available options. Such doing is, however, not culturally unbound, it is deeply embedded in the prevailing socio-economic structures. Culturally, and, therefore, also socio-economically, different people have different narratives, different customs of communication, different etiquette and relating styles (Kluckhohn 1942, pp.45–79). Ignorance as regards alternative world views, of various conceptions of human relationships, of vastly different notions of disorder and remediation, values and ideologies and the ways these affect both the imagination and expressive communication demands that perceptions about 'what may or may not be possible' are offered with substantial caution and humility.

---

5   Retold by the author. Contemporary source in Beier (1970, pp.1–2).

Happily may they come with
you.
Thus you accomplish
your tasks.
Navaho

Practice vignette: no longer a silent witness

Many years ago I facilitated a brief (10 sessions) storymaking group with homeless women and men. The building where the group took place was situated in a derelict part of town, along a major traffic artery. It was grey, smelly and hollow with a pervading sense of poverty. In this environment we tried to create the experience of containment and thoughtful interpersonal care. In that particular session, Terry, a middle-aged man, dishevelled and weary eyed, with a long history of recurring emotional problems, listened to group-talk about those occasions when, upon seeing your face in the mirror, you suddenly wonder: 'Is that really me? Is this what has become of me?' Voice hoarse with smoke, drink and unscreamed sorrow, he cut across the group and, addressing me in particular, said: 'You want us to talk about that? That gets you locked up. You don't know what happens to people like us when we think thoughts like that.' Scrimmaging through her bag, Sonya, a woman with years of street experience behind her, retorted: 'Come off it Terry, she is not that crazy'. She handed him a crumpled piece of paper, adding: 'Here, read it'. He read: 'We're not dangerous, we're frightened. Won't anybody hear us.' Terry sighed at her words, then, at my invitation to reflect on what was so frightening about the group's theme, he talked about his experience in psychiatric hospitals and, above all, about his great fear of the night during his hospitalizations. His fear reminded me of the words spoken in a Xingu myth of creation, which says:

In the morning the day is born,
in the afternoon it fades,
then it disappears all at once.
When this happens
don't think we took it back,
don't think that.
The day appears,
Then comes the night.
It will always be this way.
Don't think it will always stay

dark when night comes.

That we stole the day from you.

Don't be afraid

It will always come back. (Gersie 1991, p.114)

I wondered briefly whether to refer to the myth but decided not to, reminding myself that the level of trust in this group provided Terry with sufficient support to pursue his telling. Sonya's action had already given him the vitally needed assurance that self-revelation was both possible and worthwhile (Buie 1981). The story simply resonated in the background of my mind. In the course of Terry's talk about his life we soon encountered his deep shame related to his emotional difficulties.

In every psychiatric hospital people live in daily contact with their own and other people's illness. Intense pain is witnessed. Many participants in TSM groups talk about the unbearable burden into which such pain has combined. They wonder how they can ever re-tell the tales of suffering that have touched their lives whilst they stayed in psychiatric hospitals, prison, or day centres. Terry preferred sleeping rough, partly because the events he had encountered on the wards still terrified him. The memories of other people's distress, and of having been a silent witness to the death by suicide of fellow patients, had turned his own trouble into an unbearable burden. These multiple sorrows had not healed. He was still unable to sleep in a so-called safe place – shelter or police cell alike (see Smith 1986).

When he finally addressed his memories in the group, Terry's speech did not fail him, nor were the listeners confused by his words. None of us attached greater importance to his diagnostic label than to the actual recounting of his experience (Levontin, Rose and Kamin 1984). The group's response was not inspired by considerations such as those encapsulated by Von Franz (1980) who wrote: 'Very often the reason for schizophrenia is not so much the invasion of unconscious but that it happens to someone who is too narrow for the experience either mentally or emotionally. People who are not broad minded enough and have not enough generosity and heart to open up to what comes are exploded by the invasion of the unconscious' (p.217). Terms like 'broad-mindedness' or 'lack of generosity' were not pertinent to our understanding of Terry's experience in a dimly-lit hospital ward; of his response to hearing screams of terror and of having felt utterly unable to do anything. Our listening to his account of having been so frightened made a difference to him, as did the responses he received to his telling. The word images of terror, care, numbing and sympathy which other group members created after he had told his story gave his experience a context and a home.

His loneliness had been relieved; his response normalized. Fear, rage and frustration exercise a tragically damaging effect on both the imagination and on the capacity to act. In any therapeutic process which involves imaginary activity the issue of how to generate genuinely envisioned action-options for participants who experience deep emotional turmoil lies at the heart of the therapeutic encounter.

The generosity of, at times, very unwell people like Terry or Sonya is as kindly or unkindly rooted in their lived experience, and includes a similarly wide range of feelings, relationships, desires, hopes and thoughts, as the generosity of those less unwell (Ussher 1991). Sonya was hurting sorely not merely because of her own illness but also because of the intense psychic and physical pain she had witnessed in people with whom she had shared many a terrifying night on frightening wards. When she had tried to help these other patients, sometimes friends, sometimes people alien to her own heart, she had, once in a while, succeeded. However, she also felt that she had failed more than once, for, after all, Tina or Peter or Liz had ultimately died through suicide. The memories of these experiences were still open wounds that combined with her very own trouble that already had such great trouble healing. This combination of sorrows had not yet healed, not merely because too frequently her speech had failed her but also because too many listeners had failed to hear her speech, which contained its attempt at wellbeing in its very lack of wellbeing, seeking merely the means to lead its life.

Like Kate in Shakespeare's play *The Taming of the Shrew*, Sonya too had once vowed to say only what 'Daddy, Auntie and Mr Neighbour' had told her to say. When she safeguarded her determined subversion of this vow through the conscious adoption of a language overflowing with vagueness and a relentless flurry of metaphoric illusions, she had not been understood. Nor had she understood the price she would pay for electing to live in an idiosyncratic never-never land (de Campos 1993). Later, much later, when her process of recovery from chronic childhood sexual abuse and years of treatment as a schizoid depressive was well under way, she said: 'I was so busy trying to say that I couldn't say anything, to let them know that I was sworn to secrecy, that they just couldn't decipher the code. Do you think they tried? I was taken at my words and my words suggested I was mad. I wasn't mad, I was lonely.'

In my experience, clients readily invite each other and me to explore their involvement with how life makes sense to them, to trace their implied beliefs about the support that certain modes of life deserve or merit and to become more aware of the changing perspective upon the life that is worth living in order to examine with each other what might be useful about these truths in practice, through action as well as through contemplation on action. In therapeutic storymaking (TSM) the 'how' of life is consequently privileged over the construction of answers to the question 'why'.

And they wandered on, reflecting
How they might perchance discover,
How they might succeed in finding,
Where the fire had just descended.
Kalevala

Learning to contemplate and to act

In therapeutic storymaking groups I try to comprehend how intentional states such as believing, longing or grasping a meaning manifest themselves in a participant's life. When I search for a modicum of understanding of what, for example, hope or desire might mean to Terry or Sonya, I presume that however torn-to-pieces a person feels, they always express something that is pertinent about themselves to themselves and to others. I enable clients to clarify their experience of themselves in their situation whilst I attempt to create the widest possible perspective on that situation, so that alternatives become emergent choice-options. When I try to grasp what, for example, the feeling of 'longing' might mean to a group member and how it is rooted in their inner world, I rely on the concept of agency. Agency implies that actions and inactions occur under the influence of intention. I also presume that however unwell a person is, they still have something to say or to express about their situation. In this manner I accompanied Patricia, a woman who wrote the following words after some careful preparatory work around the theme of homecoming:

> My name is the Bird. I am born of conflict. Many years ago there was a struggle which was not resolved. The struggle was two struggles and there would be no end. But out of struggle the sky grew dark and the land became angry and there came a void. In the void there was silence and out of silence and knowledge and understanding grew wisdom and wisdom was free. And freedom soared into the sky and looked back on the struggle and the turmoil and knew that it must return. I returned and I am freedom. I can leave at any time, I can stay. I am the Bird.

When she wrote the above words she knew which conflict she referred to. I did not. It took the passage of time and the growing trust of relationship to move from metaphoric reference to actual description; time in which the group in question grew to work more closely together to re-establish the crucial, purposeful link between language, action and a workable everyday interpretation of this relationship. She learned to let her words become truly indwelling, which means connected with her knowledge about life – to incorporate both its traumatic occurrences and the ordinary events. Bruner (1990) suggests that language and action are always situated in terms of time, the cultural setting and in the mutually interacting states of therapists and clients (p. 19). Well or unwell, both therapist and client are inevitably involved in a world of images, meanings and social bonds (Rosaldo 1984, p. 139). When clients who feel disconnected from their words, as if their language belongs to somebody else, join a therapeutic group, they bring to it other important assumptions, such as:

> 'It is not worth responding to anything for if I do it still doesn't get me anywhere.'

> 'I'm definitely powerless.'

> 'I cannot influence anything or anyone in any way let alone in the direction I desire.'

Participation in story-work appeals to them because the structured use of various tasks supports their willingness temporarily to lay aside their dark imaginings. The story-work helps the client:

- to concentrate upon something or someone other than themselves as well as upon themselves
- to exercise choice and to sustain an activity
- to move from the paralyzing timelessness of 'ever-land' into time-boundness, which involves purposeful retrospection and prospecting
- to dare to anticipate again and to learn to trust this capacity once more
- to develop a communicative language which involves communicating about what was considered unmentionable.

As noted before, the imagination is exercised whenever we envisage possibilities, work these out in detail, formulate their viability and make what is believed possible an available option. People who experience severe emotional illness endure greatly curtailed imaginative horizons (Wethered 1993).

In systematic work with stories and storytelling these horizons can be expanded. In a TSM group for depressed adults which was in the throes of pain linked with acknowledged neglect during childhood, I once worked with the following story:

> A long time ago there was a land. In this land a great war raged. At first the people fought with arms, hands, feet and nails. But after a while they used stones and slings to cast the other down. Many people died. Then a great drought came upon the land. At this time an evil spirit who hated both warring factions whispered in their ears: 'Set the land on fire and your enemy will perish.' Fires were started everywhere. The land was set ablaze and all, nearly all, died.
>
> Only one couple had stayed apart from this most bitter of wars. When they heard about the planned destruction of the land they had dug themselves a deep, deep hole and made their dwelling in that dank, damp darkness. When flames ate the grass and trees above them, they were safe in the earth. When the great fire-storms had ravaged the lands they pushed a little stick above the earth. When it caught fire they knew the time had not yet come to return to earth. A little later they pushed another stick just above the soil and again it caught fire and again they knew their time had not yet come. When the third time came and the stick did not catch fire, they waited still a little longer. At last the moment came when they felt safe to venture out of their hiding place. What they saw was terrible to behold. All around them dark ashes lay. As they stood and gazed at that ashen landscape a strange voice came to them and said: 'Are you certain you want to live in this place?' 'Oh yes,' the couple replied. Once more the voice spoke, 'I tell you, the earth will again be consumed like this.' 'Oh yes, we know', the couple replied. 'In spite of that you want to live here?' 'We do', they answered. And as they affirmed their desire to begin anew they noticed that a soft green sheen enveloped the charred trees. Again the voice came to them and said: 'You will have only each other.' Once more they nodded and said, 'it will suffice.' And so it came to be that out of the great destruction there emerged just one small new beginning.[6]

The couple's decision to try to survive in hiding and, after time had passed, slowly to test a return to a more viable life, mattered. Their capacity to face the reality that their new, old world would continue to present them with both difficulties and uncertain blessings, aptly described the dynamics of the

---

6   Retold by the author. Contemporary source in Baumann (1975, pp.152–3).

group during its own recovery from despair. Group members were only too aware that much had been ravaged in their individual lives as a result of misfortune, malice or neglect. Yet they also knew that their very presence to each other constituted a new possibility. The story supported the group's engagement with the theme of fragile, but determined hope (Rivers 1912).

To take a shared authority

People with long-term mental health difficulties have learned from experience that their own understanding of what has caused their troubles becomes, in the process of treatment, subjugated to the knowledge of many different health care professionals each of whom has something pertinent to say about the client's condition (Teff 1985). Many clients are also aware that the professional team involved in their treatment may well hold opposing views about how they might best achieve improvement or cure (Hilton 1995). However, during serious illness a client needs to rely on professionals' knowledge about the best possible treatment. This factor often leads to the client's unexamined acceptance of a doctor's statement about the nature of their condition or of a social worker's or arts therapist's pronunciations about the 'cause' of their predicament. During the profoundly confusing experience of mental ill-health the client cannot but subjugate their own understanding about their predicament to that of people in special authority (Kellerman 1992). When clients' decision making power is fragmented, frequently all that remains is their occasional use of the remaining constitutive element of power – namely to withhold co-operation. Such withholding of co-operation involves substantial emotional and actual cost. Through the withholding of co-operation a client may aim to safeguard a crucial thread of dignity, yet it actually prevents the client from taking more shared authority for their healing process.

I have found that group members who are initially reluctant to accept authorship for their deeds, let alone responsibility for their process of healing, can grow towards such acceptance when they are initially enabled to tell about their experiences obliquely, within the protective analogy of a fictional story. It is as if the 'fictional realm' allows client and therapist the space to learn one another's language, to translate implied understanding into actual understanding and carefully to test the reality of the implied commitment to negotiating truth and meaning. Through such shared exploration important processes of healing are activated. As Greenberg and Stone (1992) observe, the long-term gains of confronting emotionally upsetting events in story form are substantial in terms of positive effect on the person's psychological and physical health. Story-work combines the open expression of troubling emotions with exercises which enable group members to give voice to painful experiences in a storytelling format. At the very least, people participating in such a group hear a new or old story, become (more) able to create and tell meaningful stories at will and gather evidence of other people's interaction with their own created narrative. This first, observable level of group work practice model constitutes the most obvious and, therefore, also the most necessary level of change, namely the level where a client is able to do something new and different and experiences the practice of newness in the presence of concerned others. In addition to such explicit 'learning to tell again' group members often become more aware of the extent to which they are consenting participants in their stories, to build an informed relationship with such stories and derive greater personal meaning from their interpretation of their life's events and their place within these, ultimately to become both more able and more willing to consent to the never-ending process of attempting to transform desired change into actual change. Given the emphasis on learning, TSM can best be described as a therapeutic pedagogy of kinds.

When group members explore a story's content and its stated or implied assumptions they soon discover that all of us use logic to figure something out and that this logic has a tendency to be constructed in a manner which matches the logic of the thing to be understood. This awareness is achieved by helping group members to think more systematically about:

○ the way a story-character gathers information and, by inference, how they themselves set about this task

○ how a story-character formulates goals, pursues these and which end they themselves aim for

○ the links between goals and starting situation – this runs parallel with enabling group members to think about how they started something and how this relates to what they hope to achieve

○ those unstated assumptions or propositions that might otherwise easily be taken for granted.

Many years ago I put this fairly standard structure of logical deliberation to Julie, a bright teenager who lived in an extremely tough inner city area. In response she growled: 'but that way of thinking doesn't make a wrong right does it? When you know more about where you want to go because you've understood how something's gone wrong, then that doesn't mean that you will get there. Nor does it mean that things will change. It doesn't mean at all that anyone is ever going to take the blindest bit of notice.' When I retorted that this depended, amongst other things, on whether or how she or I would take notice, she shook her head saying, 'You don't know nothing yet. You're a stupid, hopeful cow.' The pressures to which she had been exposed at too young an age and the extent of her disillusionment at that time still prevented her brightness of thought from inspiring possible, constructive action. A determined school refuser, she lived through a sad plight. But things changed. She joined an alternative learning programme and made great headway. When group workers help adults or children like Julie to become more judicious critics of the nature and quality of their thought and encourage their internalization of a habit to evaluate, they often discover that these thought processes were once familiar to these people. Many of those who need treatment for mental health difficulties surrendered their sense-making to the pressures of miseries which just could not be alleviated by excellence of thought or well-argued critique of circumstance alone.

Whenever I offer a storymaking group in an area of substantial urban deprivation, I meet the kind of despair that is partly engendered by the actual conditions in which the participants live. When we decide together to aim for a return to given-up-on excellence of thought and experience, our path inevitably leads to outrage and despondency. Many so-called mad, bad or despondent clients decided early in life that it was in their interest to be seen to be giving up on critical thought and to let go of systematic reasoning, either because the feelings it evoked could not be endured or because the helplessness it engendered was too painful and, above all, because the consequences of speaking out were too dangerous (Hilton 1995). 'Better to numb out man', one of the young boys with whom I worked once said. 'Or prove to me that thinking about things again will really, really change something.' It was not difficult to understand the profound need for self-protection which under-pinned his words. It hurts to think again. It is painful to re-consider options believed foreclosed, to sustain hope and to reflect upon action or inaction when so much has been out of reach for so long. When discussion and argument have led only to rejection, divisiveness and hostility, it takes faith to try out an idea and to risk controversy.

> *Trumpet Shell,*
> *Restore, Restore.*
> *The hunger exhaustion.*
> *Trumpet Shell, Restore.*
> Trobiand

Practice vignette: On passive action and becoming pro-active

This brings to mind a young woman, Joanna, who attended an open evening group in a drop-in centre for women with wide ranging life-difficulties. As so often happens with drop-in groups, this one had actually built up quite a steady membership. During the warm-up exercises Joanna had a persistent scowl on her face. She choose not to contribute when the group sat in a circle to reflect on this early work. However, during the story writing which followed the group-sharing, she did record her answers to a brief series of verbal questions which I had designed to help each person to write their own story based on a shared story-structure. The questions were:

- In which landscape does the story take place?
- What kind of dwelling place is there in this landscape?
- Who (animal, person or creature) lives in this dwelling?
- What kind of predicament does this one presently experience?
- What makes this particularly difficult?
- Who unexpectedly offers help?
- How does the character use the help offered?
- Which further minor obstacle then presents itself?
- How come this obstacle surprises the character?
- How is this additional difficulty overcome?
- What is the final outcome?
- What does the character gain from the experience, if anything?

The group was familiar with this story-evoking question–answer procedure, though not with this particular sequence. Each woman wrote or drew her full story on the basis of the brief answers recorded in response to my questions. That week, sixteen women attended the group. I realized that I would not have the opportunity to work with everyone's story individually in front of the whole group. Though the group was large, there were no actual newcomers that night. Many occasional users were present. I therefore decided that it was possible to invite participants to work with their stories in pairs. I aimed to work with the overall group process whilst remaining available for any specific dynamics between the pairs of story-sharers.

I proposed the following activity-sequence for the development of the participant's engagement with their respective stories:

- ○ Select a partner. Preferably someone you do not yet know that well.
- ○ Choose a large enough working space for the two of you with as much privacy as possible.
- ○ Decide who will be A, who B.
- ○ A will read her story, B listens.
- ○ Then A reads her story again. This time, B enacts, dances, mimes the story.
- ○ After the miming activity, A will give her story to B who now reads this story. During this reading (the third), A will enact her own story.
- ○ Then change over. Try not to discuss A's story. Use the same reading-enactment sequence for B.
- ○ When both partners have gone through the reading-enactment procedures, take some time to discuss your experiences and responses. Then return to the circle.

I designed this three-fold intensification/enactment procedure in order to enhance emotional involvement in a distanced way. The sequence parallels certain aspects of structured learning therapy, such as the modelling of behavioural interpretation in behaviour actualization procedures, witness reactions and the structured increase of access to a wider behavioural repertoire. All pairs worked well together. They finished their reading, story-dancing and reflection sequences at more or less the same time. When the group reassembled after the pair-work, we still had ample time to process the experience together. Some women wanted to read their tale to the whole group, others spoke about links between their story and specific life experiences. Towards the end of the session Joanna, said: 'I was kicked out of my job this week. And you know, I've just realized, I don't do anything until I get kicked. I never knew that. I never did.' After the session she approached me to ask: 'Next week same time?'

The subsequent week Joanna opened the group by saying that she was still 'bowled over' by the realization that she was a passive kind of person (her words). She added: 'I've had a really good week. I've sorted all kinds of things. All because of that story. I now know that I've made so many things actually happen to me. It was there in my story. I've been really passive...!'

When invited to reflect on how this realization had emerged from the story-work, she mentioned that during her mimed enactment of her own story the previous week she had felt annoyed with her character for letting things happen, even when she saw them coming. Joanna had thought: 'This is how it's always going to be. Nothing will ever change if she (the character in the story) goes on behaving like this.' At that moment she had started to feel physically a little strange, off balance. She had apparently been close to dropping out of the exercise, but had thought: 'I know the end, so I might just as well carry on.' The unusual physical sensation had stayed with her until she had spoken up towards the end of the group. She had apparently not known what she was going to say. The words had tumbled out of her. Her story's essential meaning had unveiled itself, not during her first reading but in a pre-verbal way during the danced enactment which followed the reading and also in the immediacy of speaking to the group.

The story offered a concretization of Joanna's experience of her everyday world. The feelings aroused by the recent sacking, the intimacy generated in her encounter with an involved other, and the confrontation with the seemingly relentless inevitability of 'the same story, all over again' moved her from self-denial and denial of the world into a recognition of the immediate usefulness of her story: the realization that she waited to move until she got kicked into movement. Her behavioural change was also a concomitant result of the carefully structured pair work. As far as Joanna was concerned, she simply made an irrepressible connection between the basic events as portrayed in her story and her quality of life. The story reflected her common response mode. The story-processing procedure, through a combination of engrossment and reflection, facilitated the emergence of a change-activating realization. In answer to a question from another participant about their experience of the exercise the previous week, both Joanna and her partner had said that there had not been any obvious parallels between the story and her dismissal. They thought that the story had provided perfect cover for this life event. Others might have disagreed with this interpretation had they known the story, which we did not. Joanna added: 'At that point (i.e. early in the session) I would rather have died than have had to admit that I got sacked.'

The story had not addressed her life events (causality) but had expressed her position in life (instrumentality). The synthesis of telling and doing had allowed her to feel safe enough to share her experiences, both the sacking and the passivity insight, with the group and to move beyond shame and stuckness. She no longer had to say: 'When I get up in the morning, my daily prayer is: grant me today my illusion, my daily illusion' (Zipes 1979, p.124). She had become strong enough to bear another aspect of her reality.

Joanna's story had dealt with possible events happening to an imaginary character. The imagined nature of the story-character and the storied events eased the exploration of future possibilities because they did not demand direct commitment to action. The structure of the pair-exercise had purposefully generated this commitment. Joanna experienced the paradox of acting passive. The fact that she was acting suggested the availability of options. The enacted awareness of behavioural options exercises a *prima facie* motivational force. As Joanna had been the first person to read and to act her story in the pair, the influence of her partner's tale upon her has to be considered minimal, though the actual choice of person and the partner's enactment of Joanna's story as well as any voice-qualities used in the re-reading will all have played a role in facilitating the emergence of change. Joanna never shared her story with the whole group, it remained an evocative mystery.

Joanna gradually stopped coming to the group. However, we met again for an individual follow-up meeting about six months later. We had arranged this meeting because, in this form of supportive therapeutic group work, I think of the termination of participation as maybe a temporary ending in the context of a possibly longer term therapeutic contact. Endings and beginnings are particularly important in drop-in groups. In these groups it matters even more so to help participants to acquire a sense of the ongoing nature of human development by providing them with a sense of the agency's continuing interest and availability for him or her in the future, if this is reasonably possible (Dewald 1994).

During our follow-up meeting we reflected on the session in which Joanna had realized that she acted passive. Joanna said that it had been as if a hand which had concealed herself from herself had suddenly been removed. She had seen a possible future and had not liked the vision. She had also felt the reality of the paradox that here she was voluntarily acting a part she no longer wanted to play. Once the paradox was noted, the rest had been comparatively plain sailing. When I asked her permission to write about her experience she inquired: 'Does it really matter to you how I think I came to realize all this. Isn't the most important thing that it happened?' Conspiratorially she moved her head towards me: 'I'll tell you... I haven't a clue.'

> The story of Nasruddin, who late at night lost a key, came to mind. He was seen searching for it in the circle of light at the base of a street lamp. A kindly stranger asked if he could help. They both looked everywhere but there was no key to be seen. Finally the stranger queried: 'But where did you last have it. Where were you when you

lost that key.' 'In the back garden' Nasruddin sighed. 'Then why are you looking for it here?' shouted the exasperated stranger. To which Nasruddin replied: 'Because here there is light.'[7]

The mystery of change is not merely the mystery of sharing a substantial transformation in another human being. The lasting difference which was generated in Joanna was not a mere fluke. I have witnessed it in other people and have learned that over years such changes often become stable. The question 'What made this change possible and what made it last?' cannot easily be reduced to statements about the practice of alternative behaviours, or about the process of witnessing an enactment of one's story. Nor can it necessarily be attributed to the problem-solving format used to facilitate the emergence of a semi-autonomous fictional story which provided her life story with a restructuring coherency.

Joanna emphasized that she treasured the story she wrote during that session but was unwilling share it with me. It was clear that the story was personally important, and equally clear that any re-telling would attract a new context and thereby new interpretation. Why risk that much when so much has already been gained? Over time I have learned how much the quality of listening clients receive from other group members matters above and beyond the listening they receive from a group facilitator. Self-disclosure is an interpersonal act which takes place within the culture of the group and within the context of the larger socio-political framework. Therapy groups function optimally when its participants not only recognize that they are an important source of support, healing and information for one another but also that they need to engage with each other in a manner that expresses and enhances these capabilities.

From nothing the begetting,
From nothing the increase,
From nothing the abundance.
The power of increase, the living breath.
Maori

The use of warm-up techniques to support reflexivity

During periods of intense emotional illness, it is hard to think. Intense pain pushes our reflective capacity out of gear. We become preoccupied, absent-

---

7   Retold by the author. Contemporary version also in Aylwin (1989, p.5).

minded and impulsive. However, limited reflectivity also makes us more vulnerable. We need access to inner space where we can take stock of a situation, review options and prepare alternatives. In the Camel story neither father nor son differentiated between thought and action. Their solution to the experienced predicament of critical comments from passers-by was to adjust their behaviour instinctively and immediately in the direction the criticism implied. They had not yet developed the ability to cope with a broadened understanding of the problem at hand. Such broadened understanding would have involved learning to consider various alternatives to any immediately apparent solution. They did not think and ended up carrying their camel.

The stimulation of a person's reflective capacity is, somewhat paradoxically, best enhanced through therapeutic support for the capacity to become engrossed. This is not that strange. After all, we cannot reflect on imagined or actual possibilities unless our thinking is informed by trust, relaxation and the ability to concentrate. Internal authority over spontaneous fantasy relies on the person's capacity constructively to employ changes in the flow of relaxation and attention. In the inner and interpersonal worlds of troubled people this capacity is dangerously reduced. Their inner realm is often characterized by vague inactivity or sudden, uncomfortable emotions. Without a developed capacity to pause and ponder, they become a victim to circumstance and a hostage to impulse – both of which lead to personal and interpersonal difficulties. In such a plight, creative-expressive work can help the person not only to redevelop a basic faith in life's more pleasurable aspects, but also to strengthen their capacity to think about what they feel, intuit and want from their situation, to scan possibilities, to review options and to develop strategies to achieve some wanted aims. As noted, reflectivity evolves from instinctive behaviour when rudiments of the following developmental indicators are present:

- the ability not to respond in the usual way to a trigger situation
- access to a central memory store in which functional relationships between various remembrances are maintained
- some capacity to abstract or to generalize.

The presence or absence of these capacities fundamentally affects the developmental possibilities available to a client. In therapeutic group work many troubled clients initially need to participate in activities which provide for immediate impulse satisfaction, offer quick goal attainment, pose little demand as regards postponement, and have a high drainage value for tensions dominated by impulse patterns. At the same time, each activity needs to promote a sense of mastery and resourcefulness. The warm-up exercises need to expand the participant's fluency at sensory-motor, symbolic/iconic and reflective/lexical stages of development. The capacity to move flexibly through these various developmental stages vitally supports the emergence of more healing ways of being and behaving.

After a particularly involving series of warm-up exercises, Derek, a group member who attended a group in a drop-in centre for people with mental health difficulties, wrote:

> I remember being a kid, but I don't remember specifically the closeness and fun that these games provoked. Something held back then, something blocked my sense of fun. How easy it feels now. How good it feels to have this closeness.

He was a relative newcomer and had not yet consciously noticed the protective interference offered by the clear ceiling I had set on aggression, the insistence on some routines – such as the use of a circle for the sharing of reflections – or the various benefits of my therapeutic role consistency. He was in the midst of a somewhat golden glow because he felt that he had entered a comparatively safe place for exploration, as well as a set of relationships in which trust could be engendered and self-esteem developed. This was, amongst other things, facilitated through the careful recapitulation of some of his words, the tentative use of interpretations and my maintaining of awareness that the therapeutically significant moment is the one when the group member surprises him or herself.

In Shakespeare's play *Hamlet*, one of the watchmen, Barnardo, urges his colleagues to explore what is happening around them. He proposes that they sit down awhile. Then that they assail their ears that have become so fortified against their story. When people are emotionally unwell, it can be safely presumed that they have both a strong need to tell their stories and that they are fortified against such telling. The group worker needs to nurture a troubled person's willingness to truly listen to their heart's stories. I learned that the willingness to embark on such listening can be strengthened by enabling group members to become more aware of sensory experiences. In an ancient Korean folktale it is said that:

> The eyes are like precious stones, they can move and roll and see so many things. The ears have been given hollow spaces so that they may hear. The nose has channels by means of which smell is noticed. The mouth is a flat open space. Air can easily pass through it. Sound and talk arise from the tongue. But all of these are as nothing without the heart. It differentiates between the good and the bad. Without the

heart, even though you have eyes, you cannot see, though you have ears you cannot hear. Though you have a nose you cannot smell, and though you have a mouth you cannot breathe, so they say that without the heart seeing you cannot see, and hearing you cannot hear.[8]

As the story indicates, we are seeing blind and hearing deaf unless we are informed by the heart's knowledge. Yet the heart's knowledge cannot find expression when the means to do so have long since been blocked. I believe that it is important to be aware of the implication of this understanding. It suggests that our current life situation is most readily interpreted on the basis of the following aspects of experience:

- how the body feels now
- what is remembered about past experiences
- what is thought, felt and intuited about the current situation
- which options are believed to be available.

However, these processes are but brittle signposts when unsupported by a capacity to invest some degree of trust in one's reading of a here and now experience of a particular situation. In group work such trust is critically connected with group members' perceptions of the reason behind the introduction of various creative-expressive exercises. Fear that the activities will be used only for diagnostic information purposes limits or stagnates involvement. The fear is legitimate in so far as every activity provides both the client and the therapist with new information. The elicitation of mere information is, however, a very weak reason for the inclusion of creative-expressive exercises in a therapeutic repertoire of activities, particularly as this justification tends to enhance a troubled group member's dominant sense of the lack of inherent value in whatever they undertake. Other arguments to support the use of creative-expressive exercises in therapeutic group work are equally valid. The most pertinent amongst these are:

- the disruption through action of maladaptive ways of communicating between people
- the enhancement of relationships through affective expression and participation in a joint creative-expressive activity (Greenberg 1974)
- giving primacy to here and now experiences, and thereby to bring these into the therapy room (Oaklander 1988)
- enabling people to gain access to emotional expression without dwelling too much on either the past or the future. (Oster and Gould 1987)

---

8   Retold by the author. Contemporary source in Bang and Ryuk (1962, p.210).

Each group's atmosphere is profoundly influenced by whatever occurs in non-verbal exercises or encounter techniques. Certain poignant exercises enhance group members' emotional awareness by stimulating an intense desire for intimate disclosure. If a therapist is too information-focused, group members are frequently not given enough time to reflect on personal reactions, or are not granted an intervening opportunity to share their memories with others. The feelings which emerge then leave the group members in a state of frustration. The effect of such frustration on behaviour during and after a session can only be guessed (Snortum and Ellenhorn 1974). Vital opportunities may well be lost when a therapist uses expressive activity primarily in order to construct a more elaborate theory about a group member's functioning.

To seed the potential for change

I use warm-up exercises for most of the reasons noted above and, above all, to emphasize certain experiences early on in the therapeutic process in order to provide a basis for later work (see also Haley 1976). I structure each creative-expressive activity so that it optimally energizes each client's potential focus for change within the broad terrain of desired change. During the warm-ups, certain concepts or experiences are rendered emotionally and cognitively accessible to the clients. The exercises are early ventures into playful states which, only at a surface level, do not seem to matter that much. Thereby the client is also helped to bond with the mode of working. Small, seemingly insignificant emotional events are then, later during the session, linked together. The brief exercises are made to fall into a clear overall pattern without this necessarily having been anticipated. In the literature of experimental psychology such purposeful seeding of change potential is sometimes described as priming. It consists of

- *direct or repetition priming* which is used to enhance a person's accuracy of response and/or to decrease latency

- *associative priming* which is employed in order to decrease the time a person needs to make decisions about lexical matters and

- *indirect priming* which is relied on to generate change in a particular behaviour which was previously linked with exposure to some kind of stimulus. (Zeig 1980)

In priming, various exercises, particularly non-verbal ones, are used to concretize feeling and to enhance interpersonal competence, self-acceptance, self-esteem and social skills. The effect of such priming has been shown to be remarkably comprehensive, particularly because it influences how a person interprets events and which actions are preferred as well as what a person actually thinks about. If, as Bartlett (1932) suggests, memory schemata are controlled by affective attitudes, which are rather like a thumb-print of the schemata which construct them, the creation of access to both the affective attitudes and to these memory traces is of fundamental importance in the therapeutic situation. Priming or seeding is one of the concepts that can be used to describe how this process might work.

In TSM the selection of warm up techniques is guided by the following criteria:

- whether they generate focus on the here-and-now
- whether they facilitate contact with those feelings which the group member has difficulty in expressing verbally, although these feelings are effectively present
- whether they enable focus on clear inter-personal dynamics or intrapsychic material.

The warm-ups not only have to support feeling, they also need to provide sustenance for feeling good. As noted above, emotionally unwell people often find it difficult both to use abstract verbal communications and to express feelings, let alone feeling good. Non-verbal and verbal warm-up exercises allow the expression of a wide range of feelings. They need to meet a group member's felt needs for communication, expression and understanding where words alone would not have sufficed, thereby to permit not only a therapeutically vital degree of letting go and initiate crucial relief but also to ease a troubled person's entry into a network of community (Bowers, Banquer and Bloomfield 1974). This second factor may ultimately be as beneficial as the former, if not more so. For these reasons it is useful to think of warm-up techniques as tools only in so far as words are tools.

Group workers who are uncomfortable with warm-ups sometimes express fears about group members' anticipated reactions to the introduction of such techniques. Beneath this fear may lurk anxiety that spontaneous expression might undermine traditional professional boundaries. When faced with a group member's reluctance to participate in an exercise, the facilitator might feel like they're giving a party and nobody turns up. An inexperienced facilitator may also realistically dread that if a reluctant group member were to be cajoled into participation, he or she might lose control. Any of these fears are certainly realistic for therapists who are themselves ill at ease with a play position, who are preoccupied with issues of authority or concerned with the maintenance of dominant, interpretative power. Warm-ups are, after all, frequently experienced as community expressions of feeling. They reflect emotional tensions and, by means of mimesis, elicit the forces which stir such emotions, whilst they direct a group's energy towards a trans-personal sense of union. This emotional engagement is achieved by means of the simple commitment to action and not bestowed by external mercy, grace or authority. This is also potentially unsettling. However, as Bates (1986) pointed out, the lust for life does seek expression (p.108). When people are emotionally unwell it fights for its imperilled existence by seeking access to stimulation of the senses. Warm-up techniques can provide multi-sensory satisfaction and generate a wholesome lust for life. It is self-evident that a group worker's personal relationship with such joy of living is more clearly at stake when play exercises are introduced into a group's activity portfolio.

The task of a group worker who uses warm-up exercises is best described as that of a dynamic administrator (Foulkes and Anthony 1957). It involves dealing with issues of space, time and boundary-setting as well as the maintenance of the group's sense of identity. When these tasks are success-fully performed, the group member's relief about the survivability of the experience of being with others reinforces their willingness to accept mutual responsibility (Foulkes 1964). Purposefully constructed warm-up exercises support this process by enhancing early awareness of boundaries, the experience of safe involvement and of togetherness and separation. Winnicott emphasized that an optimal balance of benign parental contact and the creation of opportunities to be alone seem essential to the development of a rich imaginative life (Singer 1973, p.46). Group workers could do worse than to design the warm-up exercises in accordance with this dictum, thereby to provide some raw material with which group members may fashion their progress.

Look not with indifference upon me,
I call upon thee, O answer thou me.

Hawaii

5. The Intricacy of Listening and Responding to Stories

Once a story has been told, a momentary silence reigns. Between one teller and one listener this silence is rarely translated into talk about the story. Occasionally the listener may beg for more tales, but if the story has satiated the listening hunger, teller and listener tend to part ways (Gardner 1971). With a 'good night' or 'see you later' the participants in the storytelling occasion make ready to re-inhabit a more separate world. Talk about the story is likely to be postponed to another time and place. In a group the transition from involvement with the story to talk about the story is much more readily made (Zipes 1995), if only because a casual comment about a particular story-aspect or characteristic soon prods listeners who still linger on the threshold between fantasy and reality into awareness that the story is finished; even a most casual observation can trigger a sudden (and not necessarily welcome) jolt back to everyday sociality. Before long, the listeners judge, query and elaborate the storied events; they become embroiled in the negotiation of different opinions, different life experiences and different assumptions.

Whereas storytelling in a pair tends to generate emotional confluence, with discussion of differences in perception being left to another occasion, if they are discussed at all, stories told in a group generate both confluence and divergence (Gotterer 1989). Groups thrive on the constructive exploration of difference. The largest possible tolerable variety is the material upon which democracy and well-functioning organizational or interest groups are built. When a story is told to such a group, it will have in its midst some people who did not appreciate what the tale was about, some who discerned one meaning and others who saw this quite differently. These alternative understandings and interpretations grant group members ample opportunity to explore other ideas, beliefs and experiences. In such groups the following scenario might easily ensue.

Imagine a group of eight or ten people, plus one facilitator. They sit around a large table. In the centre of the table you can see sheets of paper in different colours and sizes. Open pots of fingerpaint and clay for modelling are within easy reach of each participant. There are boxes of crayons, glue-sticks and some pairs of scissors. The participants have recently finished writing a brief story. Some re-read what they have just written and make the odd amendment, others have put their paper on the table with a gesture that seems to convey 'That wasn't much good' and one or two have stood up to look out of the window. At this point the facilitator says: 'Well, let's share our stories'. The group reassembles. The facilitator asks: 'Who will begin?' After a short, thoughtful silence one group member offers: 'I will.' The storyteller begins. The group listens attentively. When the story is finished lively discussion ensues in which the storyteller vigorously participates.

Group workers who use stories in special schools, hostels, day centres or hospitals probably smile wistfully at the above description and think: 'If only it were that easy'. They might agree with Berne (1966) who says: 'Anyone who wants people to listen to what he is really saying and to get a really pertinent answer in such a situation is likely to be disappointed' (p.71). They know from experience that in these settings the majority of group members cannot contribute steady listening or an easy willingness to share, especially not so soon after they have been involved in their own creative work. The few group members who have developed a strong sense of self, ample curiosity, a firm enough belief in the value of their own work and trust in turn-taking are probably ready to leave the setting.

When painful memories, fear or physical pain permeate the present moment, it is hard to show interest in others and to trust in the benignity of encounters. Concentration on something or someone beyond oneself is difficult. The capacity to attend to outside stimuli fluctuates immensely and unpredictably. Without additional support, intermittent listening is all that can be offered. When the inner world is already confused, exposure to telling which cannot be followed because the attentive capacity is weak can make an already unwell person feel even more inadequate. This happens especially when the person would have liked to have understood what was told, yet found that they missed a lot.

Sarah lived in a residential home for frail older people. Her grandson had just visited. He had tried to tell her about some things he had done that week. Looking at me tearfully, Sarah said: 'I couldn't listen to what he told. I wanted to, but I couldn't do it. What's happening to me?' Though she had picked up some aspects of what the boy had told her, she knew she had somehow missed the stories. The disjointed nature of what she had received only confirmed to her that all was indeed not well. Speaking about an earlier period of mental ill health, John, a middle-aged man, described how at that time he had forgotten that there even was a whole picture and that he had only discerned a few pieces of this whole. He said: 'I thought the pieces were the picture. They did not make sense. I was right. By the time I could acknowledge that I only had a few pieces that did not hang together, I was already on the road to recovery.' The experience of knowing that you have only been able to catch the odd sentence adds to a person's sense of perceptual disorientation. Not being able to make information cohere becomes yet another failure to notch onto an already low self-esteem.

In the early stages of a TSM group few members are able to listen to lots of stories, whilst every one would, in their heart of hearts, like to have their own story listened and responded to in enjoyable ways. The motivation to listen and the willingness to tell are, amongst other things, inspired by considerations such as: 'Will anybody listen? Will anybody value what I have to say and how will I know this?' The perceived quality of attention is assessed through careful observation of audience behaviour, which includes

- direction of gaze, exemplified by thoughts such as: 'Do they still look at me?'
- distractibility, including coughs, fidgeting, playing with objects, checking the time and body stretches and signs of boredom, such as yawning or nodding off.

A TSM group listed the kind of audience responses they dreaded. These included all of the above, as well as the following:

- when the group laughs loudly and what you have said isn't funny at all
- when they are soaking it up as if you're telling something really important and you know it's only a little story
- when they whisper to each other or give each other winks
- when they look at you with disbelief, as if you're lying or making it up.

It is not difficult to identify with these concerns. In the throes of stage fright before a public speech or performance, most of us entertain similar thoughts. During performance we watch out for kindred signs of audience disengagement or disapproval. As Borden (1980) has shown, fear of speaking before a group is rated greater by many people than fear of loneliness, heights or sickness. The willingness to tell and the preparedness to listen are informed by memories of past experiences, current preoccupations and the anticipation of future satisfaction or dissatisfaction. Audience lack of interest intimidates most people *without* mental health problems. The fear of exposure to such lack of interest becomes even further magnified during most forms of emotional or physical illness.

The fear of listening

Many users of mental health or special education facilities have a painful history of non-constructive listener or audience feedback. They continue to cradle potent memories of important people who said or did things in response to an offering that hurt them badly. The anticipation of imminent storytelling triggers memories of occasions when the client had wanted to please a parent, teacher, friend or lover. Clumsy timing, unclear offerings or insensitive reception had made their hope of successful performance go astray. The child or adult had longed for recognition, affection, approval or support. Instead, they remember experiencing rejection, manifest disinterest, misunderstanding or derision. In many of my clients' cases the pain this caused did not go away. It became a broken memory about a torn-up drawing, a returned present, a story which had spelling corrections scribbled all over it, or a flower left to starve for water on the teacher's desk.

I vividly remember Patricia, a middle aged client who told me she had not painted since the day she had put her heart and soul into a watercolour of two people climbing a hill. She had been sixteen years old. The art teacher had not only scorned her painting, but actually taken it from the easel, shown it to the class and then thrown it in a dustbin, saying: 'In this school we don't paint like that.' The very presence of fingerpaints, crayons and felt tip pens in the room where the storymaking group took place initially terrified her. It also secretly excited her. I later learned that during her years of profound depression she had also nursed an unspoken hope that one day she might regain access to the joy of painting. When audience fear predominates, the group members anticipate unfriendly comments or indifference in response to their stories, visual images, dramatizations or poems. This pattern of sombre expectation is a constitutive aspect of their emotional illness. Their learned expectation exercises a potentially dark influence before creative work is even begun, whilst it is undertaken and, especially, as soon as the work is finished.

In addition to a *fear of telling or showing*, many TSM participants also bring a *fear of listening* to the group. The reluctance to listen is often informed by concern that a story's content might challenge them in unwanted ways.

Troubled group members have a range of specific sounds, voice qualities or words which continues to evoke startle pain. Screams, fights, the dull thump of accidents or sarcastic or furious words have configured into sound and memory patterns that still hurt. Michelle, a participant who suffered from depression, initially put her hands over her ears whenever a group member tried to imitate a loud voice. Memories of her mother's drunken ranting and raving interfered with her ability to listen to what was actually said. Whilst Michelle was sensitive to tonal variations, Adrian was terrified of what the stories might contain. Within a few years he had suffered several traumatic losses. He was able to listen to a story as long as it took place in familiar, happy-tinted surroundings. But when the slightest hint of danger entered the tale, he withdrew his listening attention. He explained: 'Too many bad things have happened. I cannot bear to hear about more unhappy times. I will not listen.' As he was in serious danger of re-traumatization in a group context, he was advised to discontinue his participation in the group, to create a good ending with the members, and to engage in individual therapeutic work instead.

People with mental health problems have often experienced prolonged periods of social isolation. Many were exposed to threats, severe punishment or torture at too young an age. They heard what they were not allowed to hear, and saw what was denied they had seen. When told to 'dis-remember' many such clients learn effectively to hide both their attention and their critical thoughts. Abbie, a man who had sought refuge from a country with a violent, repressive regime where he had been tortured, once sighed: 'I no longer know what I think.' Quick as a flash a fellow group member responded: 'Just as well, it would have cost you your head.' Abbie momentarily looked surprised. His eyes filled with tears. Clients like Abbie paid a high price for speaking up during their childhood or adult days. Not only was their perception of reality frequently denied but they were also beaten, ignored or mocked for being who they were or for saying what they saw. Whereas initially they may have protested about their situation, the reaction they received soon taught them that it was safer just to watch.

In my experience, many people with emotional or behavioral difficulties have become true masters of apparent disengagement whilst actually observing the interactions between people in meticulous detail. Such clients are ever watchful, yet uncommunicative about what they perceive. Their outward behaviour is structured to lead others to believe that they are blind to emotional exchanges, immune to neglect or unresponsive to reward. Initially this behaviour may have been an effective way to minimize harm and to maximize survival chances in certain specific situations or environments.

Over time it became generalized to a way of being in most situations. In the long run the acquired habit of responding diffusely is unhelpful, both to themselves and to others. The solution has become a problem. The persistence in communicative habits that no longer work increases interpersonal discomfort and leads to further diminishment of interpersonal efficacy (Ganster and Victor 1988). The complexity of 'apparent disengagement' is often brought to a TSM group where it needs to be addressed and, above all, surmounted.

Social loafing

Attentive group listening to the telling of a story by one person is not easy to achieve. Group members are tempted to ponder their own story under the motto: 'as long as I appear to be listening no one will notice if I don't.' Such non-attendance is, however, acutely sensed by the storyteller. It reinforces their impression that they are not important enough to be granted attention. Whilst the habit of absent-minded listening may derive from several of the factors noted above, in group work it can also be attributed to a phenomenon called 'social loafing'. Social loafing is the tendency for individuals to expend less effort when working collectively in a group than when working individually. In groups, the motivation to put in your best effort is reduced. The hope that people might invest more energy together than they would do individually or co-actively is unrewarded. Unless special measures are taken, people do not give their personal best when asked to work collectively. Life experience, corroborated by research, has shown that continued engagement of individuals in a group task demands that:

- there is an identifiable aspect to individual input/output
- that this input can be potentially evaluated
- that there will be a standard against which output may be compared
- that the group is sufficiently rewarding, harmonious and successful for the individual to want to continue to contribute. (Karau and Williams 1993)

As soon as a person thinks that their contribution is dispensable they are tempted to grant attention to themselves over attention to others. In order to continue to listen to someone else's story the group members need to have a clear sense that in some way or other a valued outcome may be obtained. The tendency not to pull one's weight in a group supports the proposition that special measures may be taken to maximize the potential healing effect of group storytelling. For in spite of the fact that fear, shame or guilt dominate clients' self-awareness, the longing for acceptance, praise, commendation or appreciation is rarely completely submerged. An ample dosage of good enough responses to the sharing of creative work can create a fertile soil from which participants may draw the strength to address those experiences that have been resistant to development (Bronfenbrenner 1979). All of us have a need for connection with other people, for intimacy, closeness and meaning. In the context of a healing relationship, the sufferer has, as Jackson (1992) points out, 'a yearning to be listened to, to be valued and to be understood. And the healer has his own need to listen, to understand and so to bridge the divide between the two persons in the potentially healing dyadic relationship.' (pp.1623–1632).

When considering how or why to support the capacity to listen and respond to stories in groups, apart from the above considerations, another factor may be born in mind. In the professional therapeutic community it is generally accepted that the repeated exposure to clients' life stories has an impact on the therapist. Consequently, most therapists use established procedures for the retrospective narration of such stories through professional supervision, the writing of papers and during both formal and informal talk at meetings or conferences. The therapist's need to retell their clients' stories in order to give further coherency to their understanding of distinctive events in clients' lives and to the long-term suffering these entail, is well documented (Hawkins and Shohet 1989, pp.153–7).

The same cannot be said as regards a client's need to integrate and to retell the many tales of turmoil and trouble they hear in a group. Though the therapist's position within the group differs from the client's as regards overall responsibility for the facilitation of healing, and though it could be postulated that a degree of retelling automatically occurs whenever a client recognizes his or her own story in another person's tale, there is also an inevitable surplus of difference between their own and another person's story. In spite of the fortuitous overlap of coincidental similarity between life stories or fictional stories, which gives birth to the experience of universality, the impact of the surplus of difference is something clients must learn to manage (Yalom 1975). As discussed, many people run into trouble when their stories cannot be adequately told. In the daily life of the average person there is generally little space for the retelling of tales of sorrow or delight, whether these are one's own or received tales. The term 'quality time' is nowadays used to describe those occasions when friends or family members feel truly present to each other and listen wholeheartedly to each other's tales. The lack of access to 'quality time' experiences and the reality of substantial silence about emotionally laden issues holds particularly true for people with mental health difficulties. The limited availability of meaningful re-telling situations can add to the sense of inadequacy a client may feel when invited to listen to a range of stories in a TSM group, simply because the person may not know what to do with the stories and especially when they are invited to listen and to respond to stories which are surplus to their personal experience. All of us feel inadequate when demands are made which we cannot yet meet, when we face an overwhelming situation, when we cannot quite process information about ideas or occurrences that are well beyond our own experience or when we believe that any remaining response ability would not be good enough anyway. However understandable such feelings of inadequacy might be, it is not therapeutically useful for clients to feel like a dumb witness to another person's life story, unable to validate its interpretation or to affirm its value.[1] If the telling of tales matters, and if witnessing and helping to order these experiences can be of therapeutic value, as Kleinman (1988) suggests, then it is important to do this in the best way possible.

These various considerations led me to formulate the queries:

○ what (if anything) might prepare group members better for the experience of listening to a story

○ what (if anything) might support their capacity to continue to listen once it has begun

○ given that what we perceive depends in part on what we are ready for, how might it be possible to enhance group member's preparatory set for the anticipated demand to respond to a story. In this situation they would hold certain kinds of responses in readiness, somewhat like a runner who is ready to respond to the sound of a starting gun.

I searched for the answers to these queries through practice. I soon learned that specific interpersonal exercises may be purposefully employed to enable participants to practise alternative ways of responding to stories and thereby of interacting with one another. Because therapeutic storymaking is a time-limited, structured group work method, active intervention to support

---

1   Aziz (1990, p.24) notes that in his analytic practice Jung was exposed to indelible impressions of hellish meaninglessness which were linked with his experience of his own father, about whom he writes in his autobiography: 'My memory of my father is of a sufferer stricken with an Amfortas wound, a 'fisher king', whose wound would not heal – that Christean suffering for which the alchemists sought the panacea. I as a 'dumb' Parsifal was the witness of this sickness during the years of my boyhood, and like Parsifal, speech failed me.' These unhealing wounds in the parental generation are paid for heavily by the next generation. The sense of having been impotent to alleviate the parents' illness permeates many a TSM group member's life.

both the ability to listen and the ability to interact is a logical extension of facilitator style. It fits the group culture which aims explicitly to create an experimental ground for testing out new approaches to sociality in a low-risk environment. A teenage member of an East-End gang once succinctly observed that: 'You have to learn, not only copy. It's like learning to walk, you waddle about, fall on your ass, you get up until you can walk properly. You learn your own style of doing it. ...It is interest mainly, you 'ave to 'ave interest to learn' (Daniel and McGuire 1972, p.48). Most TSM participants bring a hesitant interest to the group, but initially they have real trouble with the getting up bit after the fall. It therefore seemed to make sense to provide steady support for their fragile ability to explore alternative behaviours and to try something once more, especially because it didn't quite work out the first time round.

The self's identity is sensed in the act of experiencing it, whilst the ability to contemplate arises from the experience of having felt present to oneself. I believe that a therapeutic/educational group which aims to enhance people's capacity to become more of a 'listening teller' can provide planned opportunities for participants to learn to do just that (Reid 1971). I therefore use various response procedures which turn uninvited criticism into invited contribution by using visual images and text-based metaphors as viable instruments for social negotiation. By eliciting specific creative–expressive responses to a hesitantly shared story, various 'understanding hypotheses' can be gathered. This emphasis on 'harvesting the listeners' responses whenever you tell a story' reframes the dynamics of performance anxiety in the storytelling situation in useful ways.

> *I listen, I simply listen.*
> *Watching for a story,*
> *A story I can hear.*
> *That it may drift towards*
> *me*
> *Along my road.*
> Bushman

Once the story is made: the survival of the object

Group members bring fundamental uncertainty about the value or relevance of their work as well as real doubt about the value of sharing what they have made. Rollo May (1977) suggests that creation needs to be understood as a process in which a poet, composer, painter or writer knocks upon silence or formlessness in the hope of finding a responsive answer. The story or painting is the gift which emerges out of this persistent knocking upon the silence. In the act of writing or painting, the storymaker discovers that he or she not only uses the medium to mold the silence into communicable expression but also that the medium uses them. As such, the experience of painting, dancing, writing or music making entails both control and submission. The creative product grows from an encounter between the subjective pole of the inner world and the possibilities which the person is able to grasp in the world beyond him or herself. Each picture or narrative is born out of the dynamic interaction between a person and their world. Though filled with poorly or exquisitely veiled representations of events, beliefs and hopes, the makings are more than projections of earlier experience. They contain facets of the present, reflect available knowledge, imaginings or information, are built out of accessible materials and skills, and display direct or indirect reference to a personal past as well as the greater context of human history and expectations.

In TSM, group members are helped to down-key aspects of a potential story's building blocks by quickly responding to a series of purposeful questions. They are then invited to expand their tale. After some initial hesitation, the writing or drawing of the full story begins. Soon the atmosphere in the room changes. Everyone's breathing becomes deeper and more intense. The rhythmic movement of hands is interspersed with brief thoughtful breaks, which convey that the story is written or drawn in an atmosphere of heightened intensity. This involves a degree of self-forgetfulness and momentary reduction of self-consciousness (Maslow 1977). During the process of writing, the storymaker experiences, in however limited a way, some sense of good enoughness. Though the story writing may have felt more or less okay, emergence from the writing renders the person vulnerable. When invited to share their story, the participants remember all the more vividly that their tale was born out of a not yet understood mixture of private fantasies, actual memories, felt disappointments or desire. Individual writing and drawing activities performed in a group are profoundly private experiences in which awareness of the presence of others is pushed into the background. When the storymaking is finished and the writer realizes that they are but one storymaker in a group of storymakers, their attentional focus rapidly shifts from the internal world of habits, dreams and knowledge to the interpersonal world of the group. This can be an unwelcome surprise.

Told stories enter a group's public realm. Audiences inevitably evaluate one's contribution. Whereas the story was made in the presence of others, and even though a responsible group worker will have suggested that the stories would be shared after the writing, awareness of the audience fades during the process of storymaking. The invitation to share the story can come as a bit of a shock, however well prepared the storymaker was. They cannot but wonder whether they want to expose their private story to public scrutiny. May (1969) points out that this vulnerability results from the regressive aspect of a sojourn amidst symbols, as this brings into our presence infantile, archaic and unconscious longings. The contradictory feelings which surface in response to the invitation to share a story link with the re-emergence from engagement with a symbolic world. They are informed by feelings the person has about the requirement to let go of the transcendence of the self–object dichotomy which can be so intensely felt during a time of creation. Group members have described what they felt as follows:

- sudden fear that guidelines for writing the story might have been inadequately followed
- satisfaction and excitement that they were able to write a story
- fear that their story would prove to be too simple, too predictable or too weird to be understood
- a sense of relief that at last something had been put down on paper
- fear that their story's theme might be thought boring
- fear that the emotion or deeds recorded in the story would prove to be unacceptable to the group
- a sense of shame about having written the story at all
- a sense of guilt at having described a family or personal secret in thinly disguised form
- a profound longing to be understood
- fear that the language used would be too poetic or insufficiently poetic
- real pleasure that something had been described accurately, that words or images had surrendered to intention
- fear that their story would turn out to be much shorter or much longer than other people's stories.

This miscellany of feelings pulls both at the willingness to tell the personal story and interferes with the listening available for other people's stories. Their intensity can be worked with, but it often takes a while. During my early work as a general arts group worker with deprived people I grew to understand the fear, shame or fury a person may feel about their actual or anticipated audience. I found it initially shocking to see how, at the end of the session, a child or adult who had written a story or made a clay sculpture with exquisite attention and apparent satisfaction, would suddenly tear it up or scratch all over it, then throw it out. Whilst there are many intra-psychic explanations for the dynamics of such attacks on their work, I also became aware that some explanations belonged firmly and squarely in the person's interpersonal realm.[2] When we talked about the whys and wheretos of this kind of action, the participants told me that they destroyed the work, amongst other reasons, because they felt annoyed that they had made something beautiful which confronted them with the reality that their perception of the world as 'only' awful was no longer valid. Unable to tolerate such ambiguity, the work was undone. Sometimes they said that they would rather they themselves destroyed their object than that someone else would do so. That would have caused even more hurt. Many undid their work because there was nowhere for them to take it; no place in the home to keep it safe; no one to look at it with pleasure and encouragement. I learned that we had (at least) five tasks:

○ To enable participants experientially to learn the difference between the act of conscious, precautionary, respectful unmaking and the act of blindly destroying something that has just been made.

○ To create a safe place in the centre where their work could be temporarily kept and/or displayed and to nurture satisfaction in the experience of re-encounter with a left-behind object.

○ To help the person to find or make some kind of safe place in their home where they could keep something that was important to them (this often meant reducing the scale of the work, as the only safe place they could reasonably secure might be a box or a small folder).

○ To help the participant to invite the people with whom they lived to offer acknowledgment, appreciation and reward and to co-operate when such a response was forthcoming.

○ To accept that the centre needed to work simultaneously with these important others and to provide them with enough positive feedback

2   Redl and Wineman (1951) offer an illuminating discussion of the behaviour of children whose disturbance pattern centres around hate and aggression. They note that a certain amount of destruction must be anticipated and tolerated before basic change can take place. This containment needs to occur within clear limits. Their understanding of newness, panic and disorganization in the face of guilt offers the group worker who is faced with object attacks both understanding of the events and insight into how to enable clients to find constructive ways beyond the terror such destructiveness also evokes in them.

experiences, so that they might be able to use constructive interaction patterns during their daily life with the group members with whom we worked more intensely (e.g. carers or parent groups).

I learned that there is a distinct experiential sequence to a troubled person's process of relating to their creative work, which is reflected in changes in behaviour and mood. This sequence has the following signposts:

° creative work is quite suddenly destroyed or carelessly abandoned towards the end of the session

° the work is allowed to stay intact during the session and is consciously left for safekeeping

° the work is taken away from the session but, in spite of earlier stated intentions that it was to be taken home, it is discarded immediately outside the room or building, there to be found by the worker

° the work is taken home and put away without being shown to anyone

° the work is taken home and left around for someone to see. It is frequently accidentally thrown away or damaged

° the work is taken home with the intention of showing it to an important other. It is shown. However, there is a reported invalidating response

° the work is taken home, shown, valued and put away

° the work is taken home, shown, valued and displayed for a brief or longer period of time, then put away or discarded.

By being attentive to what happened to the product someone had made I not only learned a great deal about the participants' relationship with their own 'makings' and with their home environment, I also discovered how I could best support the participant to achieve what they most wanted. More often than not this included becoming able to value what they had made for themselves. Such learning was crucially facilitated through consciously receiving feedback about other participants' relationship with what they had just been shown or told. In other words, if other group members were clearly interested in one's painting or story, posed stimulating questions or showed pleasure or surprise, the maker would, within even a short time span, start to show similar appreciative behaviour – both towards their own and other people's work.

In TSM a person's capacity to appreciate their own work is systematically developed through the use of structured responsive interaction with others in the group about their story or image. When group members experience that the facilitator's and the other group members' task is not primarily interventional or corrective in terms of re-editing a 'faulty' story or changing a dysfunctional one, they gradually acquire different ways of understanding their own interpretation of their stories or image-work. Their identification with memory-stories of failure moves towards the articulation of self-stories which emphasize exceptional, good outcomes (White and Epstein 1989). In such a group's atmosphere both fictional and self-stories are expanded by means of co-operative dialogue, where different points of view are allowed to co-exist and in which no one perspective dominates. The facilitator takes care simply to participate in a conversation with the story and attempts not to have his or her interpretations wield more influence, power or authority than the clients' interpretation (Gergen and McNamee 1991).

During this process the facilitator knowingly safeguards a responsive climate in which it is possible for participants to experience relative belonging amidst support for exploration and dealing with challenges. Menninger (1963) observed that the intangibles of love, faith and hope are crucial determinants of the process of effective healing and sublime expressions of the life instinct. Next to the TSM facilitator's professional responsibility to assess the participants' situation and to create the best possible development programme, the safeguarding of the vivid presence of these intangibles provides the basic philosophical ground upon which TSM practice is built. Yet it is vital to remember that however much a facilitator may wish to minimize their authority and to delineate its influence, it is never quite possible to do away with the authority exercised by expertise, setting, context or the explicit purpose of the TSM group.

❧❧❧

And we will be
frightened to use words.
But it will happen that the words we need
shall come to meet us.

Inuit

Developmental support for the capacity to listen through the structuring of structured feedback

Stories invite the listener critically to examine what he or she hears or sees. This includes the negotiation of perceived meanings (Brook 1988, p.235). The negotiation of meaning demands that people feel free to utter an opinion, know themselves capable of listening to others without becoming over-whelmed or threatened, are secure enough to consider differences and wise enough to review ideas or beliefs concerning themselves and others where appropriate. These capabilities parallel the kind of skills for which Daldin (1994) proposes therapists might need to provide developmental support. They include:

○ helping a client to understand and to clarify the external realities of life, thereby to explore fantasy and realistic expectation

○ assisting the client to separate thoughts from feelings

○ enabling the client to recognize thought as thought and to label feeling as feeling

○ promoting the use of words to translate non-verbal behaviours and expressions where necessary

○ promoting participation in a co-operatively shared reality.

A safe, facilitating environment in which people listen to a story and explore the ideas encountered in the story can promote Daldin's developmental aims. In TSM all manner of stories are told. Facilitators must therefore take care not to aggravate participants' memories of earlier overwhelming situations by exposing them to the recitation of a whole series of stories without creating opportunities for the processing of the storied material. The working through of feelings, thoughts or memories which the stories have evoked can be created through the provision of explicit support. This not only means helping group members to notice the impact of another person's narrative upon themselves within the here and now context of the group but also to translate this noticing into purposeful interpersonal responsiveness. It is not enough to experience someone's story passively. Group members can do much more to make the story their own and to provide the storyteller with feedback. Such tasks might contribute to:

○ renewing a person's confidence in being able to respond quickly and to turn out something adequately

○ building confidence in the capacity to express feeling or thoughts precisely

○ building trust in the ability to pay back for a pleasure received

○ building confidence in the capacity to develop an opinion or position

○ learning to use a given opportunity to exercise influence

○ learning to offer consolation

- ∘ learning to make something for the moment
- ∘ learning to contribute to the creation of knowledge in the group
- ∘ learning to invite constructive criticism and to use it
- ∘ regaining access to an appetite for attention and response.

In this process the storyteller who is also a storylistener can strengthen their habit of autonomous, reflective being. Real listening involves taking conscious note of:

- ∘ what you feel about a story you have just heard
- ∘ registering which associations/memories the story evokes
- ∘ being able to notice how you felt recently as well as that moment
- ∘ pondering what you feel about your relationship with the teller, and remembering its events and dynamics
- ∘ being aware of what you feel about the facilitator and/or the group and how this influences the listening to the story
- ∘ linking the story you have just heard with others like and unlike this one.

When structured support is offered for group members' abilities to listen to storytelling, to reflect upon what has been noticed in the story and to give expressive form to such noticing, they soon become aware that attentional drift happens when uncomfortable feelings or important associations surface in their own inner world (Spence 1984). Once this realization lingers on the edge of awareness, it can be shared and explored. In addition, the ability to listen, to formulate an idea and to present the idea for contemplation to the originating speaker supports emerging leadership capacities in each group member. The fostering of distributed leadership not only contributes to an atmosphere of mutuality in which both vulnerability and strength may thrive but also strengthens a group's commitment to their chosen tasks (Beck and Peters 1981).

Response tasks as interpersonal requests

Response tasks are individual or whole group exercises which are initially set by the facilitator and, after a while, by a storyteller before a story is told. The tasks are completed immediately after the story is finished by all group members (the listeners), including the storyteller him or herself and the facilitator. Each response task takes the form of a specific creative/expressive exercise of approximately three to five minutes duration. The exercises include primarily written or visual tasks. They are formulated as interpersonal requests, such as:

- Please record the sentence in my story which means most to you.
- Paint the image in my story which you saw most vividly in your mind's eye.
- Please describe an event in your own life of which my story reminded you.
- As you will hear, the main character in my story has an unusual… (e.g. musical instrument, coat, bag). Please make a drawing of this.
- As you will discover, the main character in my story is given a present by his mother before he sets out on the journey, which he particularly values. Please imagine what this present is and describe what is special about it.
- Towards the end of my story the character suddenly feels very… (e.g. elated, angry, determined, sad). Though this subsequently changes, I feel uneasy about this. Please think about why she feels like this and write about it.
- At the end of my story my character wonders what has been gained from all these adventures. Please write a poem about the meaning of the journey.
- Whilst you listen to my story you may think: 'If only…' Please record those moments.
- Record something that you want to remember about my story.
- Write a wish that you have for the main character.

Occasionally a storyteller may ask a group to undertake a whole group task. These group-responses often have a performance aspect, with a visual or sound-based demonstration or clarification purpose, such as:

- Please show me through mime the place through which my character will travel, e.g. forest, mountains, town.
- Can you make up and sing the song my character heard when she arrived?
- Would you please dance the welcome dance the characters (e.g. creatures, animals, court officials) danced when my main character returned home.

Due to the performative nature of these latter tasks, the storyteller will only have a memory of the response-performance to serve them in future and not a piece of paper with some words or an image which they might otherwise be able take away as a relatively constant reminder of the group's involvement with the response task they have set. Such an ephemeral gift is sometimes precisely what the group member needs. However, the timing of this kind of response work is important. When response tasks which are based on the ephemeral arts of music, drama or dance are introduced too early in the therapeutic process, the storyteller may experience profound disappointment. Once the response performance is completed, the group member/storyteller tends suddenly to realize that they will have an internal memory to carry away from the group, whilst other group members are laden with visual or written images. When this is therapeutically unhelpful, the facilitator may invite the storyteller to reformulate their task to include two components: the first, a brief, performative group response and the second, a concise representation of the group effort by means of painting or writing.

In my experience early explicit help with the real difficulties people encounter when they try to offer attentive listening to other people's stories results in both anticipated and unexpected gains, whilst few unwelcome results emerge. Kleinman (1988) states that empathic witnessing is a moral act, not a technical procedure (p.154). In the response tasks I try to teach easily distracted group members ways of listening and responding to other people's stories, and therefore ultimately to their own stories, both as an act of commitment to interaction and as a technical procedure. These techniques aim to support the group members' capacities to stay emotionally alert and present to their listening experience, to give immediate, expressive form to what was felt or thought in relation to their own as well other group member's stories and to the impact these stories have upon themselves, to clarify images or associations and to recall personal memories linked with their own/ another group member's story, and to recognize and to manage genuine as opposed to avoidant disinterest. They learn experientially that judgment is always based on fragmentary evidence, that it takes courage to expose oneself to the experience of recognition and that it is joyous to be affirmed as a performer and enriched as a spectator.

She sucketh white flowers
For to keep her voice clear,
And the more she singeth cuckoo
The summer draweth near.

Anonymous

The rhythmic sequence of telling, responding and reflecting

More often than not group members are informed about the particular response task which a storyteller would like them to perform in relation to their story *before the story is told.* The group's listening to the story is thus informed by the particular task which the storyteller has set. The task-centredness of the listening supports group members' ability to engage in consentful listening. As each response-task takes approximately three to five minutes, the storytelling and response task combined take about seven minutes. In my experience this is about the maximum period of time a group can initially focus on one particular participant (Stanislavski 1980, p.225). The rhythmic sequence of telling and making is guarded by the facilitator who invites the next storyteller to inform the group of their specific task for the story they are about to tell before the group has lost its momentum of engagement. The rhythmic sequence of telling and responding is as follows:

- The group is informed about the specific response a storyteller desires.

- The group listens to the story whilst this is born in mind.

- The group completes the response-task, which is then momentarily put aside. (i.e. The response is not yet given to the storyteller. As further stories are told, a small pile of responses accumulates near each listener. This provides confirmatory evidence of their capacity to listen and to create.)

- The group prepares to listen to the next story.

- They are informed which new response is desired.

- The telling begins, etc.

This process of alternate telling and responding continues until each group member has told a story and responses have been created for all participants – even those who decided not to tell their story are asked whether they would like the group to perform a response-task, for example by creating a gift for an unknown story character. Though at first such a group member might refuse this offer, they often accept the suggestion and are comforted by it.

The repetitious pattern generated by the rhythmic alternation of telling–responding–telling allows for reaction to become more reliable, proportionately less conscious and potentially more repetitive. Frequent repetition of a rewarding performance enables changed behaviour to sink in and to be absorbed. Effective functioning relies on the integration of frequently repeated situations, particularly because the same or very similar situations tend to repeat themselves. In TSM both the storytelling and the response tasks make use of sufficient repetition to contain the anxiety that narrative generates (Tambling 1991).

Once all the stories have been told and responded to, the group is invited to take careful note of who is located where in the circle. This signals the delivery of the responses and is greeted with anticipatory delight. It feels good to have quite a few responses to give away and, equally, to know that in your absence (because you're busy distributing your own gifts) a whole range of responses will be left near your place. In the early stages of a TSM group participants often exclaim at this distribution moment: 'It is like Christmas', or 'I have not gotten so many presents in years'. Once all the responses have been delivered to the respective storytellers, the viewing begins. It is important to note that most responses are unsigned. They are merely other group members' individual contributions to the story's development and not, in the strict sense, personal gifts from one group member to another. This anonymity is found to be important. It frees members' willingness to explore ideas, both on the giving and on the receiving end. I shall return later to the subject of the sharing of responses but first want to expand on how group members learn how to formulate response tasks.

Initially most group members need supportive help with the formulation of a response task. The facilitator encourages each group member to phrase their response task in such a way that it will specifically

- elicit further information about their story which they want to elaborate
- clarify a specific aspect which interests the storyteller
- link story-material to life-events.

Before group members can use this process to the full, they need to experience what it feels like to receive informative responses which satisfy. No amount of words can prepare a person for what happens emotionally and cognitively when they receive group gifts for, for example, a frightened and lonesome story character – particularly when we bear in mind that when a person creates such a story they are unlikely to feel closely connected with their group. Amanda, a woman who had been shivering with emotional cold all through the first session, received, on behalf of a similarly lonesome story character, response gifts such as

- a colourful soft blanket in which the character can wrap herself and feel really warm
- a soft pillow filled with sweet smelling herbs
- the kind of music the character likes, which gently fills the room where she is
- the quiet presence of a safe and kind person in that same room.

After she had carefully studied the drawings and writings which conveyed these gifts, Amanda chose the present of a 'safe and kind person' as the one her story character wanted most. She took care to acknowledge that the presence of all other gifts enabled her character to select the one thing she most wanted and needed. Though most response-presents are given anonymously, in this case the group member who gave the quiet presence of a person identified herself. She was herself filled with sadness about love and loss. In the response-gift she had given away something that she herself also so much wanted. However, upon having discovered that her gift consoled a fellow group member, who was like and yet also so much unlike herself, she felt twice comforted. Her sadness had been given manageable expression, whilst the welcome appreciation of her gift suggested continued interpersonal usefulness in spite of her sorrows. As this was the very thing she had begun to doubt, it made her feel a little better. Thus two people acknowledged to each other that a shared pain was, in their case, definitely a sorrow made more bearable. Similar situations arise repeatedly during the processing stage of response tasks. Most group members thereby learn very quickly *how* best to use the listening and reflective abilities of their fellow group members (see Coyne and Downey 1991).

There is a plant with a thorn.
With a thorn which may prick your hand.
If your hand obtains that plant,
you will find new life.

Gilgamesh

Learning to use response tasks

I believe that individuals act with various levels of conscious and unconscious awareness of what others see them doing. I presume that behaviour has important meanings at an overt, observable level – this applies both to myself and to the participants. I therefore clarify the effect of various forms of apparent, useful behaviour with the group and deal quite explicitly with boundary issues which concern the interface between the group and the outside world, thereby to safeguard the group as a good enough holding space. This means that as a facilitator I systematically attempt to lower defences, including my own; to give direct, honest feedback in as non-judgmental a way as possible; to recognize, name and accept feelings; and to acknowledge interdependence in the group. The emphasis in the process on promoting response-ability and participation meets Nitsun's demand for respect for a group's struggle to develop from an as yet formless, unintegrated state towards identity. Nitsun (1989) also observes that actions, interpretations or appeal may force premature activity on the group, compelling it into precocious development. He proposes that the management of the group's anxiety about who they will become and how they will do the becoming needs holding, not resolving, by the facilitator. Consequently, such a facilitator would aim for low-key participation and an unstructured group environment. From this perspective, the structured activity present in TSM might be seen to play right into the fantasized wishes and expectations of a dependent group which is reluctant to grow up.

Argyle posits that the individual needs both interaction and feedback in order for self-awareness to develop (Argyle 1972). When a group is treated as a social system, emphasis needs to be granted to overt behaviour, individual values and desires as well as interpersonal dynamics. It is then assumed that in each session many interrelated forces operate. Group phenomena are explicitly understood to have multiple causes and to exercise several and mutual influences. In terms of human behaviour, multi-causality is the norm and not the exception (Butkovich *et al.* 1975).

In TSM I find it useful to think of the group in these latter terms. In this context I understand response tasks as exercises which generate 'social reward' conditions. During any storytelling event both teller and audience negotiate the inevitable tension between separateness and attachment, change and continuity, as well as significance in the light of finiteness. Many group members experience that there is little space in daily life to articulate the complexities these tensions create. However, this material is the stuff therapeutic groups are made of. By inviting a response, the storyteller publicizes their willingness to receive suggestions for development and potential change. They are rewarded for this effort by receiving contributory ideas or options. This occurs in a climate where members engage with our most serious preoccupations: 'Why am I here? How to make sense of suffering? What is the meaning of it all?' When such concerns are uttered, they experience others' responsiveness and willingness to explore alternative approaches to the way they are dealing with their dilemma. Emerging competence to tolerate involvement with these intimate issues is reinforced through the feedback which the response tasks provide. Through the use of different response techniques, flexible resourcefulness is practised *in situ*.

The gathering and evaluation of alternative ideas and suggestions by the storyteller becomes a kind of invisible coaching. This in turn improves the quality of their own subsequent responses. Reward for the visible risk-taking of one person often encourages others to follow suit. Thereby a climate is created which is sympathetic and supportive to change efforts. The response tasks enable the listeners to hear each story 'as slightly foreign, a dialect no one else speaks, in which numerous histories animate the all-too-familiar words in that speaker's mind' (Makari and Shapiro 1993). This kind of climate is a long way removed from Nitsun's envisioned struggle for identity. In TSM this struggle is made experientially explicit whilst different creative–expressive pathways are offered to promote development. The criticism that such development may be precocious, false and therefore fragile can be countered through the confirmed evidence that there are many different therapeutic pathways by which distressed people seek and find healing change. So-called unstructured group environments are one such pathway, semi-structured groups another. Both forms have different limitations, and different advantages – whilst each can learn a great deal from In TSM the other. The facilitator supports the group members so that they may learn fully to utilize the possibilities inherent in this method of working. This help often follows a predictable developmental pattern:

> **Phase 1:** The facilitator suggests the same response task for each group member's story. For example, each time a story is told each group member creates a present for the main character in the story.

Phase 2: The facilitator offers each storyteller several suggested response tasks out of which he/she chooses one. Suggestions may include ideas such as

- each group member is invited to make a drawing of the place where their story character lives

- each group member describes in detail what friends or neighbours appreciate about their story character, however unattractive or attractive that character might seem to them right now

- each group member composes a brief poem in remembrance of their character's deeds.

Phase 3: The facilitator invites the storyteller to formulate a response task and offers coaching to ensure that the suggested task will fit the anticipated response. To illustrate:

Storyteller: 'My character will spend the night in a frightening place. Please describe what is frightening about that place.'

Facilitator: 'Might it be helpful if each person were also to describe what helps the story character not to become too overwhelmed with fear?'

Phase 4: The storyteller designs the response task with minimal or no coaching support from the facilitator, even though the responses which can be anticipated might be tough. To illustrate:

Storyteller: 'You will hear that my story character's child dies. Please describe the reason why nobody comes to comfort her.'

Phase 5: The storyteller invites the group to respond to the story in accordance with each individual member's own wishes or ideas. At this stage the group has acquired fully fledged response ability.

Some groups may never develop beyond Phase 2 or 3; however, the vast majority of groups are able over time to achieve free-flowing interpersonal response ability. In TSM participants are encouraged to observe to their heart's content. They learn to translate their observations into an expressive response, which is ultimately given to the originating speaker. Group members participate in a process of focused, responsive listening several times during each session. This reinforces a habit of responsiveness. Because response tasks rely on observation, impression and imagination, the clients learn to incorporate their understanding of the storyteller's use of para-linguistics and kinesis into their understanding of the story. This permitted broadening of their perceptive realm helps many troubled people to use a frequently well-developed tendency: namely to be somewhat repetitively preoccupied with the detail of emotions and with hyper attention to nuances of expression. As noted before, many people who suffer emotional troubles are watchful, if anything too observant of details, which tends to weaken their understanding of the whole gestalt of the experience.

I have found that the channelling of this ability into productive interpersonal activity provides focus for otherwise incommensurable impressions, which lack expressive channelling. When invited to create a symbolic interpretation about a particular event in the story, or to articulate a wish for a certain story character, participants tend to rally forth. No longer do they need to defend group members against their imagined personal influence. The permission to exercise actual and explicit, yet clearly delineated influence by means of an invited response which the storyteller has asked the group to perform, helps group members to build new understanding and new boundaries. The habit of observation becomes a true asset in the response tasks. The reframing of an interpersonal difficulty as an attribute which, moreover, is valued by the recipient of the response tasks, begins to guide the ability to note small variations in mood and behaviour into more constructive interpersonal channels. The feedback received about those response-gifts which a storyteller has particularly appreciated further develops the participant's understanding of interpersonal efficacy in a non-threatening climate. Thus they learn to speak more freely with a mind of their own in a situation of belonging.

In the course of enabling a group and its individual members to work with response tasks as a way of processing story material, the facilitator engages explicitly in a range of tasks. These include the use of emotionally supportive behaviour, appropriate modelling and focusing attention on the task in hand. Stockton, Moran and Velkoff (1987) have noted that these are key facilitator attributes. In order to make previously overwhelming feelings, thoughts or fantasies interactively useful, a TSM participant needs to learn to develop mental terms between experience and response as well as the requisite distance and communicative structure to relay these. The facilitator's role in promoting such development is expressed in the maintenance of the group rhythm, the safeguarding of group boundaries and the facilitation of group learning.

Traumatic over-stimulation, emotional neglect, deprivation and chronic illness intersect in troublesome ways with a person's capacity to make use of a facilitating environment. This is a given. Because the development of mental terms to hold and develop experience crucially affects a person's recovery from illness, it is the facilitator's task, together with the group members, to promote this optimally. Response tasks are a specific form of assisted learning which use conscious invitation of constructive criticism. Over time, the response tasks help most group members to establish a more productive habit of using new information, critique and support (Anderson and Goolishian 1992). The systematic use of story-making, storytelling and response tasks supports the participants' involvement in circles of attention which consist of thinking, creating, preparing to present an idea, presenting it, making and receiving responses, and thinking about these and reformulating thoughts, etc. During the early stages of group formation the TSM facilitator

- enables members to gain an initial sense of the group as group
- helps members to feel safe by the clear definition and maintenance of boundaries
- clarifies the group's containing and exploratory function without premature confrontation.

These three tasks are reflected in the Phase 1 and 2 response tasks as described above. The tolerance of mental states and support for a group member's ability to experience the manifestations of other people's feelings and intentions as well as a predictable social environment in which rules can be seen to apply, support, as Fonagy (1989) suggests, the development of a theory of mind. Responses within the story frame encourage mutual playfulness, the reciprocal risking of action over inaction and, especially, the practice of interpersonal attunement in a try-out imaginary context.

Problems a group member might encounter when formulating a response task

There are three kinds of problems which may occur in the process of formulating a response task:

(1) The task is too loosely defined
This may be illustrated in tasks such as:

- Just write about anything that comes to mind after you have heard my story
- Make a doodle whilst you listen to my story and then give it to me.

The non-specificness of these demands creates too many possibilities. What the storyteller specifically desires remains unaddressed and unmet. The task needs tightening up through dialogue between facilitator, storyteller-to-be and the group.

(2) The task takes too much or too little time
This may take the form of requests such as:

- Dramatize my story for me and show me three alternative endings.

- Write down one word from my story that you are likely to remember.

Here the storyteller is in danger of taking up either too much of the available time resource, endangering other members' ability to have their request met or, conversely, so little time space that they do not receive the response they actually desire. They may feel cheated when other group members use the space that was vacated by their own minimalist demand. In the first case I tend to protect group space (especially during the early stage of TSM work) by asking the group member to rephrase the request, pointing out the likely time needed to do their original request justice. In the second case I likewise draw the storyteller's and the group's attention to the time consequences of the request and invite the storyteller to amplify what they have asked for, which they may or may not wish to do.

(3) The task as formulated cannot be made concrete
This happens when a group member either tries out wild imagery or has difficulty operating in a mode of fantasy which is bound by group-norms. Examples of such requests are:

- My character floats in outer space. I want you all to float in outer space.

- My character gets beaten up. I want you to beat me up.

When this happens the facilitator works with the group member to create a reformulation of the response task which will have some components of the original request, but with a firm recognition of what is actually possible. The storyteller-to-be in the first illustration needs to become aware that the request as formulated cannot be met, though approximations of the experience of floating can be created; for example group members might be asked to carry one another through the room in ways which might mimic the imagined experience of floating through outer space. Group members could also describe or paint what they imagine such floating through outer space might feel or look like. The re-working of the second request might result in group members enjoying a strictly boundaried pillow fight. When the reformulation of a response task request is undertaken in a spirit of respectful dialogue, group members often sigh with relief, as if they somehow hoped that it would be recognized that they had moved outside the task's manageable boundaries.

هوهوهو

> *Rarely can we be together;*
> *Rarely one can meet*
> *the other...*
> *Let us clasp our hands together;*
> *Let us interlock our fingers.*
> Kalevala

Commitment to relationship

Following the selection of one or two received responses, each participant is invited to share these with the group. At this point an interesting phenomenon occurs. Each storyteller knows that they are in the group both as a recipient and as a giver of responses. They realize that they themselves have 'merely' selected a response that is shareable. They also know that they have received other responses which might be more important or pertinent, but that they decided not to mention these for a whole range of reasons, if only because a particular suggestion might be too close to the bone. Their familiarity with their own process softens any judgment they have about why others might not have chosen their particular response to be shared in the group. Each group member also realizes that their gifts/responses have been seen or read by the other group members and that they do not and will not really know how relevant or irrelevant the responses they gave away are or will be to the storyteller-recipients.

During the sharing of selected responses it soon becomes obvious that group members are fascinated by what other group members have chosen as the response they want to talk about in the group. This interest links with the hope that their own response will be selected for sharing. This curiosity again supports the creation and maintenance of a circle of attention. In this phase of group-talk about the responses the group members receive feedback on what publicly matters most to the recipient of the responses. They can set this information against what they had imagined might be of interest to the recipient storyteller, compare it with the response they offered and adjust their understandings where necessary. In the course of this process the group quietly learns to negotiate its understanding of each participant's reality. The impression of the storyteller and of the story is modified by means of hearing the teller talk about the story, especially their own understanding of their story, and by the ways in which the teller makes sense of the received contributions to his or her story. When a group member shares what he or she thinks and feels about their story and shares how he or she perceives the links between their story, the selected responses and their actual life-experiences, the group's understanding of the multiple connections between fantasy material and lived experiences is deepened. A kind of useful doubt is introduced into the group. Group members learn experientially that certainty dwells in the trust of a bond between them, in which respect, love and interest are felt presences. Such relative security also dwells in the shared willingness to safeguard an atmosphere which contains all the space that is needed to enable individuals to explore ideas as well as different ways of being. The fear of an uncomfortably sensed unpredictability of others is thereby gradually transformed into a more joyous acceptance of the rich, surprising abundance of others. Helpful doubt takes the place of clinging uncertainty. Therapeutic storymaking uses a fairly straightforward set of procedural tasks. These are:

∘ warm-ups

∘ story creation

∘ identification of an area of query about a story and the formulation of specific response tasks to be performed by the listeners-to-be

∘ storytelling

∘ the performance of the response tasks

∘ the distribution and reading/viewing of the responses

∘ the storyteller selects the most appropriate solutions/ideas after having formulated criteria for selection

∘ the responses which contain solutions/ideas are integrated into the story and cross-referenced to the storyteller's personal life situation where appropriate

∘ a new story is made, etc.

Group members have often commented that the telling-response sequence initially evokes a strange sensation. They are not used to telling a story to a group of attentive listeners, whom they have asked to listen in a certain way, and who, once the story is finished, sit back awhile to really think about the task you have set them, let alone used to seeing people reach for paper, pens, colour, scissors, glue or clay to make or write a response based on what you have asked them to attend to – after which you, the storyteller, also set to and do your own bit.

When the harvest of responses is gathered, each group member is confronted with concrete evidence of the fact that people have thought about their story or story character and persisted in thinking about this character, even though the story was finished. There is abundant evidence that the group member's felt presence by means of their story lingered. People who are emotionally unwell frequently have trouble believing that they are in some way or another object-constants in the mind and hearts of others, and to trust that they are alive in other people's inner world. The response-gifts provide concrete evidence of this reality. This itself is often deeply moving to participants.

Exploratory thoughts about a story and a story character's deeds entail divergent solutions to predicaments. In TSM this ideas-gathering stage is followed by a more evaluative stage in which the storyteller takes account of all that was generated, at first deferring all judgment. This happens when each storyteller reads all the responses he or she has received. The storyteller, with the help of the group if wanted, then selects which 'selection criterion' might best be applied to the material received, for example:

- which is the most challenging response
- which is the most comfortable
- which is the most reassuring
- which is the most dreaded.

During this phase of the session group members work alongside each other, because each has told a story and each has received a bundle of responses. The facilitator encourages each person to choose personal criteria by which they will conduct their selection of the received responses. The criteria need to be supportive of development and permit exploration. In addition to the above, group members might be invited to consider aspects such as the attractiveness of a suggested action, its feasibility, the sense of wonder it evokes, or the disadvantages of a proposed solution. The process of individual evaluation of the received responses further promotes the development of informed judgment as well as the discipline of committing oneself to a position.

Work with response tasks as a form of assisted reflection

In addition to providing awareness of relationship constancy, the group members discover that a group can be invited to function as a team of investigators which can address his or her question. They learn through experience that these investigations unearth a range of individual interpretations, some of which overlap. These are offered for contemplation to the storyteller.[3] De Waele and Harre (1979) describe how in some forms of autobiography writing a person is assisted by a well-trained team in the production of a life-document. They suggest that such assistance enables the person more precisely to formulate 'a representation of how he views his own-life course, his own knowledge, beliefs, interpretative schemata, and principles of action and judgment' (p.177). The biography, which is elaborated by means of response tasks is, on the surface, the story-character's life-story. However, the suggestion that maybe the storyteller/participants might also find something relevant in a response received that he/she might wish to ponder a while in terms of their daily life facilitates the emergence of awareness that one's personal life is also considered by means of narrative strategies and intertwined with the fictional story that was created. When people are emotionally distressed they are often so wholly in their story that it is hard for them to conceive that there may be other ways to tell and to construct the stories of their life, let alone to entertain reinterpretations that might lead to a greater sense of available options.

The making of a response momentarily frames the participant's understanding of a specific story aspect. It directs thought to one element only with other ideas having to be surrendered to the one at hand. The concentration on the task which has been set by the storyteller demands a willingness briefly to de-emphasize one's own listening priorities. The ability to catch an idea, to realize that whilst it stands for something it does not represent everything, to reflect on a story's gist, to give these reflections words or image and to offer this to the storyteller for contemplation, not only pursues the experience of the story into memory, it also allows for the emergence of 'thought about something' (Peirce 1960, p.228). This emergence of 'thought about something' against an acknowledged background of information (the story as well as the storyteller's relationship with their story) is delightful to most participants. It is like the sun breaking through on a cloudy day. The realm of ideas is, in a broadly Platonic sense, often

---

3   Reflecting teams of professional therapists have for some time been used in family or marital therapy. Following an introductory period, during which the family works with one or two therapists, the family becomes the observer of a team discussion which takes place on the other side of a now reversed one-way mirror. The team members offer informed speculations about the client situation whilst the clients listen to their discussion. In this process the family members gather the information/opinions and are subsequently helped to clarify their own ideas in relation to those of the treatment team. For an evaluation of the clients' opinions about this way of working read Smith, Yoshioka and Winton (1993).

associated with light. The most moving confirmation that 'ideas' may equal light is the smile which breaks through on the face of a troubled person when they have caught an idea in their inner world and shared it with others who then recognize the thought as interesting. Turner describes this process as the emergence of performance reflexivity. Such reflexivity is a condition in which a socio-cultural group turns, bends and reflects back upon itself, upon the relations, actions, symbols, meanings, codes, roles, statuses, social structures, ethical and legal rules, and other socio-cultural components which make up their public and private selves (Turner 1986, p.25). The encounter with a group's response-ability, the gathering and evaluating of these responses, the selection of some pertinent ones for the story character and the request to see whether any of these responses might be of interest to the storyteller him or herself stimulate new thought by the client about the storying of their life. In a strict sense, this process is not the rewriting of biography through a conscious strategy as De Waele and Harre suggest; however, over time such re-formulation strategies may be absorbed.

Group members learn to use various processes of reconstructing fictional stories. They develop new understandings of the process and procedures of change in fictional realms, which stay close to their daily, lived reality – thereby the process of continuous change becomes less alien and, above all less, intimidating. Awareness grows that our autobiographies are always assisted. In TSM groups participants simply practice how to use such assistance.

Memory has a tendency to create re-enactments of remembered events. Not only does it reproduce the past as an image, it reproduces the past as a confirmatory, lived actuality. Though this actuality does not represent the original situation, when life is troubled its semblance to the past can make it feel pretty much like the same old story. The congruence between unhappy current experiences and vividly remembered situations sustains ongoing conflicting self–world dynamics. In TSM such conflicting dynamics are of course represented in the stories people make. They cannot not be. However, every new relationship, including those with people, animals, environments, materials and exercises, offers much more than an opportunity for the re-creation of familiar, unhappy situations. They allow for the emergence of newness. The stories function as the funnel which focuses the past. They give the pretext to generate semblance. However, the way in which the group works with this story can become the anvil on which group members' new relationship with the story, and simultaneously with others, is forged. Because the focus of the work is to all intents and purposes on the story and on the response tasks, the rebuilding of new relationships happens in a setting of interest, excitement and emotion which favours the development of new images. Bartlett (1932) suggests that memories of habits of relating may become reconstructed through the provision of 'a persistent framework of institutions and customs which act as a schematic basis' (p.277). The rhythm of story creation, telling and responding establishes just such a re-framing custom. The story-work casts different light onto habitual processes of representation, recollection, reflection, rehearsing and reconstruction. By means of reflective play, a frozen, fixed interpretation of the past becomes more emotionally fluid. Such emergent fluidity provides group members with a greater capacity to make and to enjoy distinctions. The ability to distinguish, and through distinguishing to differentiate further, permits the emergence of emotional flexibility. A welcome self-supporting cycle of development is thereby set in motion.

When responses are troublesome

The facilitator needs to address the fact that occasionally problematic or unwelcome responses may be sent and/or perceived. This can be a most painful experience. The recipient of a troublesome response feels let down, attacked and misunderstood. When a sufficient climate of trust has been established in the group, they will often ask: 'Who did it?' In my experience group members mostly identify themselves as the sender of the particular response and explain why they formulated/painted their reaction in that way. The group then reflects together on the 'unwanted' nature of the gift. Often the recipient will return this gift to the neutral centre of the group. It has happened that another group member actually would have liked to have received it. Sometimes the sender has claimed it back. Either way, the negotiation of troubling responses is invariably an important stage in both a person's and a group's development.

Each response-task creates dilatory space because it allows for a pattern of communication following storytelling that is initially strategically indirect and story-centred. The response exercises deflect the group's fears away from the immediacy of dialogue, whilst a basic capacity for responsive dialogue is surreptitiously practised. By learning to make a response of kinds to someone else's story in the form of some carefully focused writing, painting or through participation in a brief movement exercise, a preoccupied, troubled person can rediscover that what they have on offer to others is frequently good enough, sometimes highly valued and mostly welcome. They also learn that what they made or wrote with the best intentions is not necessarily well received. Sooner or later the group encounters the reality that the giver does not decide whether something is a good enough response.

Sometimes a gift is spot on, sometimes irrelevant and sometimes downright awkward or wrong. During the creation of a response the capacity to tolerate the consequences of 'making something within this uncertainty' is practised, whilst the means to cope with the impact of the recipient's response to one's own response is slowly brought under ego-control. Feelings thus become less frightening, other people less distant and intimacy is no longer quite so intimidating. Once the fabric of mutual responsiveness is strengthened, a person's deeply troubling life-experiences can be brought more readily into the fabric of the temporary human community of a TSM group.

It is therefore vital that both appreciated and unappreciated responses find a place in the group culture. Not only do participants need to learn the difference between immediate and delayed appreciation but they also need to discover that it takes all sorts of suggestions – some highly applicable, some off the wall – to establish one's own truth. In my experience a response which is received as hurtful is rarely sent with unkind intent. On the one occasion that this did happen, work with group members around the issue of knowingly wanting to cause distress to another soon clarified the depth of the pain which the man, Tony, who was sending such responses to every group member, experienced. His difficulty with the management of his sadistic impulses was felt by everyone and acknowledged by him. Tony reminded me of Cyrulnik's (1993) description of a child who is nine or ten months old. At that stage a child, restrained in its high chair, first stretches all its fingers towards a toy it has previously thrown on the floor. It will look at the toy and start to yell because the toy cannot be reached. When the toy is not picked up and handed back by someone, the baby will throw itself back in the chair, arch backwards and engage in self-aggressive behaviour, such as biting its hands. At the age of ten or eleven months a change occurs. Instead of spreading out its whole hand, the child starts pointing, as if to say: 'I want that and I want you to give me that.' The other has become a known intermediary.

There was enough evidence in Tony's behaviour to suggest that others could also be used as trusted intermediaries, provided sufficient attunement and appropriate social challenge were available to him. The cohesion of the group had become strong enough to hold his illness and to work with him towards recovery. Though his participation in the short-term TSM group was fruitful for all concerned, Tony subsequently undertook longer term individual psychotherapy to work through his internal and relational dynamics.

The receipt of unwanted or peculiar responses provide opportunities for the group to practise resilience, the capacity to discern between what is wanted and what is not wanted and gratitude – gratitude for the sheer fact that other people have made an effort on one's behalf and resilience in coping with the inevitable gap between anticipation (what they imagine they could have received) and the reality of what was received (some items better, some items worse). I believe that learning to recover from disappointment and acquiring emotional bounce are fundamental precursors to emotional stability. Coping with an unhelpful response and learning to differentiate between angry intent and benign intent in a not very applicable gift further strengthens interpersonal skills and supports a participant's vital awareness of the reality that other human beings are a help much more often than a hindrance (Russell 1958, p.50).

Storymaking as a process of shared discovery

The response tasks facilitate the systematic practice of a habit of involvement in each other's stories. The group members learn to become consenting co-investigators. Through exploration of a story-character's aspirations, motives and objectives they query the apparent givens and develop alternative approaches to presented solutions. Such a process of co-investigation is not a given behaviour; it is learned or facilitated. I believe that people and their situations are changed through shared reflection on that situation, as well as through thought about *how* their thinking is structured as a result of being in the situation. The TSM group and the many realities it represents are like a unique, living code which is to be deciphered by all its members. In this work everyone aims to learn how others feel and construct their worlds and to tolerate the feelings evoked by the experience of how these different worlds affect each other. In this process of shared discovery the group reconsiders what they had previously thought, felt and sensed. In other words, the perceived realities are not only examined, they are re-constructed – including the passionate emergence of feelings this also entails, by means of continuous evaluation. In the course of such investigative evaluations the group needs to engage in an emotional way with the interactive dynamics between personal feeling or thought and group feeling or thought, between exposition, review and reorientation. Contradictions need to be noted, meaningful thematics identified and awareness of what is held important or believed to be unachievable needs to be supported. Inevitably the group encounters its own fatalism or lack of belief and needs to embrace a review of perceived limits which have actually been left untested in either thought or action for too long.

When this complex of feelings, thoughts, intuitions and perceived (yet untried) limits is openly shared by all, its thematic content becomes accessible. The growing externalization of felt and lived problem clarifies to the participants how they presently sense or perceive their world. Felt needs and articulated longings can then find a home in the group's awareness of itself and of its situation. The group's engagement with how they may emerge from this situation becomes its explicit task. The entire process of warm-up, storymaking, story-sharing and evaluation is characterized by explicit support for group members' ability to identify, describe, elaborate, explore and address problems with the aim of achieving a more productive and satisfactory engagement with their life's felt complexities. Enduring change-ability needs to become a continuous given. The member's activity in the group is characterized by reflection *and* action, thinking, sensing, feeling *and* doing (Jones 1995).

This process may be illustrated by Margaret's work in a group. When we met she was in her late forties. She was struggling with the aftermath of a difficult divorce. In the third session of a twelve-week group she wrote a story about a young deer who was cold and lost in the middle of a dense, prickly wood. The only helper who appeared, a bird, did not even see the deer. Before Margaret read her story she asked each participant to create, subsequent to the telling, through painting or writing, a safe place where the main character in her story might spend the night. Most participants obliged by describing or painting a snug shelter in a wood but one woman did something quite different. She drew the outline of two hands with the words 'a warm hug' written in a large scrawl around the drawing. During the phase when the group shared selected responses, Margaret said that she was immensely pleased to receive the gift but that she was terrified of touch or even to talk about touch. She fixed me with her gaze as she spoke. Acknowledging her fear, I pondered aloud if she might want the group to show her the comfortable abode for the deer, for example by collectively creating a shelter-like shape with their bodies where the story-deer might temporarily find some rest. I added that she might even try to go inside this imaginary shelter to check it out. She looked shocked and intrigued at the very audacity of my suggestion but refused. I immediately followed this not-yet-possible suggestion, which was primarily seeded for further use during a later session, with a possibly-acceptable idea. I proposed that the group might simply show Margaret what such a body-built-shelter for a story-deer might look like. She could then inspect it on the outside only. As Margaret pondered this suggestion, I asked the group, including Margaret, to do a brief movement exercise. This involved swaying their upper body whilst singing the words: 'Yes... No. Here... There.' There was much laughter as the group moved about. Margaret embodied her ambivalence and visibly eased up whilst doing so. Meanwhile, the very act of moving prepared the group for the possible building of the shelter. As the group slowed its sway into a steady, relaxed-breathing rhythm, Margaret said: 'Thanks for the opportunity, but I don't want to ask you to make the shelter just yet.' Pat commented: 'I know just how you feel.' Margaret snapped back: 'No, you don't.' Though initially hurt by her words, Pat responded with: 'I guess you're right. I don't.' She paused: 'I know how I feel though.' Both Margaret and she looked relieved. Soon other group members talked about fears related to seeking shelter, which was certainly an appropriate theme during this our third session. Paradoxically, Margaret had tolerated being in touch with other group members because the group had spontaneously hooked arms when swaying. Though the deer's shelter was not built, the group's function as a shelter which could contain voiced ambivalence was strengthened. Then the group moved on to share reflection on another person's selected response.

Several sessions later, Margaret commented that saying no to the possibility of seeing the shelter made had been crucial to her, adding:

> I realized when I received the picture of those hands, that I wanted to be actually, physically touched. That's what I really, really longed for. As I swayed backwards and forwards, I knew that it would have been false to build that shelter and just to look at it. But I couldn't have borne going inside of it. Not then. It would have been too much too soon. It would have been the same old story. When I said no to the exercise something changed.

After acknowledging her felt sense of gradual betterment, I queried: 'Are you also saying that you want to build a shelter now?' 'Oh yeah, please...' she said. The group laughed warmly and at a later point during the session they performed her request. The group was moving on. The imagined uncontainable longings of several sessions ago could now be firmly, yet gently, held within the stronger skin of the group.

When fear dominates a group's atmosphere its members urgently need to discover shared concerns, like the group's very personal, though brief, reflections on touch and trouble with intimacy which had followed Margaret's decision not to see a shelter built there and then. In any group it takes time to unwind from the isolation of illness and move towards the understanding that feelings are shared with most other people – unique only in so far that they are ours, general in the sense that they are common. Such a return to the fold of average, common humanity can hurt a great deal. There are gains as well as losses in the experience of isolation. To surrender its splendour can be a real ache. In parallel with the easement of imagined, somewhat cold, separateness, participants in TSM groups need to become more aware of the vital difference between an imagined response to an imagined situation (what I might do with the shelter once it is built or what I would do with the shelter if I were Margaret) and an actual response to an actual event (what I am doing with the shelter).

To illustrate: given Margaret's fears and recent life experience, she had to learn how to tolerate the very thought of a possible slight touch inside a possible shelter which might be made by other group members at some point in the future (a series of imagined responses to an imagined situation); to taste the range of associated, possible feelings through anticipation. Given that she was just about able to deal with the possibility of the hope that there might be a safe shelter somewhere, Margaret was certainly not yet ready to experience seeing how such a shelter could be physically represented by the group (an imagined situation made dramatically actual), let alone to experience going into, being inside and eventually to leave this shelter (to have an embodied experience in a dramatized situation).

During the various stories and exercises which had followed the shelter episode the group continued its process of rebuilding a more resilient connection with hope, intention and enjoyment of actual experience. In subsequent sessions the group was steadily, playfully and, therefore, nearly surreptitiously enabled to re-learn the sequence of conceiving an idea, imagining its realization, seeing it realized at a safe distance and then fully participating in its realization and evaluating it. Once Margaret and her fellow group members gained sufficient experience with identifying the various points of choice which commitment to continuing action entails, it was safe enough for her to participate in a group-made shelter. However, this was by no means the end of her journey. The comparative anonymity of the group shelter required further developmental work which dealt with her difficulties with the more challenging directness of identifiable small groups and the demands of pair-relationships. She gradually learned to share dyadic and family-sized spaces with others.

The rebuilding of a participant's trust in their capacity to make a commitment to a chosen act relies on the exploration of both the connection and the differences between feeling aroused by an anticipated reality and feelings in the present situation. What is shifted in this kind of work is not the feelings themselves but the feelings about the feelings. In other words, a person is helped to become less intimidated by the fact that they have feelings. The various stories and response tasks are stepping-stones towards achieving this.

Very wisely have you acted;
That you leave the birch tree
standing.
Leave the great, dear tree
unfallen,
That the birds may perch
upon it.

Kalevala

The therapeutic utility of response tasks

Whereas I had anticipated that the suggestion of specific response modes and the teaching over time of a wide range of response-abilities might be experienced as limiting or frustrating, I found that enabling group members to use structured tasks which relied on specific observations and the subsequent translation of these observations into a particular response was experienced as freeing. After my first puzzlement that response tasks were so much easier to introduce and to perform than I had ever imagined, I remembered that responding to a request is initially easier than making a spontaneous contribution.

When group members are invited by a fellow group member/storyteller to listen carefully to their story, to pay particular attention to a specific aspect and to work their understanding of this aspect into an observation, an idea or a suggestion, they are essentially invited into relationship. Not only is there an expectation that they will work on an individual group-task, carrying their share of the responsibility for the collective performance, there is also an explicit request that they will use life-experience, fantasy and feelings to formulate an idea and to do so expressively. In this manner the listener's response to a story they have just heard, their reflection upon the story and their interpretation of events are given digestible form. The timely utterance of ideas or impressions gives the thoughts and feelings release. It prevents un-stated responses from accumulating.

The involvement in the response tasks enables participants to isolate an issue and to transform a possibly disorganized, projected perception into a communicable expression. The act of engagement in this process provides group members with new evidence of the importance of co-operation, of the need to maintain an equilibrium between projective and introjective process and of the possibility that good enough others can be internalized and, through internalization, used. The accumulative experience of giving and receiving responses (both during a particular session and over time in a series of sessions) also permits a more ready structuring of a person's understanding of others. The group members gain clearer knowledge of how others articulate their inner world. If yet another story is told with a similar theme or character, the group soon recognizes 'the lonesome igloo in the howling wind', 'the snake that hides in the forest' or 'the wild musician who taunts the weary old woman' as a regular, thematic representation of a person's inner world. If relative constants emerge in people's stories, as they often do, the group develops a relationship with these. Such relationships are often characterized by affection and informed by the group's wish that these storied characters will also undergo development. Though an average family may find old Uncle Harry endearing as he once again grumbles his way through Christmas dinner, a TSM group initially simply welcomes such a storied Uncle Harry but, after a while, even a storied Uncle Harry will be invited to change.

Over time, the group's shared memory of story events and story characters' dispositions support a group member's attempt to understand how come their character once again dwells in an unreachable cold shelter or how come the character once more rejects help that is offered. The group generates such 'how comes' in the process of responding to areas of query which the storyteller has emphasized. The collective history and common knowledge soon become a real source of pleasure to the group. The response tasks allow the display of the ability to recall and to connect both memories and observations in so many different ways.

It is fruitful to be remembered by others for little things. In a particular TSM group Michael said to Ann: 'Didn't you tell a story about a little boy some weeks ago who threw a bottle with a message into the sea?' When this was affirmed, he continued: 'In this story you're doing something similar. Did you realize? Now, it's not a bottle, but a balloon with a message. Can you see? Your characters really find it hard to ask for something direct, don't they.' Ann, the recipient of these thoughts, became quite tearful. Shortly after she shared with the group her experience of leaving her parents behind on the quayside when she travelled alone by boat to go to school in this country. Long, unhappy separations were the story of her childhood. Her basic pattern of relating to others was most succinctly encapsulated in the metaphor of a person who puts a message in a bottle and sends it adrift in the hope that someone will find it and respond. Within the protective structure of story the group was able to encourage her to rework this habit – initially for the story characters and subsequently for herself. The additional expectation that she would be able to respond directly (by means of symbolic expression or ordinary language) to other storytellers' tales enabled her to practise speaking with a mind of her own in a situation of belonging. Due to these two factors, she began to practise greater responsive directness in the group.

Once a group has built up some experience with the structure of responding and receiving, members realize that response-items are given both for the here and now of this moment in the group and for later. They themselves have taken response-gifts away from the session to other places. Some have looked at the gifts with other people at other times. Some have simply filed them or thrown them away. If at some future time the storymaker wants to be reminded of *how* his or her work had been received, the responses are there to revitalize the experience. They convey: 'This is how you directed the group to respond to you and what they were able to do with your request. This is what people offered you.' Thus the response tasks also suggest and grant a degree of permanence to the relatively impermanent – the momentary perception of a contemporary spectator. Reciprocal commentary and self-commentary are helped to find an integrative balance (Palmer and Jankowiak 1996).

By learning to balance advice with support, concern with encouragement and reassurance with realism, group members begin to inhabit a middle road. Good attunement means giving attention to fears and wishes, defences and intuitions. When a group learns to notice the subtle energies that signal movement out of stuckness, or the emergence of a commitment to action over inaction, these are welcomed and given fruitful space. Then change becomes a real possibility (Winston, McCulough and Laikin 1993). Therapeutic storymaking is a short-term group work method. In this process the primary focus of interpretation must be on interpersonal relationships with important others over and above the interpretation of the relationship with the therapist. Work outside the transference is granted priority (Hoglend 1993). In TSM these 'important others' include the other group members and the facilitator, the fictional and actual characters they describe, as well as the memories or fantasies of animals, events and landscapes which are brought into the group. Change is brought about through the systematic healing use of relationship, through practice of the capacity to respond flexibly, by means of support for the expansion of ways of being, and through the imaginative exploration of entirely new circumstances which require different habits and new, more adaptive ways of going about things. The group work sets the conditions to illuminate our existence. It promotes development whilst members participate in change through partially ritualized patterns of social interaction (VanderHart 1989).

Wandering from place to place
Ay!
Like a feather in the breeze,
Ay!
Quechua

6. To Create a Secure Base

Under the sky, here on the earth, we begin our life. This primacy of place is acknowledged in most traditional stories. They frequently begin with the setting of a scene. However, hardly is the location, the where-aspect of the story, established before the listener is told about the character's immediate or imminent movement away from this setting. With or without their felt agreement, the story character starts a journey away from their home sphere. The act of departure from the starting situation initiates all events that follow. A princess may have been delighted to live in a palace or at the bottom of a well. A farmer's son may have enjoyed waking up in a farmhouse, a shed or a temporary make-shift shelter. Birds may have most intricately built their nest. But if they are characters in a story, before long something will happen to cause a development away from the place of beginning. The journey that removes the story character from where they are when the story begins may be commenced in fear, delight or anger, but made it will be (Bowlby 1988). Traditional stories emphasize that life itself or the urge to growth exercises a maturational pull. Every story character is invited to wake up and to grow up. Sooner or later the shed, prison, nest, cottage or cave where a story character abides is turned into a location which must be left. It becomes a home base from which initiating actions occur. The inevitability of themes of departure and possible return soon impresses itself on any listener to traditional stories.

On victim heroes and their troubles

In traditional stories home is left in one of two ways. In the first set of scenarios the story characters set out to do something, such as deliver a parcel, gather food or begin a journey. The purpose of such a journey varies. It may be undertaken because something crucial needs to be found, such as healing herbs, or retrieved, such as a treasure. There are also enemies who must be defeated, lovers to be liberated or, simply, experiences to be gained. Though some travellers may be eager to start their journey, they can face serious opposition from those who will be left behind. Take, for example, Dobrinya, Nikita's son. His mother pleads as he makes ready to depart: "Oh, my Dobrinya, why must you ride to the Saracen's Mount to kill the dragon and free the Russians imprisoned there? No one who has tried to swim the Puchei river has ever returned. It is a fierce beast of prey, with fire leaping from its first rapids, a shower of sparks from the second, and columns of smoke rising from the third.' But Dobrinya, Nikita's son did not listen to his mother. He rode out...' (Baumann 1975, p.20). Though his mother tried to prevent him from going on a dangerous journey, Dobrinya persisted. This hero passed his first test: a challenge to his commitment.

In one category of starting situations the story characters freely choose to leave the dwelling place for a shorter or longer period of time. They even insist on doing so against substantial opposition. In the opening phase of the story they show determination, intention and volition. These basic behaviour traits crucially affect the subsequent storied events. In a second set of scenarios the story characters are thrown out of their dwelling place, often during a spell of rough or cold weather. They are rudely sent into a wide unfriendly world. They are barred access because they have broken a rule, violated an interdiction or have become unwanted. A more powerful being, such as an evil giant or a cruel stepmother, deprives the hero or heroine of the right to return. Sometimes tragedy takes this role. In such stories home is lost due to a natural disaster, to war, or because of the death or disappearance of a parent. These tragedies generate the same effect: a stunned hero or heroine has to come to grips with a different kind of life, for which he or she is ill-prepared, amidst portentous circumstances.

Jane's story succinctly encapsulated this theme. She wrote:

> When the boy was six years old his grandmother died. They had lived together in a small house. She always sang him old songs and gave him sweet things to eat. He didn't understand why she would not wake up. Why he stopped living in her little house. He cried for his grandmother to come sing to him and scratch his back. But she never...'

Her fictional story stopped at the point where it bordered too closely on the felt events of her own life. It paralleled her own 'great missing'. When she later elaborated her tale about this little boy, it became saturated with a violent event that befell an essentially helpless story character. Her fictional story, in common with other victim-hero stories, emphasized the child's inability to understand the events. Such non-comprehension is a poignant characteristic of these tales. In stories which begin with involuntary departure the cast-away is unprotected and slow to recognize that a different phase of life has begun. Their new circumstances require a more active approach than that proffered by their habitual attitude. A sharper thoughtfulness and planning as well as initiative are needed. No longer do the Cinderellas of this world passively have to endure an unpleasant or violent home situation. The casting out has removed them from that situation, albeit against their will. The story invites some kind of change in their relationship with their world. This change in the dominant way of relating to life's events from reactive to proactive is a tall order for many such characters, particularly because any protest they might earlier have felt about their treatment had long since been silenced.

Propp (1984) calls these two dominant types of characters the seeker hero and the victim hero. Whereas the seeker hero is spurred on by volition, the victim hero is overcome by the shock of abandonment, banishment, bewitchment or exclusion. Though some seekers commence their journey suddenly, most prepare for their adventure. They take the necessary accoutrements and their going forward into the world is often blessed. Their haste is measured. Their goal fairly clear. Assured of a warm welcome upon their awaited return, these travellers trust that the home fires will be kept burning whilst they are on the road. Their solid base grants them the advantage of confidence for the tasks they need to complete.

Victim heroes, on the other hand, are often truly surprised that they have been excluded from a cold, unfriendly place. Instead of being relieved, they endlessly ponder what has gone wrong and how they are not even acceptable to bad people in a bad place. Their childhood years were characterized by making do, not by preparation for a life with greater freedom, independence and kindliness. They are ill prepared for the journey that lies ahead, if only because they did not decide knowingly to leave. Even when the home is saturated with pain, the victim heroes in stories rarely consent to their departure. During the events which follow the leaving, these reluctant heroes and heroines find it difficult to gain some kind of inner perspective on the events of their life and to develop a sense of agency. They do not easily arrive at inner consent to their journey, act on the basis of knowledge, take responsibility for their actions and inactions or act with foresight. They dream away, unable to behave in accordance with the demands of time and place and unwilling to query their understanding of things. An old European teaching story illustrates such foreclosing of thought:

Each day a certain fisherman is given one of many rowing boats by the harbourmaster of the village where he lives. One day he has taken a boat out to sea. He finds a particularly good spot for fishing. He wants to return there. After much reflection he decides to mark the location by cutting a notch in the boat. When evening falls he returns the boat to the harbourmaster. As he walks home he suddenly realizes that he does not know if he will get the same boat tomorrow. He frets all night that someone else might now find his fishing place.[1]

In the grips of their interpretation of reality, and deprived of the help of useful doubt, the victim heroes' actual knowledge lies forgotten and ignored in the rag-and-bone shops of their heart. There it waits until at last they are strong enough to face their reality, their hurts, longings and possibilities – thereby to be transformed.

Practice vignette: That place called home

Irrespective of their original starting mode, the call to adventure or, what Campbell (1975) called the opening of destiny heralds that something is on the move, things will not continue as they once were (p.52). The time for crossing the threshold into a wider world is at hand. A reluctant or gutsy heroine or hero needs to set forth into the world. Distant horizons call with greater or lesser urgency, more or less attraction. Fortified in castles, isolated in pristine towers or hidden in caves deep beneath the surface of the water, sooner or later each story character must face the challenge to wake up to their relationship with their world. When that moment comes the character can adopt a few basic positions: consenting exploration, reluctant acknowledgement, the denial of the importance of the journey, protest at being expelled into a strange world or trying to dwell forever at the place of ousting. The nook of earth from where the journey started is the inevitable companion on any journey through life (Timmer, Eitzen and Talley 1994). Proshansky, Fabian and Kaminoff (1983) describe the confluence of the individual and their environment as place-identity. Who we are and how we behave is not simply defined and expressed by our relationship with other people. It is also deeply reflective of our relationship with the physical settings that surround our daily life. Our home-sickness, home-fondness or home-painedness travels with us. It cannot not be so.

In a TSM group which explored the theme of homecoming, Mike asked Sarah why she had left her country of origin. She replied: 'A

---

1   Retold by the author. Story circulates in oral tradition.

broken heart.' Turning to him, she queried: 'Why did you *not* leave your country?' He retorted with a sigh: 'A distinct lack of courage.'

Whether we stay put or go away, the place we call home accompanies us wherever we are (Douglas 1993). The location, design and placing of our home in relation to other dwellings profoundly influences who we think ourselves to be and how we are perceived by others. However much we may try not to be identified with a certain area, we are also people of a place (Belk 1991). Many years ago I worked on a grim inner city housing estate. Its residents endured countless troubles, not the least of which was their deeply felt shame at living in a slum. Theirs was the land behind God's back: noisy, violent, ugly, dirty and thoroughly miserable. They were well aware that their home and streets contained their history, created their memory and conveyed their social status (Gillis 1996). They did not like where this placed them in both their internal and external world. As one of the residents said: 'We may clear the streets of rubbish, repair the street lights, clean up the balconies. We might even begin to feel less ashamed of living here. Yet I'll always be a man from a troubled council housing estate. For me that is not a good thing. It hurts.' He needed to explore his grief of having had to endure the years of violence and shame linked with living in a deprived inner-city area. It takes time and physical effort to rework a pained and troubled home environment into a good enough place of identity. It took courage too.

Fred, a lonesome bachelor in his mid-forties who lived in a similarly tough inner-city area, once wrote the following story:

> Whipple is a fox who lives in a wood. The wood is beautiful with many trees, flowers and ferns. He would very much like a home. He has a friend who has a home. She will help him build a home. Whipple collects wood to build a lean-to based on his friend's house. Together they collect sheets of flat supersoft moss to sleep on. His friend brings him a plant to put in his house.

The tale spoke of his developing relationship with the group and with myself as its facilitator. It also expressed his pleasure in nature and the memories of his childhood in a village far away from the city. It conveyed his emerging realization that in order to get some of what you want, you have to work for it and to co-operate with others. Above all, the story carried his longing for a better kind of place; a home in which he would feel less alone and more dignified. How he was actually going to make that happen escaped him at that time. However, the story signalled to him that some kind of action to improve his living environment needed to become a concrete goal.

People who use mental health services often associate their original environment with a great deal of pain. They long to build a better kind of home for themselves and their kin than the one from which they emerged. Yet they also know that in order to realize that dream they somehow have to tell the story of the place they want to leave behind.

During childhood, Karen, a woman in her early thirties, lived in various towns and villages. Irrespective of where she lived, the same events occurred. After a brief period of sobriety her mother would drink again. Each day, walking home from school, Karen had dreaded the moment when she had to turn the corner of whichever road she lived in. She described how once she crossed the emotional barrier into her street, she would become all ears. On a good day the street was filled with ordinary sounds: birdsong, voices, laughter, cars. But on a bad day she would hear loud music. When the music raged across the pavement towards her, she knew what to expect. Her drunken mother would be in the front room trying to conduct her gramophone orchestra and shouting at her musicians to perform the music just like she wanted to hear it. The absent orchestra never obliged. Once the front door fell shut behind her, young Karen was exposed to the brunt of her mother's frustration with those stupid, stubborn musicians. Until she was big enough to fight back there was no escape from the carping voice, the demands and the beatings. Whatever she did, she would get hurt. Home was a place of violence and broken promises. Occasionally it meant sobriety, excitement, mother playing the piano and showers of sudden, passionate care. But those occasions were rare. During her own adult years Karen moved from room to room, unable to settle anywhere for long. Her childhood pain needed acknowledgement and working through.

Karen is not alone with her painful memories of home. More often than not, the people who use mental health facilities or the children who draw a teacher's attention have a troubled relationship with their home base. They are only too aware that the physical/emotional place called home could be associated with security, constancy, personalization, welcome and stimulus, but they know from tough experience that somehow that is not their situation. For them home is irrepressibly associated with potential violence, unpredictability, exposure to overwhelming events, absence of warmth and discontinuity. They often wonder why. When someone is unable to make sense of the confusion these experiences generate, their bundle of troubling home memories grows into a profoundly felt sense of alienation, of not belonging. With such memories deeply ingrained they do not become oriented with relative security towards some kind of stimulating road through life. Because they cannot yet articulate where they have come from, they cannot possibly discern where they might be going. This generates further difficulties in attachment, spells trouble in intimate relationships and interferes with the development of an overall sense of direction in life.

Paul, a participant whose childhood home had been as tortuous and unpredictable as Karen's, wrote:

> The seven-year-old boy came home from wandering outside and his mother had baked him some cookies. And his father had made the best hot chocolate in the world. And they all three sat down to an afternoon treat with the sun shining in through the windows and open door. And you could see the orange flowers on the path outside and the dark green trees of the forest further away. The air was cool and fresh and he and his parents laughed and talked together. Peace.

When he finished reading these words he looked extremely sad. I asked: 'Sometimes?' He replied, holding my gaze: 'Not once.' Upon which another group member queried: 'Maybe you can be the man in this story one day and make the hot chocolate.' Smiling wistfully, Paul retorted: 'I already know how to make hot chocolate. I need to mourn what I never had.' During his adolescence Paul had left home. He restlessly moved from hostel to hostel, unable to settle down. Unbeknown to himself he remained faithful to his idealized image, as yet unable to mourn the harsh reality of having been an only child at home with a single mother who was severely depressed. In order to survive he had constructed the storied image of a boy's life, which he so passionately desired. The story protected him against his pain. When Paul first joined the TSM group he wanted happiness always. He was not yet ready to be reconciled to a life with occasional chocolate, occasional storms, times of unease and of common happiness. He aimed for lasting bliss and was always disappointed. When the longing and the pain his memories engendered finally arrived within his emotional grasp, he became alive to his hurt. His subsequent inner position is succinctly described in the following Tewa Myth of Creation.

> The early people live in a dark, cramped underground world. They want to find more of a world somewhere. On his travels Mole has sensed that the soil which surrounds him feels different in some places. He knows he can feel the change. The people decide to follow behind him, to claw their way towards newness. As they dig their path, the earth which is gathered in their hands is passed down the long line, back towards the final person. Thus the tunnel of newness closes behind them. It is forever closed. On their perilous journey towards another world they lose the old. When at last they arrive in the new world the light washes over them like a blessing. But they are blinded

by the light. Screaming with fear they hide their eyes in their hands, wishing, wishing they could go back. They argue and fight and despair, until at last they hear a tiny voice which speaks: 'Be patient my children. Take your hands away, but do it slowly. Take your time. Cover your eyes again, and rest, and take your hands away again.' Four times they moved their hands, four times they rested. Only then were they able to open their eyes and see the strangeness of their new world.[2]

Paul's recovery process took time, patience and a growing understanding of the process of healing from the grief which is engendered by the necessary loss of an idealized home. His journey reminded me of Mary, a sad young woman in her early thirties, who had been just such a child. She told the following story:

A long time ago there was a child, a girl. She is five years old. She lives in a tent in the forest. She is all alone. She has run away from home. It is night. Angry wolves howl outside the tent. She is thirsty. Very thirsty. She had run away from home…

The story halted. Mary fixed me with a lost and weary gaze. It seemed to hold an as yet unspeakable request for a resolution of kinds to some intensely felt dilemma. Her story and her way of telling it spoke of so many different realms in her past and present life situation and reflected the dynamics of her inner world. It succinctly described her way of functioning within the group and characterized key elements of her relationship with me, whilst it also spoke of her dread of the future as well as her way of relating to the anticipation of future life events. The interpretation of any of these pathways into the story's knot might have been fruitful. I decided that it was of paramount importance to promote improvement within the story's frame, in a way which might mirror most efficaciously the kind of working through and maturation Mary needed. I therefore tried to work out, together with Mary and by means of dialogic storytelling, who might be able to help the story's little girl in her predicament.

Struggling to surmount her wish simply to abandon the girl to her tent in the forest, Mary hesitantly continued her tale. The group listened attentively, both to Mary's resistance and to her fragile efforts to find a way through. She told the group how 'when morning came the wolves moved away. Then an old woman chanced to come along. She gave the girl some of the food she carried with her. However, the old lady then continued her journey.' I expressed concern that even though the old woman's arrival had

---

2   Retold by the author. Contemporary source in Marriott and Rachlin (1968, pp.225–241).

brought some temporary relief, we were still confronted with a little five-year-old alone in a tent in a forest, unwilling to go home and yet unable to survive alone at so young an age. Mary picked up the thread of her tale. She said that 'after the old woman left, a young friend found the girl. She pleaded with her to go back home but still the girl refused to come out of the tent.'

Though we had made some emotional progress, Mary was still in trouble. We had imaginatively established that the tent was not too far away from the girl's home, otherwise the friend wouldn't have found her. She had also stated that the girl in the story was able to accept care from someone – the strange old woman. A group member voiced her bewilderment that the parents in the story didn't seem to worry where the girl was. Mary immediately replied: 'They're too busy with the baby. They haven't noticed she has gone.' Another group member persisted that at least after a while they would have noticed that the girl had disappeared, after all a full night had passed. They surely would have missed the girl in the morning. Mary shrugged the comments off and, with some irritation, said: 'I don't know, I just don't know.' Then, with tears quickening to her eyes, she added: 'Her daddy is trying to find her.' When I asked why the girl's daddy couldn't find the tent, when the little friend knew where it was, Mary elaborated her tale: 'The father cannot see where the tent is. It is invisible to him. Only when the father realizes that the little girl has run away because of the birth of the baby will he be able to see the tent.' Playing a hunch I queried: 'Did you yourself ever feel like you were in a tent, just like that little girl?' Mary nodded. The fantasy story bridged the referential gap to the life story. Then she told us, bit by bit, about the premature birth of her first-born child and the terror she had felt whilst her daughter lived in an incubator for the first three weeks of her life. She spoke too about her sense of having failed to provide her child with a warm enough home, and of herself as having needed to camp out, attempting to stay close to her child whilst meanwhile feeling dislocated between home and the hospital. I asked: 'How come this is hurting quite so much now?' She quietly wept: 'I so want another baby but I don't know if I can go through that again. I don't know.'

It did not take that much work to help Mary to gradually unravel the trauma which had accompanied the birth of her daughter five years earlier, the life complexities which had ensued and their links with her present state of being. It will also come as no surprise that the story contained profound resonances with Mary's own childhood, including unresolved sibling rivalries and grief about her mother's death about a year before Mary's daughter was born. As such, her story reflected the intertwined pathways of both present and past. It also contained a clear directive towards the resolution of these complexities by means of imaginative and reality-based reflective processes. In the imaginative realm the girl in the story needed to become aware of the dangers of withdrawal, of the need for co-operation with potential helpers, of the depth of her longing to be rescued and her rage at the loss of a position of primacy in the home. In the reality-based realm Mary needed to come to grips with similar dynamics.

A good enough shelter

Because our sense of place is of vital importance to us, we need to pay scrupulous attention to the kind of dwelling-place described in a story – whether this is a traditional tale or a self-authored fictional story. In one group we explored several images of possible dwelling-places. The group enumerated a range of real and make-believe homes for story characters such as animals, creatures, animated objects, aliens and human beings. The dwelling-places included: nests, caves, palaces, tents, prisons, cottages, a hole in a tree, a gap beneath a roof tile, a pocket and a stately home. We then made group sculpts of some of these dwellings. In this technique several group members work together. They use their bodies to create the physical contours of a space, for example a nest, a church, a cottage, a cave. The group created an oak tree which had an animal's shelter in a hollow between its roots underground. During reflection on the possible weakness and strengths of such a dwelling-place, they expressed the following concerns:

- Maybe the tree will fall down or be cut.
- Is the space open to other animals to use?
- How many of them have to live in that hole? Maybe it is overcrowded.
- Does it have firm walls and a firm ceiling or will it collapse?
- What happens when it rains? Does it fill up with water?
- Can the animals store food there?
- Is there another way out of the hole, otherwise the animals could get trapped there?

The strengths were listed as follows:

- It could be really snug, particularly with several animals.
- You could feel really protected by that big oak.
- They could feel nicely hidden there.
- It could feel like a secret place.

Then one of the group members said: 'You see, it all depends. If it's a friendly world they'll be okay. But if not, they'll really have to take care with choosing the right kind of home. It all depends on what they need and what kind of world they live in. It all depends.' This was a remarkable insight for a young woman who until then had shrugged her shoulders with depressed indifference whenever the thought arose that dwelling-places might matter. I have learned that thoughtful, patient attention to the physicality of the imagined dwelling-place and the exploration of its good enoughness as a possible shelter for the night, as well as its facilitating characteristics during the day, leads group members in a quiet yet direct way towards exploration of their own concepts of a good enough place to be.

Dwelling-places in stories are most often described at the beginning of a story and occasionally in the middle in the form of other characters' homes and towards the end when the character may face the need to return home or to find a good enough place to spend the night. Sunny hillsides, cool breezes and wattled skies may have encouraged the traveller to rove the land with a light load of contentment, courage and commitment in her heart but when darkness falls or driving winds break through sweeping woods, the wish to find a shelter of kinds will once more become paramount. The need to create a good enough dwelling-place returns to the surface of awareness. Though during daytime or fine weather hours this thought might be have been ignored, sooner or later the story character will again need to address the question 'where will I sleep and will I be safe there?' In stories the need to find a good enough resting place is as inevitable as the departure. Though a story character may be an essential wanderer, a rolling stone, at some point they too must lay themselves to rest somewhere. The Crow sleepy-story reminds the listener: 'In the fall whenever there is a little wind, when we lie in some shelter, when dried weeds rub against each other and we listen, we generally get drowsy, is it not so' (Lowie 1935, p.135).

The process of 'tucking a character up for sleep', which engages the story's author in a dialogue about their character's sleeping place, is often experienced as surprising and comforting. Such a dialogue may take the following the shape:

> Nigel, a depressed man in his thirties, had ended his story about a mountain-climbing traveller with the words: 'He came to a plateau high up in the mountains and decided to go no further. He decided to spend the night there.' When the group appeared to be waiting for the rest of his story, Nigel added: 'That's where it ends.' A group member asked with a concerned voice: 'Did he have a warm sleeping bag?' When he responded affirmatively, the following group dialogue ensued:

Another group member: Was the ledge wide enough for him to be safe?

Nigel: I don't know.

Same group member says encouragingly: Think about it.

Nigel: Yes, yes. It was quite wide enough.

Me: Was he experienced at sleeping out like this. Had he done it before?

Nigel: No, he has never slept out like this.

Another group member: So, how does he know he'll be safe?

Nigel: I don't know. I guess he had heard other people talk about what they did.

Another group member: What kind of advice had they given?

At this point Nigel broke the story frame. He burst out: 'What do I care. So what if he falls off the ledge. Who the hell cares.' Then he began to cry. After a while he spoke about an unnoticed suicide attempt some years earlier. One night he had drunk too much. In the grips of a depression which had been unrelieved for weeks he had swallowed many tablets of aspirin, vaguely thinking that this was not a good thing to do but hoping that all his troubles would now be finished. To his surprise he woke up the next day feeling terrible and with a growing awareness of what he had tried to do. He told nobody. Yet the fear and shame of his capacity to attack and destroy himself, though deeply hidden, were still vividly alive. The story and its subsequent elaboration enabled him to speak of something that had needed to be spoken about many years earlier. Not only did the breaking of the silence bring relief, it also enabled him to begin to explore the inner and interpersonal dynamics that had culminated in his blind act (Gersie 1991).

In another TSM group I also raised the issue of creating a good enough, safe resting place for story characters. We pondered what that meant to the group members in question. They suggested issues such as momentary security, being cared for, having a chance to sleep and gain strength, feeling protected and acknowledging that there is such a thing as 'the next day'. When the group returned for the following session, several members commented on how they had cherished the image of a safe sleeping-place all through the week. Some had changed something in their bedroom to make it feel more secure. Some said that they had felt sad; they had remembered how throughout most of their childhood they had not felt secure at all — always waiting for footsteps on the stairs and the subsequent intrusion into their bedroom, for the sound of raised voices, their hearing acutely attuned to the perception of imminent danger. The very engagement with the theme of a good enough shelter evokes profound feelings and calls forth a wide range of memories. The facilitator and the group need to feel that it is safe enough to share these with each other, secure in the knowledge that feelings can be contained, reflected on and reworked. Whether this happens is affected by a wide range of factors, such as:

- what the group is about in terms of its explicit and implicit goals
- the context within which the group meets
- the typical character structure, histories and predispositions of its individual members
- the skills, spirit and understanding of the facilitator.

In this process I try to be mindful of the fact that every session is but an interval in the development of a person's ongoing life. I explicitly acknowledge that group members have varying experiences in the in-between time. If a group meets once a week for two hours, a further 166 hours have passed before the next group takes place. A great deal happens in that period. This is succinctly demonstrated by Muriel.

To share the great human dilemmas

In a brief TSM group for people with a history of depression, Muriel once created several stories. These stories centred around a small bear who lived alone in an igloo. Though long ago someone had left this little bear with a supply of food, this was now beginning to run out. Whenever someone approached the igloo, which was rare as the igloo was situated far away from any other habitation, the bear would hide in a hole in the ice. Thinking that the igloo was abandoned, any visitor would wander on.

The group had quickly noticed the themes of isolation and avoidance of interaction in her story. Muriel had been depressed for a long time. She was, however, reluctant to share more personal aspects of her life. In the response phase of the work, the bear was given a range of gifts that might enable him to greet a passing visitor. One day Muriel returned to the group looking a great deal more energetic. Following some introductory warm-ups, I asked group members what kind of experience of feelings they brought into the group this week. Muriel said: 'I have eaten, slept, talked, wept, been bored and I've thought of this group. I don't know where to begin.' To which another group member retorted: 'Just tell us something that you feel like sharing now.' In response, Muriel described how she had told her husband some days earlier that their marriage of thirty years was in deep trouble and that if it did not improve she might seek a separation. She added that she was in her late fifties and had been treated for depression for twenty of those years. No health professional involved in her treatment had ever made an explicit link between the state of her marriage and her depression (see McGoldrick, Anderson and Walsh 1989). When asked how come she had made this link this time, she said that the group's concern about the bear being all alone in an igloo and their involvement with helping the bear to develop new habits so that it might be able to greet a visitor had made her realize how profoundly lonesome she felt in her marriage. Once the link was made, it had been relatively easy to talk to her husband. As the sessions progressed, Muriel learned to re-animate the fictions of her inner world with more benign possibilities and kindlier creatures. Over time her story characters became more capable of interaction, learned to seek their fortune, tackle difficulties and recover from apparent defeat. She developed her own strengths in parallel.

The factors which influenced Muriel's growing capacity to articulate her needs, negotiate those with the needs of others and defend her wants were numerous. Some of these could undoubtedly be attributed to the work in the group. She was offered acceptance of her emotional state, support for interactive behaviour, reward for making a contribution or being willing to have a go at something, encouragement to lower her defences and acknowledgement of the value of her contribution whenever she gave feedback to others in a non-judgmental way. In other words the group did aim to function as a good enough nest. Here she received firm support to recognize, label and accept her feelings and learned not to be governed by feelings alone. Her developing capacity to acknowledge her interdependence with others enabled her to shift the dynamics in her marriage. Not long after her initial discussion with her husband, the couple agreed to seek marriage-counselling. The attunement which Muriel received in the group had offered her some clarification of her wishes and fears. Over time, the process of reworking the storied material helped her to inhabit a different internal and interpersonal world (Winston, McCulough and Laikin 1993). The continuing application of new insights in the process of responding to story material in a range of creative ways further sustained adaptive behavioural change. To say it simply and respectfully, the group encouraged Muriel to move from distressed sulking to kindly assertiveness. Inevitably, this change had an impact upon her marriage, which needed to be refreshed. In this TSM group she learned to notice and to reflect on the dynamics of her interpersonal relationships as these went through the predictable phases of idealization, withdrawal, attack and re-integration. The more direct work which was needed to address the dynamics between herself and her husband was successfully undertaken in couple therapy.

As most TSM groups are short term (average 8–12 sessions), I keep the primary focus of interpretation in these groups outside the transference – though clear transference phenomena are interpreted (Hoglend 1993). Because the relationship between group facilitator and group member is enacted in the group and reflected in the stories, it is possible to restructure and to interpret these dynamics through analogy (in the story frame) and only occasionally directly through interpretation. In my experience both levels of intervention are useful. The near-truth of a good analogical response by a group's facilitator provides extra delight because it signals attunement at a double language level, i.e. both in the literal and in the metaphoric realm. For Muriel, as for many other group members, the first facilitative task is to provide steady support for the re-awakening of the experience of a good enough base in which hope can emerge. Hope is a fragile intangible which allows for the birth of positive expectations in a studied situation. It travels beyond the visible facts. There are many conditions which can be taken to be good for a human life. These include health, security, companionship, freedom, meaningful activity, accomplishment and autonomy (Frankel, Miller and Paul 1992). Maslow (1962) defined our general motivational needs. He placed at their base our physiological needs, swiftly followed by safety needs, the need to belong, and the need for love, esteem and self-actualization. In general, the motives at the lower end of this hierarchy are activated through deficiency. They become urgent determinants of behaviour when satisfaction is lacking. Folktales often address such urgent themes, as the following Persian story illustrates:

> A rich man once invited several of his friends to his house. As usual they conversed awhile, expecting dinner to be served shortly. The host interrupted the flow of the talk by asking his friends: 'What do you think is the sweetest sound?' Like hungry dogs they set to discussing the topic. Each one fiercely defended their choice. 'The harp! No. The Flute. Never. The violin.' They could not come to an agreement. Still hotly disputing the matter they sat down at the dinner table. The food had not yet arrived. The guests wait and wait. Hours pass. They still talk about the sweetest sound, but with less animation and growing irritation. At last the rich man calls for the food to be served. He softly drums his spoon against one of the pots which is filled to the rim with

sweetly smelling vegetables. He says: 'In the ears of a hungry person, the ting of cooking pots is the sweetest sound.'[3]

In TSM it is possible to attend to deficiencies within the framework of a story. Sufficient safety in the group gradually enables group members to tackle these issues and how they are entailed in their illness. By paying scrupulous attention to a story character's physiological and security needs, the possibility of reparation of felt lack in a client's real world is engendered. This process often includes sympathetic explorations of the three great anxieties which, according to Tillich (1952), all people must face. These are themes of fate and death, emptiness and meaninglessness, guilt and condemnation. They evoke our recognition of the great human dilemmas. Speaking about the principle of hope, Ernst Bloch expressed his faith that 'Once human beings have grasped themselves and what is theirs, without depersonalization and alienation, founded in real democracy, then something comes into being in the world that shines into everyone's childhood and where no one has yet been – home' (Zipes 1979, p.129).

Engagement with these themes can help a group member to reach a place of homecoming. However, such explorations can only occur when a sense of a good enough base is created in the group. The exploration of what might constitute a safe and comfortable imaginary shelter for an imaginary character and the vivification of the dwellings a story character encounters play a crucial role in this process.

---

3 Retold by the author. Contemporary version in Yolen (1986, p.413)

Thence I ran,
as the darkness gathered,
in fluttering darkness
to the singing place.
Pima

7. In Search of Re-narration
Narrative detail and ethical choice

As a therapist and a teacher I am privileged to share many people's intimate life experiences. They have taught me how to recognize the highly specific ways in which we convey 'this is what it is like to be me' or, more accurately, 'this is what I'll let you know right now about what it is like to be me'. Frequently my clients and I can understand one another lightly, as if, amidst the turmoil of change, we do not have to work really hard to preserve the thread of congruent empathy between us. Occasionally both of us struggle to maintain healing contact beyond their fear, the screams, the frozen silence, the battles and the hurt. Once in a while I have felt that someone's life would be truly at stake if we were to be unable to re-establish a human place of encounter.

Such a moment occurred in a group of distressed adults with whom I worked in a community centre which catered for adults and children with a wide range of emotional and mental health difficulties. They participated in a brief therapeutic storymaking group (14 sessions). The seven group members – five women and two men – represented a true melting pot of strengths, coping styles and troubles. They shared the experience of profound emotional pain. Moreover, they were relative neighbours. All lived on or near a somewhat grim local authority housing estate. Most clients expected to make use of the centre as a home away from home for some time to come. In the following discussion I shall describe some dynamics of this group and in particular lift one client to the fore in the hope that thereby the group's narrative may be seen in sharper focus.

Pamela was a childless single woman in her mid-forties. During most of her adult life she had struggled with prolonged periods of severe depression. She attributed the depression to childhood years spent in a internment camp during the second world war. Though seven years old when the camp was

170

liberated, she had no access to memories of the period – saying, with forceful emphasis, that she simply knew that all had changed during the years of living in the camp. Following a troubled adolescence, her adult life had consisted of revolving-door stays in psychiatric hospitals and independent living in a flat on the estate. Here she tried to gather the fragile threads of a life permeated by substantial darkness. When we first met she said: 'I'm really a no-hoper, Alida.' And, nearly proudly, she had added: 'Quite a few social workers have given up on me. Please don't expect me to change. I'll come to the group because I like stories.'

During the first three of the fourteen sessions the group worked around the theme of 'beginnings'. We also addressed and reworked interaction styles linked with giving and receiving attention; we tried to build more effective mutual attentiveness. In the fourth session the group had 'the experience of surprise' as its central theme. This theme was chosen by the group during the previous session when concern had been raised that mental ill-health makes people feel predictable to themselves. They had described their inner world as stultifyingly unchanging. During this session I aimed to help the group members to access stories which emphasized behaviour other than that which they traditionally attributed to themselves. In the warm-up part of this session we worked with specially designed exercises around the themes of wonder, change and courage and the various feelings surrounding these.

I then asked the participants to select one memory of a time in their life when they had acted in a somewhat unpredictable manner and to write a few lines to describe the occasion. I suggested that the memory needed to relate to a moment when they had behaved in a surprising way, maybe nobly, or somewhat outrageously or possibly even a little unkindly. Before group members set to work we discussed the fact that autobiographical truth is more a matter of verisimilitude than verifiability. Whilst I had given this instruction I noticed that Pamela seemed to become twitchy. Though I had expected some resistance to actual work around the theme of surprise, given that it embodies both the fear of the sudden as well as a longing for it, she seemed to find it more threatening than expected, as if on hearing the word 'surprise' something had jarred inside her.

The group members each took a sheet of paper to jot down their memory. Pamela did so too, but without much apparent enthusiasm. When the brief writings were completed I suggested that we might share the memories. Once this was agreed I invited each group member to take a new fair-sized sheet of paper and to paint a colourful boundary along its edges, as if creating a frame for an as yet unknown picture. In so far as the resurfaced memories had aroused strong feelings in people, a degree of calming inevitably occurred while group members looked around for the right size and colour paper, for crayons and paint (Case and Daley 1992). With my ongoing encouragement, each person made the kind of border they liked. The open space in the middle of the sheet of paper, the group and inside the group member had thereby become a little less intimidating.

I suggested that they might now divide the space within the border into seven smaller spaces, one for each group member. Once the memory sharing began, they would use these spaces to draw a picture of their immediately-felt response to another group member's memory inside it. Everyone would simply paint or draw something which expressed their response to the story or a mnemonic image of the story on their sheet of paper. Sometimes someone might feel like adding a few words to their mini-drawing or painting. I assured the group that it really did not matter quite what was done, as long as a response was recorded on the still blank sheet of paper with its now colourful outer border and seven inner spaces. Once made, each mini-painting would be a personal record of the impact of first hearing about a surprising event in a group member's life.

I then reflected on the reality that when we listen to a person's memories we might hear something that this person has never before told to anyone else. Alternatively, we might hear an oft-told tale with which the person is very comfortable (Ruthrof 1981). The listener is not necessarily told upon which side of the line 'oft-told...first-told' a memory belongs. I noted that this potential for disclosure demands an additional sensitivity in our listening. With these words I alerted group members to prepare for a possible encounter with intimate and maybe disturbing disclosures. As Bion (1985) said: 'In every treatment room there ought to be two very frightened people, one the client, the other therapist. If not, one wonders why they are there bothering to find out what both of them already know'. (p.4). I also prepared each person for the act of sharing their memory by offering a notion of the kind of receptive listening they would receive.

In my experience this pre-description of imminent aware listening temporarily increases some participants' defensiveness – namely those who are not yet ready to receive such hearing because the feelings it evoke are as yet too uncomfortable – whilst it encourages others who may already feel more able to bypass their self-silencing structures to speak in greater depth about their situation. I have learned that this awareness-raising of what listening may be about enables participants to function with greater ease within their comfort zone. In therapeutic group work many stories are told. The participants would like to retell these tales to acquaintances, family members and friends, yet ground rules about confidentiality and respect for the privacy of each person's tale mean that little or no retelling can take place outside the therapy group. A degree of retelling occurs whenever clients embark on 'me too' stories part echoing, part competing with another group member. This kind of competitive storytelling is characterized by the rhythmic telling of one similar story after another, with an increase in incident intensity and likely exaggeration. Such serial retelling easily emerges in all forms of group work, without it having been purposefully called into existence as in this exercise. However, there are distinct disadvantages to uninvited serial 'me too' stories. Not only does the third or fourth story tend to go astray in terms of authenticity, compactness or relevance but the listeners also become emotionally absent, absorbed in the construction of their own contribution. Absent-minded listening means that the inevitable surplus of difference between individuals' experiences remains unacknowledged. People with mental health problems often find it particularly difficult to talk about their inner world. The propensity to generate one illness narrative after another can increase a sense of helplessness.

Because life tales need and must be told, it is important to enhance group members' ways of accessing and expressing responses to other people's life stories (Gergen 1992). This means helping group members to notice the impact of another person's life story upon themselves within the here and now context of the group and then translating this noticing into purposeful interpersonal responsiveness. In this case the cumulative response paintings or drawings would be made within a clear pictorial boundary or frame. By introducing this task I reminded the group that disclosure of personal material is meant to happen in a therapeutic context and that it needs to happen at a pace and in a space that feels comfortable. The preparation for listening and the giving of feedback is as important as the preparation for telling one's tale.[1]

I had registered how, after much sighing and bag-searching, during the writing-exercise Pamela had quickly jotted down some words in the notebook she had first brought to our second meeting. She had on that occasion shown it to the group saying, with the slightest hint of pride in her voice, 'I prefer to have everything together'. This time, after writing just a few sentences, she closed her notebook demonstratively, making sure I noticed. Whilst waiting for other group members to complete their writing, Pamela began a pattern of furtively looking at me, then looking away as soon as our eyes touched. Whilst she had appreciated the brief painting exercises in earlier sessions, she now waited for a group member to pass her a sheet of

---

1   See Chapter 4 for a discussion of response tasks

paper, saying pointedly that she didn't particularly care about the colours. Any crayons would do. She did not reach out for crayons either, but accepted what eventually was handed to her. This was in contrast to her lively engagement with visual expressive work in earlier sessions.

A memory of feeling surprised by yourself

The sharing of writings began. Laura, a tall woman in her mid-thirties, told about how she had played truant from school to embark on what sounded like a much-needed adventure. In the previous session she had described herself as a very lost person hidden in a big, big body. Momentarily she slipped out of an otherwise somewhat down mood to recall a day when she had skipped school to go window-shopping with some friends in a nearby town. They hadn't bought anything, but she had loved it. She also said that home was at that time the place where mother was dying a long slow death from cancer and where father spent his days at the kitchen table, drunk. The next day, when her teacher, whom she adored, asked her where she had been, she had lied, saying she had been needed at home. 'That lie made all the difference,' she said. I looked at her. It was not difficult to see in her the young lass she had been, holding together the pride, despair and privacy that had combined into the lie. She held my eyes steadily when I said: 'I'm glad that you were able to treat yourself to something. Life was hard in those days.' A brief flicker of suspicious hope rushed through her gaze. I had seen that look before. It is the prematurely wizened, yet longing gaze that I have seen in many clients' eyes. The group members sat back a while to register the thoughts and feelings aroused by Laura's memory. Then everyone recorded their own response. Images of windows, shoes, empty glasses, shopping bags and a broken bottle appeared, as well as the words 'white lie'.

Jane continued the telling process. She said that she had found it difficult to get into the exercise because, as she put it, today she felt particularly upset by the bad memories, adding that as far as she knew there was no particular reason why. The group already knew that 'bad memories' referred, in Jane's code, to the experience of the still-birth, three years earlier, of her first and so far only child. Then Jane talked about how Laura's memory had reminded her of something. Normally an over-conscientious girl, one afternoon she had not returned to school but simply taken herself for a bike-ride in the nearby countryside. It had been a beautiful afternoon. She looked somewhat wistfully at the high, blocked-up window of our barely-carpeted room in the community centre. I said: 'What longing...?', 'Yes,' she responded, 'What longing...!' The group registered the images that had been evoked by Jane's tale. The word 'forbidden' appeared, flowers, a bird, and a bike.

John, a burly man in his early forties, asked to go next. He described how, still a boy, he and a friend had gone for a swim in a fast-running river. After a while his friend had shouted that he was in trouble. Instead of swimming towards him, John had swum away, laughing, teasing. A little later he had looked back. He could no longer see his friend. When, after what had felt like forever, his friend's head surfaced above the water, he was struggling for his life. John had written:

> I swam towards him as fast as I could. Grabbed him. Dragged him ashore. Just when we got to the side he kicked me in the groin. I never knew whether he did that on purpose. We laughed and fell back into the water.

When he spoke those last words his voice cracked just a little, which alerted me that he was moved. The group already knew that following the death of his young daughter about eighteen months earlier in a traffic accident, John's life had run into serious trouble. He had started to drink and embarked on a tumultuous affair which had badly damaged his marriage, though he and his wife were now attempting a reconciliation. He had started to attend the community centre some months earlier following a nearly successful suicide attempt. He had tried to kill himself by leading a tube from the exhaust pipe back into the car whilst the engine was kept running. Some walkers had chanced across him in the woods where he had parked the car and rescued him. Now he told us how he had rescued a friend when he was a child. Once more John attempted to place the themes of death and near death on the group's agenda. The group did not seem to pick it up. They showed little visible reaction to John's story, in the same way as they had not been able to do much with their awareness of his daughter's death, which had been common knowledge since our first meeting.[2] Nonetheless, once John had finished speaking, everyone, including Pamela, picked up crayons to record their responses. I noticed various images of rivers and what looked like whirlpools. Pamela struck a brown crayon hard on the paper, making some fierce cutting marks. Was she expressing something about the kick in the groin?

Death's reality, its experience and impact were unsettling to this group. For John's and for the group's sake the link which I imagined existed between this particular memory, his daughter's death and the suicide attempt had to be made a little more accessible. I looked at him and asked: 'Was it summer when you swam in that river?' He nodded. I then ventured to continue: 'Was it again one of those fine summer days?' He immediately heard the reference

---

2   For a moving description of the experience of tragedy and felt unfair loss see Kushner (1981).

behind my words. Sorrow ran across his face. Other group members looked alert, as if they too heard my partial repeating of John's words during our very first meeting, when he had said: 'Death comes to me on fine summer days.' Holding my eyes steadily, first nodding then shaking his head, he mumbled: 'August.' Again he shook his head, then he briefly rested his face in both hands. The group, nearly collectively, sighed, undoubtedly recalling their own still unexpressed grief for the people they loved who didn't stay around, for their unlived lives and also for the helpless rage at life being as it is. Cathy, a young woman who sat next to John, lightly touched his shoulder. He looked up, saw that she knew something about trouble too, and said: 'I can't, please, please carry on.' I reminded him that we would carry on soon, but that it might be helpful if he could first make a mark on his own piece of paper to reflect his own response to his memory within the here and now of this group. Still shaking his head he said, pleading through reprimand: 'You won't give up, will you now.' Then, vaguely smiling, he wrote the words: 'Not dead.' He then indicated to Cathy that he really wanted her to take up the fragile thread of searching for continuity by allowing the past a place in the present.

Cathy began by apologizing that her memory might be a bit distasteful to people. With one reproachful eye on me she added: 'It might get us out of the death trap.' She described how one night, when she was working the streets as a teenage prostitute, a particularly sleazy man had approached her for sex. Though trade had not been good, she had refused him eloquently and with fondly remembered gusto. This had been deeply satisfying. It had been great to show him the back of her tongue: 'In a different kind o' way. Well, you know what I mean, don't you.' Though John and Jane looked warmly at her, the others tried their best not to condone too obviously her challenge to the group to address issues related to sexuality, by avoiding eye-contact. I asked Cathy about the specific aspect of this experience that surprised her. 'Saying no,' she answered. Eros and Thanatos were as yet the uninvited guests in this particular group and like the excluded fairy-goddess they exercised their potent influence. My interpretation that at some point we might need to talk with one another in greater depth about the themes of death, life and sexuality met with acknowledging but rather reluctant nods. I was allowed to note it; as yet that was all.

Susan, a woman in her mid-forties, asked to go next. She recounted her feelings of utter helplessness when, shortly after she had been diagnosed with Multiple Sclerosis, she had gone to the Post Office to cash a cheque. On her way back home she had felt a push against her back. As she fell, her handbag, with what little money she had, was ripped off her shoulder. What had surprised her about herself was that she had not screamed. 'Not a sound', she said, 'Just silence'. She had picked herself up and had walked home and hadn't even called the police or mentioned the incident to anyone because, as she said: 'I couldn't. So much had already happened. If I had told them that, all the rest would have come out.' Though urged by fellow group members to say a little more, she refrained.

Laura, Jane, John, Cathy and Susan had so far shared one memory. There were two more speakers to go: Pamela and Tom. Already the five who had shared a tale were bursting at their inner seams with the urgency of other untold stories which needed to emerge, yet not quite knowing if or how they could embark on such telling, particularly because the consequences of telling were becoming more clear. Could they bear to listen to more stories and still stay present to the experience of the other? I pondered whether the sequence of telling and re-telling of painful memories was not in and of itself creating a further trauma, reflecting too that at this early stage of the group a degree of competitive pain probably also occurred under the motto 'my suffering is greater than yours'.

Five group members had used the opportunity to share some aspects of their life experience with one another. However, the sharing was combining into a burden which seemed nearly too great to carry in a meaningful way. As the I-Ching, says: 'The ridge pole stretches to breaking-point. It furthers one to have somewhere to go.' Somewhere to go indeed, but where, back into withdrawal and isolation? Back towards a decision that difficult experiences cannot be talked about because they cannot be adequately contained? The group was collectively holding its cry of fear and outrage at life having been, and promising to continue to be, hard. Was there no relief? There was. It pointed forwards to the continuing process of testing the waters of mutual trust and containment, but presently that too terrified the group. The group's longing for change was tempered by a substantial investment in maintaining continuity, which expressed itself as a joined and as yet semi-conscious desire to make the burden of pain feel unbearable. If it were to prove to be unbearable then this would constitute renewed proof that containment was beyond reach, had been beyond reach and would always remain beyond reach. It would be reaffirmed that their suffering was too great for any healing to occur, ever. Sorting out this muddle and helping the group to make some sort of sense of it all was likely to be high on the agenda. The opportunity arose immediately.

Pamela had not made any marks on her paper in response to Cathy's memory. Instead, she restlessly attempted to hide her chin as deep as she could in the hollow of her right shoulder. Alternately she touched, in rapid sequence, first her lips then her forehead and once more her lips with the cusp of her left hand, consoling and encouraging herself in a strange ritual of desperate and furious containment. I expressed my concern for her apparent distress, and asked the group as a whole to reflect on any feelings currently present but not expressed by them, as these feelings which were also rightly theirs might now be embodied by Pamela. This immediately brought her some relief. It was as if the group struggled with a profound sense of 'If only'. I noted too that terrible events had occurred, none of which had been wanted, most of which they were just beginning to protest against, and little of which had, as yet, been worked through to a place of recognition, let alone acceptance or forgiveness. We still had a long way to go together. However, we were on the road. By taking the responses to the recounted events, which manifested themselves as withdrawal and fear away from those events, I not only placed the group's present emotional state in a larger context of time and change processes, I also normalized the range of emotions associated with traumatic experiences – thereby to begin the laying-out of an emotional map of kinds. Even though the details of the map were not yet filled in, the fact that there are maps of human journeys through suffering was reassuring. Though most group members became less tense after my interpretation of the possible dynamics and possible future development of such dynamics within the group, I was not entirely surprised that Pamela withdrew further into her own ever more frightening world. She was holding the group's battle with destructive despair. I had an inkling of what might be at stake (Gersie and King 1990).

The ambiguity of aware experience

In the previous session we had focused on the theme of 'consent to trying a different approach'. We had worked with a Cherokee Native American light-bringing myth which tells how Grandmother Spider brings light to a dark world.

> In this myth it is said that in the beginning the animals live in darkness. They know that somewhere there is a sun but the sun keeps its light to itself. When they are worn out with darkness, the animals call a meeting to discuss what to do. How might they get hold of light for their world? After some discussion, first Possum and then Buzzard set out to try, hoping to grasp a piece of Sun. Possum tries to hide it beneath his tail but when he gets badly burned he has to let it go. Then Buzzard sets out. He steals a bit of Sun and puts it bravely on his head. He too gets burned, and drops the bit of Sun. Both are wounded in their effort to bring light to earth. The animals become

very upset that two of their strongest and most determined have tried and not succeeded.

Then up piped a tiny voice. 'Who is talking?' the animal people asked. 'Let me try.' A woman's voice had spoken very gently. It took a while before the others listened to Grandmother Spider, for it was her voice the people could not hear. She said again: 'Let me try'. They let her. Feeling about in that great darkness, Grandmother Spider searched until she found some damp clay. She made a thick-walled pot. It was a small one. She started eastwards, the same as Possum and Buzzard, but she spun a thread behind her so that she knew her way home. No one even saw her when she came close to the sun. She was so small. She reached out one of her hands and gently took a small bit of sun and put it in the bowl. Holding the bowl safely in her hands, she made her slow way home along the thread she had spun. The light shone before her. It shone everywhere. The people were very happy. Grandmother Spider had made this happen. Even today you notice how the spider always spins her web before the sun has fully risen. Spider Woman brought the sun to the Cherokee as well as the gift of fire. More so, she also taught the people the art of pottery.'[3]

There had been a lively discussion about this story, which focused particularly on Grandmother Spider's success due to her insight that an altogether different solution had to be found. She had the wisdom to interrupt the attempted solution (to carry the fire on one's body) and thought up the crucial transition to instrumentality (the making of the bowl). Astute connections had been made with people's personal battles with enfolding darkness, with our own repetitious ways of trying to solve these battles in the same old ways and how this did not work. We had also explored the group's and individual's need for containment and for developing the skill to contain. No one had doubted any longer that change-journeys took a great deal of courage. The emergence of the desire to bring light into a dark world, the willingness to try and to fail, the spinning of a thread of kinds – all these demanded a willingness to commit. The story had also offered us indirect comfort that even though the mission to bring some light into an

---

3   Spider Woman is a powerful, nearly always beneficent character, in the myths of many Plains, South-Western and Western Native Americans. Sometimes Spider is the creator, sometimes a trickster character. In this myth Spider Woman is an astute culture-hero who brings the art of pottery as well as weaving to the people. The stealing of light (or fire or summer weather) for people who otherwise live in darkness is a common theme in stories. In these tales the journey to get the light frequently involves successful and unsuccessful attempts as well as wounding.

otherwise sombre world might not be immediately successful, it was an effort worth undertaking.

Pamela had talked about liking the Grandmother Spider story. With some pleasure she had made a small clay bowl, which she had planned to get fired in the Centre's kiln, and had written a few 'I will try...' statements. These had said:

'I will always try to open the curtains.'

'I will try to clear out the rubbish more often.'

'I will always try to be kind.'

My heart had sunk a little when I heard the word 'always'. I sensed that she tried to be seen to be making compliant progress. Maybe she was compelling herself to move rather quickly, too quickly probably, to the culturally-valued positive realm of the emotional spectrum, towards kindness, joy and happiness. When the group had done a further exercise, during which each participant was offered further suggestions for possible additions to their 'I will try' list, Pamela had, amongst others, been given a statement which said:

'I will sometimes try to be kind.'

Towards the end of that session she had drawn the group's attention to this particular suggestion, adding that she liked it that someone in the group seemed to be granting her the permission to feel a range of feelings. As is so often the case in therapeutic group work, my own concerns had been shared by another group member, and Pamela herself had picked these up too. That was promising. However, it also meant that we were likely to see some testing of the group's ability to contain her darker side in the near future.

That future was closer than it had appeared the previous week. Pamela now seemed to struggle with her longing for containment. I wondered whether maybe her self-ideal, which had that week expressed itself as a desire for permanent kindness, had been tackled too soon. Had her inner organization been too rapidly queried? Jung's words about the therapeutic caution that needs to be exercised as regards the challenging of self-perceptions and self-stories came to mind. Referring to a particular client, who was convinced that his present troubles were of an exclusively sexual origin, Jung wrote: 'I would not disturb him in his opinion because I know that such a conviction, particularly if it is deeply rooted, is an excellent defence against an onslaught of the terrible ambiguity of an immediate experience.'

Witnessed compassion

Pamela's body certainly spoke the vivid language of such an onslaught. I then also recalled the rest of Jung's statement: 'But if his dreams should begin to destroy the protective theory, I have to support the wider personality' (1978, pp.54–58). The previous week Pamela had chosen to present the difficulties around her 'always-sometimes' dynamics to the group. Contradicting her earlier statement: 'I'm a no-hoper, Alida', she had implied that she desired a degree of personal change. Our mutual determination to help her to tolerate the contradiction inherent in ambiguity, as Jung put it, was now certainly being tested.

Keeping the various images of her life that she had presented to the group in the forefront of my mind, I quietly talked her through her fear and rage, thus enabling her to become less intimidated by the feelings and to recover some much needed inner space. My speech bath achieved the desired effect: she became much calmer. I noticed how my thoughts wandered towards Pamela's childhood years in the internment camp. I wondered how she had coped with that troubled world. Meanwhile the group held its breath, trying to stay with her fear of whatever was frightening her so very much. A comment on the superficial breathing in the group and encouragement for deeper breathing surmounted the tension. Then Pamela whispered a response to my request to articulate what she wanted from the group so that she might be able to shift herself out of this seemingly terribly lonely, and maybe also somewhat angry, place. With her head down and her eyes firmly fixed on the floor, she said: 'I need to look at someone'. Tom, a young man whose battered childhood had left him with a hearing impairment, heard her plea beyond the sound of her voice. He moved forward to sit opposite her. Breathing quietly, he just sat there and looked, his face illuminated by a most tender passionate concern, whilst the other group members and myself kept a watchful vigil. We waited for the emergence of contact in the awareness of aloneness. Together we sat, each in our own way wrestling to keep faith that a way through could be found, continuing to believe that in spite of years of depressed inner aloneness, benign contact with another human being at a time of inner trouble could still be made. At last Pamela raised her head. Steadying herself, she looked Tom in the eye. Then she wept. Others also cried. Not long after, Pamela shared her memory with the group. She had written:

> 'In the camp I made a drawing of the tree and I showed it to the guard. My mother scolded me.'

I asked her what had been surprising about this event – the drawing, the showing, the scolding, or all three. She said the showing. There was obviously a great deal more we could do with this memory, but now was not the time. On her own response-painting she drew a tiny image of a tree. Other group members too drew tree images on their paintings.

Then Tom recounted his 'surprise' story. He told how he had recently met a young man in the street, who begged for money. He had stopped and they had talked together a while. The man had realized he had hearing difficulties and had simply spoken quite loudly. This had pleased Tom immensely. He felt surprised that a brief conversation with a passing stranger could give him so much satisfaction (Finkelstein 1993). The negative self-image conferred on him during his troubled childhood had kindled his delight in having a chat with a stranger. I requested that people added their response to Tom's story to the painting.

As he had been the last person to share his memory with the group, I suggested they would take some time to complete their work, to find a way of integrating the various images into a, for them, more or less meaningful whole. For some minutes the group worked quietly, adding colour and shape where wanted, until a place of inner and imaginable satisfaction was reached. With the pictures placed in the circle between us, we talked a little more, reflecting on both the content of the memories, the paintings and the procedures we had used. We acknowledged that we had worked hard. Many feelings and memories had been evoked. I then asked each person to title their overall painting, to help condense the experience of the group's stories into a personal metaphor. John called his overall painting 'Not dead, not yet alive.' Pamela called hers: 'Glimpse of the other side.' There was a great deal more work to be done, but crucial openings had been established. The newly-surfaced memory of the time in the internment camp, the dynamics of the interaction between Pamela, her mother and the guard, were merely noted during this session, as was John's grief, Jane's grief about her still-born child and her longing for exercise and fresh air, Laura's feelings about her inability to tell the teacher who actually cared for her about what was going on at home, Cathy's pride in being able to set boundaries and yet her lostness, Tom's lack of self-esteem and longing for contact, and Susan's furious fear. These themes were to be extensively worked with during later sessions. However, it had been of vital importance that seven very pained people and myself were able to stay truly present to each other, thereby allowing the actual experiences of troubled lives to enter the here and now of the group. The difference between 'then and now' was beginning to become correctively established.

We need to hear who has seen them:
Shadows thrown back by the night.
We need to hear who has seen them.

Gabon

The story behind the story told

In the above presentation of a segment of TSM group work practice, I made use of three readily distinguished types of narrative. The first of these is the use of stories as presentations of a group member's personal recollections. Such stories reflect our propensity to think about ourselves and our lives in story form (White 1982). Each memory exemplified our tendency to construct as it were a mini logical system out of the recollected, represented and restructured experience. This structure provides a provisional model. The model guides what the individual tries to convey or to demonstrate. It supports the person's effort to grasp some kind of insight about themselves in the here and now of the group (such as thoughts about the possible meaning or implications of the event).

I also described work with a narrative in the form of myth, in this case from the Cherokee Nation, Native American tradition. This story has for centuries been part of the Cherokee people's sacred literature. The story was used to illuminate and accelerate a drama of deeply personal interest to this group. It portrayed aspects of the group's felt reality, both what was and what might be. I chose this story from a wide range of possible tales because it succinctly encapsulated the group members' fears that they would forever dwell in darkness. In addition, the story contained information about procedures of change as well as processes of change Radin (1957). It imaginatively mapped out possible ways of moving forward, whilst providing implicit support for people's as yet fragile hope that somehow beneficence and a change of kinds might be possible. The story also offered a realistic warning as regards the actual costs involved in creating change.

During this group session I did not use a third kind of narrative, namely self-generated fantasy stories (Singer and Schaefer 1993). These are coherent products of an unfolding series of private responses which describe possible events that have varying likelihood of actually happening. Here it merely matters briefly to note some of the potential such stories entail, such as the exploration of future possibilities without having to commit to action, or to alter emotional states in anticipation of future situations. The process of telling self-made fantasy stories, including the experience of the teller–listener responses, provides interpersonal feedback which enables further adjustment and self-regulation of behaviour. Some of these potentials are, of course, also present in work with memory stories or with traditional tales.

In addition to the two familiar narrative structures in the form of memory as personal story and myth, I employed a narrative pattern to discuss this brief moment in the life of the group and its important events and protagonists. In order to present the material, I selected a beginning-middle-and-end of kinds whilst I created a parallel exploration of the experiences and relevant professional considerations. This telling, too, has a history.

My first writing of the group's story consists of detailed case-recordings, which I wrote immediately after each session took place many years ago. The notes were annotated following what might be called a second retelling of the group's story during the clinical supervision sessions which accompanied my practice. As a result of the supervision work, the story which I recorded about the group was re-visioned on a weekly basis. The writings you have just read describe the early part of the group's history. The current retelling reflects the usual limitations of clinical vignettes, which are chosen to amplify a particular position or point. However, such clinical vignettes serve not merely an illustrative function of certain therapeutic moments, they also carry explicit or hidden information about preceding and succeeding episodes (Higgins 1993). They are vitally constructed by information which the therapist possesses about preceding and succeeding events, including the group's further progress and ending (see Sartre 1965). Because I know how the group proceeded and ended, and also how members fared during the year after the group finished as a result of follow-up interviews, my presentation of the material is inevitably coloured by this awareness.

In order to write this book I re-read the annotated case-notes. Many years have passed since I facilitated the work. The revisiting of the case-notes became a journey of rediscovery of the events, of my memory of the events, of my ways of conducting my practice at that time and, above all, of my present ideas, feelings and desires. The act of creating this retelling, including the choices I made about inclusion and exclusion of material, made me reflect again on the ambiguities and internal contradictions which are part of any group's actual experience. In addition, my own further experience, both personal and professional, changes how I interpret the events and experiences now versus then. This too has influenced the story I have presented.

Though the above delineation of four separate and unstable kinds of narrative – namely, memory as story, story as folktale or myth, self-generated fantasy story and story as case description – is frequently used and therefore readily recognizable, the assumption of separateness is also a little problematic. As was obvious in my account of the group, each story and each layer of storying entails, as Schieffelin and Crittenden (1991) precisely observe, 'constructing an analysis and interpretation of the material itself, which emerges in the way the story is told, in its narrative strategy'. They continue: 'The narrative constructs the account in two ways: first, through the juxta-position of voices; and second, through the exposition of a complex series of events that uncovers the underlying forces that brought them about' (p.250). Though I attempted to separate the narratives, the connection and interdependence between the various stories and modes of storying is substantial. The narrative modes are mutually entailed. They belong together because they are co-constructed. It would have been hard for them to have been anything else, given that they emerged in processes of human interac-tion. As such, each tale contains the tales.

In my storied account of the session, the visible and the invisible surface of the group was occupied by several different voices: the clients', my own, the internalized voices of supervisors and trainers, as well as people who are important to us, and the lingering voices of authors, whose words pertained to both practice and reflection on practice (Page and Wosket 1994). As yet unmentioned, and therefore seemingly invisible, influence was exercised by the physical environment of the community centre, the weather and time of year and, above all, by the prevailing socio-political climate that surrounded the group. These invisibles may have left substantial gaps in and between my stories. These gaps might reflect not only my limitations of knowledge and style in presenting therapeutic narratives, but also the rough edges of what we can know. I propose that these narrative gaps, apart from also being the inevitable concomitants of any attempt at representation, constitute a vital difference. They occupy the potential, transitional area in therapeutic practice where insight, discovery and change happen. The felt space between the words and beyond the images vitally contributes to the unfolding, and ultimately imprecise, process of change. It draws attention to the indefinable qualities of relationship, experience and intuition, and helps us to hear beyond the talk presented, the laughter, the groan and the wail.

To include or not to include

Without detracting from the validity of the above arguments, I believe that it is also necessary to cast a more doubting light on the omissions in my narrative, and therefore by implication on the practice of the group's work as presented so far. The most obvious of these failures is the absence of any reference in my account of the group to the daily consequences of the fact that every individual is also identified, and partly constituted, by socio-po-litical and economic structures. Although these issues may not have been actively spoken about in the group, they were undoubtedly present in the para-linguistic signs of voice, gesture and communicative style. Did my clients' experiences of these socio-political and economic circumstances matter? Do such factors influence the clients' illness in important ways? It could be argued that I rightly emphasized key aspects of a client's life, because the dynamics of immediate personal situation cause the greatest suffering, whilst it is also necessary to delineate a field of concern and influence. Were we to accept this argument, I could simply have been encouraged to improve my case-presentation skills by presenting some further identifying data regarding etiology of their illness, previous treatment interventions, their family relationships, education, employment or lack of it, quality of housing, access to affordable child care, travel and entertainment or the absence of any of these in so far as any of these areas were felt to be problematic for the client.

Once stated, it might have been acceptable to disregard these data and grant them no actual status of importance in the therapeutic narrative. I could have justified doing so by arguing that these experiences were not immediately relevant to the here-and-now experience in the group, which concerned itself with intrapsychic and interpersonal suffering of a different kind. Even if I acknowledged that data, such as those referred to above, do willie nillie enter a group as para-linguistic signs, or as reported experience in the world 'out there', I could still have worked with these issues in a manner which suggested to the group members that I believed them to be solely responsible for their success or failure in socio-political and economic terms – especially because this appears to suggest that the locus of change as regards difficulties in the socio-political and economic realm also resides with the clients.

The assumption of such a position would have had profound consequences for my therapeutic practice. It would have excluded from the domain of therapy the potential to help the client with the exploration of connections between felt helplessness and factual disempowerment. Power is here defined as a person's means to obtain some apparent good, as something that is open to increase and which assures the satisfaction of desires. Many clients in therapy, who cannot directly purchase therapeutic support through private financial means but rely on state provision of therapeutic facilities, are also the very same people whose daily experience is that their capacity to exercise power, as defined above, is extremely limited. They are often unable to buy access to affordable child care, or afford adequate heating, cannot shop freely for food, buy necessary winter clothing, or respond enthusiastically to their children's request for money to join a school-outing and, even more painfully, are unable to visit a sick relative in a hospital several hundred miles away, just because the money for the fare cannot be found (Davis 1995).

Realities such as these do, in many a client's mind, crucially affect their well-being; yet financial trouble is but one of numerous socio-political and economic constraints. Felt powerlessness also manifests itself in clients' lives through lack of access to educational opportunities, decision making processes, and the demonstrated inability to defend oneself against unjust accusations, effectively to have pleaded one's cause and, above all, adequately to have protected one's interests. If we acknowledge that all of us are the objects as well as the subjects of power, are parts of systems of institutions which allocate and absorb varying degrees and levels of authority, we may conclude that people who run into serious emotional trouble have issues around power and powerlessness entailed in their suffering. The examination of how these themes are engaged with in our practice then becomes particularly relevant.

In therapeutic practice we cannot but negotiate authority and put knowledge and experience first. It is therefore useful to remember Marilyn French's (1985) critical distinction between non-coercive authority, and authority that masks might or force (p.506). In her terms, non-coercive authority exists when someone possesses a special skill or knowledge which is useful to others, and where people may consult such authority but are not required to comply with the advice given. Coercive authority refers to the assumption of a position of superiority or omniscience in such a way that, though compliance is not mandatory, a compelling influence is exercised.

It needs to be borne in mind that many people who receive non-privately purchased therapy join the therapeutic process under some form of duress (Barnitt and Fulton 1994). It is becoming quite commonplace to have mandated therapy linked with school-difficulties, probation requirements, the felt threat of sectioning under mental health laws or the fear of imminent loss of a job or custody over children. Frequently the participation in such semi-mandatory therapy involves working with a white, middle-class therapist towards therapeutic goals which are partially negotiated with or on behalf of the client and partly on behalf of the therapy-commissioning agency (Collins, Rickman and Mathura 1980). In these already constraining circumstances the emotional difficulties the client faces need to be linked with their everyday social realities – which frequently consist of grossly inadequate housing conditions, long-term unemployment, overcrowded schools and a general physical vulnerability due to the violence of poverty (Whitehead 1991). These are not defects to which our clients have purposefully exposed themselves, nor are they circumstances without any bearing upon the here and now of the therapeutic situation. Equally, the emotional

and economic effects of racism, sexism and classism are not merely indicative
of some individual or familial deficiency (Admad and Will 1993, p.92).

The group's story revisited: to name the unnameable

In terms of the dynamics of the group described above, it mattered a great
deal that Susan's parents had owned a bakery in which they had worked
extremely hard. When they died, the bakery was sold. Susan, an only child,
was now financially comfortable, as she put it. The two men in the group
were white, Anglo-European.

John's father had been an unskilled factory worker. John had for some
years owned a small but relatively successful building company which had
gone down the drain, as he said, in the recent recession. He and his family
survived on social security benefits and some insurance money, which would
shortly run out. Looking back, John realized that rather than going into the
building trade, he would have preferred to stay on at school and study a
subject such as engineering or preferably English literature. 'But that was not
the kind of thing our kind of people were expected to do', he added wistfully.

Tom's father had recently retired as a minister in the Church of England.
Family life in the small-town vicarage had added its own complexity to John's
battered childhood. Ministers aren't supposed to be violent. Tom's breakdown had occurred whilst studying history in Oxford; it happened around
the time when he first acknowledged that his homosexuality was real. 'Given
my background', he said, 'this was hard.'

Cathy, who reached out to John when he struggled with his encounter
with death, was the youngest of seven children. She had grown up on a tough
inner-city housing estate. Both parents had long since given up the struggle
to find work because there just weren't any jobs in a town where unemployment had been at a record high for years. She left home in search of work
at the age of seventeen. Finding that opportunities were not as golden as she
had imagined, she was walking the streets as a young prostitute before she
knew what had become of her. 'I was a bit of a sensitive and I was good at
what I did', she explained. But following some attacks in the course of 'my
profession', as she called it, she had started to see things. During one session
she described her understanding of what happened as follows: 'Mind, I don't
think I was crazy. They were just happy images like. But they got a bit out
of hand. It didn't help that jerk hit me, and that I drank and took pills. So,
one morning I woke up in the hospital. I kicked and screamed. I'm a fighter.
I now wish I hadn't. Hadn't fought so hard. It took me months to get out.'

Pamela's parents had moved to the tropics shortly before she was born.
She was an only child. Her father, a civil servant, had spent the war in a

different internment camp than she and her mother. Following their release from the camps the family had returned to Europe. Her parents' marriage had never recovered from the prolonged separation.

Pamela, John, Tom, Susan and Cathy were white Anglo-European; Laura was the child of parents of different race. She identified herself as black. Her mother's family was of middle-class Afro-Caribbean origin, whose family had lived in this country for several generations. It was still part of Laura's weekly experience to be asked: 'Where (meaning in which country) were you born?' Her father was also white Anglo-European, from a middle class background, who had started drinking when his wife, whom he adored, became ill.

Jane was a black African woman from a high-ranking family, who had been sent to this country at the age of three to live with relatives. Her parents had arrived when she was eight years old. Re-integrating into this old-new family, whose social status had changed dramatically upon arriving here, had not been easy for her. During one session she shared that she had never asked her parents why she had been sent ahead. 'Somehow I never got round to asking, and no one ever bothered to tell me. I wonder why?' she pondered at last.

I believe that these group members' emotional difficulties were intimately linked with the real socio-political and economic complexities they faced. The particular equalizing circumstance of mental illness throws together people from many different cultural, racial, religious and economic backgrounds (Medical Ethics Committee and Mental Health Committee 1990). In therapy groups such people meet not only one another's intimate personal pain, but also the various practical situations which each individual has experienced and continues to experience. When explicitly dealt with, the explosiveness and emotional surrounding themes like the distribution of opportunity bring to the group's surface our society's volatile tensions (Atkin and Rollings 1993). Of these volatile issues, race, sexual orientation and religion are probably the most tempting ones about which to assume silence (Grainger 1995).

In most therapy groups which take place in mental health establishments, people whose lives are scarred by the circumstances as well as the consequences of different skin colours, differences in sexual orientation or alternative belief structures are cast together with the unnameable other. As there is already an abundance of miseries, the desire to deny the consequences of racism and sexual or religious intolerance is extremely strong. To require people who are already unwell also to think about the consequences of racism on people's lives might feel overwhelming. I have heard clients say: 'It's hard

enough to change myself' and therapists plead: 'How can I change society?'
They thereby create a frequently heard but ultimately therapeutically unhelpful separation between ourselves and our worlds. Referring to racism, James
Baldwin (1966) writes: 'In great pain and terror, one enters into battle with
historical creation, oneself, and attempts to recreate oneself according to a
principle more humane and more liberating; one begins to attempt to achieve
a level of personal maturity and freedom which robs history of its tyrannical
power and also changes history' (p.183). Just such an attempt at recreation
lies at the heart of the therapeutic process.

Many therapy groups experience the dilemma of how to begin to talk
about those experiences which divide, whilst finding that it is relatively easy
to share those experiences which unite. It takes both courage and determination slowly to de-construct our understanding of how the pain we endure
is personally and socially connected, or to explore the ways we are influenced
by the dynamics of class, race, gender, sexual orientation or physical
endowment (Wilson 1996). When conflict and confrontation have impacted
upon one's life in deeply troubling ways it appears to make sense to avoid
further trouble-arousing situations and therefore to avoid what is perceived
as 'a similar theme' in the here and now of the group. The desire for an
alternative, cosy form of oneness predominates. Most groups wish to leave
the nasty subjects of intolerance and economic differences to the harsh world
out there, whilst keeping the goodness of untested tolerance and benignity
in here. Yet, in order for any realistic healing to occur, feelings of confusion
and anxiety related to unequality and unfairness need to emerge and the fear
of exploring the impact of difference tamed. As Baldwin said: we then
encounter further pain and terror. However, at least the terror can then be
consciously engaged. As early as the 1950s, Slavson (1950) emphasized the
need for a cross-culture modification of group psychotherapy, given that
individuals are in constant transaction with their specific socio-cultural
milieus. Systems of care-taking and care-giving differ widely across cultures.
Adherence to a fixed set of principles derived from one milieu only needs to
be avoided in work with people whose roots provide the group with a wide
range of socio-cultural milieus. In group work it must be recognized that
each social environment not only demands specific adaptations, it also offers
unique characteristics (Sedgewick 1982).

Stereotype, prejudice and the changing story
The urgency to recreate ourselves through engagement with themes of
racism, classism, religious intolerance and the exploration of dominant
hetero-sexism was amply evident in our group in the community centre.

Numerous unspoken prejudices critically influenced how we were with one another. Laziness, meanness, unreliability, trouble-making, and so forth were mildly, yet blindly, allocated to different group members in neat concordance with prevailing stereotypes. Thus Laura's or Jane's lateness was initially, and without any of the Caucasian group members explicitly saying so, attributed to 'racial difficulties with time-keeping'. Had such a passing, casual sideline been unnoticed and left unchallenged, the disaster of racism which affects all of us would have remained unhealed. Over time the group needed to learn to work with such problems in order to establish real tolerance and actual mutual respect. This was not easy (Ferron 1991). In the early stages of the group the noting of any issues regarding differences in race, class, sexual orientation or religion aroused panic. The process of mutual stereotyping, which had for so long supported already fragile ways of being, had to be unravelled softly but firmly. But it had to be unravelled. The challenge was not only how the group might learn to tolerate the expression of intrapsychic pain but also how it might contain interpersonal pain linked with these issues. In order to achieve this we needed to acquire a new, effective language which would lift us beyond silence on the themes mentioned above.

The learning happened when I drew our attention to something John said to Jane in a friendly voice in the sixth session: 'Ah, welcome Jane. You're late, but I guess that's what you people are like.' As the tone of voice had been light-hearted, most people laughed, Jane joined in with a smile, seemingly double-bound between the desire to be welcomed and a barely perceivable annoyance at the racist nature of the words. When she had settled down, I asked the group to revisit John's suggestion that 'lateness and racial identity' were linked in some way or other. I wondered too how it felt to realize that passing words about someone being late might not only be an awkward way of welcoming someone, but actually a racial comment. The group was at first shocked that I had mentioned the unmentionable word. John was quick to ask both Jane and Laura what they really felt about his greeting, adding that of course he had meant no conscious harm and apologizing for any hurt his thoughtless words had caused. He queried how they did or did not cope with similar comments.

After some initial testing, Jane and Laura realized that the group truly wanted to explore this issue. Then they talked, and their talk hurt. However, it did much more than hurt, it also shifted Susan's reluctance to explore her memory of the mugging on the way back home from the post office. The brevity of her comments on this incident had not been merely informed by the troubles she experienced. She told the group for the first time that she was Jewish. The attack had reminded her of her family's history as Jewish refugees from Poland, who had left just in time to escape the gruesome horrors of the Third Reich. It also resonated with recent damage by extreme right-wing groups to graves in the Jewish cemetery. This had informed her decision not to tell strangers, such as people like ourselves, that she was Jewish. Above all, she had not mentioned the fact that the teenager who had pushed her and stolen her handbag was a young, black male, a detail she had omitted to mention for fear of offending Laura and Jane, yet a fact which profoundly influenced her interaction with them in particular. As she said: 'I just avoided you.' It clarified her way of being with the entire group. Until she felt free to share the fuller story, the underlying fears and the racism the event evoked had been too shameful and too painful to address. 'What with my background', she later said, 'I now see an attacker in every black boy. I know that would not have happened had the boy been white.' Thus we slowly learned to share with each other how our racism, when left unexplored, becomes a malfunctioning of kinds. It warps the very thoughts we would like to express and wounds our souls and limits our healing (see Seiderman 1974).

Such wounding is concisely articulated in an African tale about Bat, who lives with his mother. Bat's mother becomes very ill. Antelope tells Bat that only the sun can help him find a cure for her. Try as he might, whenever Bat is able to catch up with Sun, who tends to set out early on his daily track, Sun says that he cannot give Bat the medicine he needs, because he has not met him in his own house. Again and again Bat is asked to return, until finally Bat's mother is extremely weakened. On the seventh day Bat's mother dies. The story continues:

> Many people came to share Bat's mourning. They mourned the whole day. Then Bat ordered that his mother's body be carried to her grave. This happened. When they came to the grave, the beasts said that they always looked at a person's face before burial. They wanted to look upon Bat's mother too.

> When they saw, they said: 'No, we cannot bury her. She is not one of us. She is not a beast. She had a head like us, but she also has wings. Therefore she looks like a bird. Call upon the birds to bury her.' Thus they left.

> Bat called the birds, and they came, all of them, and they too asked to see his mother. Bat let her be seen. They looked very attentively. Then they spoke and said: 'Yes, she looks like us, for she has wings as we do. But we do not have teeth. None of us has teeth. She is not one of us, because she has teeth. She is not one of us.' The birds flew away.

Much time had passed as they talked. Meanwhile the ants had come. They had entered the body of Bat's mother. There was nothing he could do to drive them away. To make matters worse, one of the birds said: 'You should not have postponed the burial. I warned you that such a thing might happen.'

Then all the birds and the beasts had gone.

Bat was all alone. He spoke to himself and said. 'I blame the Sun for all my trouble. My mother would still be alive if only he had made her some medicine. I shall never look upon the Sun again. We shall never be friends. I shall hide myself when the Sun shines forth. I shall neither greet him nor ever look at him. Then Bat spoke and said: 'I shall grieve for my mother for all time. I shall visit nobody. I shall always walk in darkness, lest I meet anyone.[4]

The horror of Bat's decision is not only that it was made, it is also that we can so easily understand how he came to his conclusion. When the animals and the birds failed to recognize his mother, and, therefore, him as one of theirs, Bat was effectively placed beyond the recognition of society. He merely tried to grant himself some desperately needed authority by constructing the belief that he had the power to isolate himself. In reality, the decision to isolate him was made by the others. He was sent and did not choose to go into a lonesome wilderness. By turning his anger inwards, Bat still protected those who rejected him.

We recognize Bat's response because it can also be ours, and the more so ours when we are exposed to the horrid face of prejudice or stereotype. Then we have trouble realizing that there is a process of fusion at work between the negative images held up to ourselves by a dominant majority with the negative identity of ourselves we believe we are purposefully cultivating. When a person unknowingly attempts to live up to bad expectation, they tragically become most like whom they are predicted to be, but whom they are not, thus adding inauthenticity to the harsh impact of personal and cultural betrayal.

A gentler humanity

The recognition of the desire for self-esteem does not mean that someone will find it easy to wrestle free from the plethora of deprecating images of their racial, gender, sexual or class group. Such images are widely distributed and influence life on a daily basis. In any process of gaining self-esteem,

---

4   Retold by the author. See also Gersie (1991).

which includes the exploration of the impact of negative expectation on one's life, people experience substantial, emotional pain. Prejudices and stereotypes are not taken as inevitable givens, they are challenged. New experiences demand a willingness as well as an ability to tolerate the temporary disarray of one's working knowledge of a certain kind of reality.

It was not easy for Tom to hear John's initially hidden anger at not having been to university, or for that matter for John to move beyond his envy of Tom's 'wasted opportunity at Oxford', or his prejudices as regards gay men. Jane, who was a devout Christian, had difficulty accepting that Tom's father had not made a one-off mistake when he hit his son, that violence was a fact of life in the vicarage and that there had been little repentance after the beatings. This unsettled her deeply and caused a degree of crisis of faith. There were many other tensions and conflicts which reflected the involvement between our individual and social worlds. Group members engaged with their emotions about these issues and reflected on the relation between the assumed causes of the emotions and the beliefs taken to justify them, not only because they experienced emotional illness, but also because judgment of the rationality or appropriateness of an emotion involves conceptions of normality (Szass 1961). Such conceptions have an inevitable normative force, which necessitates, as Oksenberg Rorty (1988, p.355) points out, the exploration of disagreements or agreements about what is wholesome or right. At first such stirring up feels like losing something, and of course we are. The unfamiliar ways feel wrong; the old ways feel comfortable and right. All movement to a new plane of respectful acknowledgment of otherness, whilst acknowledging that antagonistic respect may be all that can ever be achieved, takes more than commitment, it takes faith.

During the process of gradual development towards a gentler humanity the group discovered that it was useful to address the consequences of individual encounters with the untender embrace of unequal power relations. Once we truly listened to one another's stories, we could not help but learn to distinguish between felt helplessness and having been placed in a position of actual circumstantial powerlessness. The group's journey towards such awareness was mediated by many a story character's encounters with deliberate disempowerment in the folktales we worked with. Those stories articulated key aspects of the group's personal stories before group members ever shared much about their own positions. After all, Grandmother Spider herself had said: 'I am but a woman. If you lose me, it is not like you will have lost one of your great warriors. I am also very old. But I am willing to try.' The tale had eloquently spoken to the group about people who feel superfluous, about the presumed fragility of women and the apparent need for strong men to be strong and of the fear of offering so much of oneself and of not even that being good enough.

This group of people became committed to working with each other through the miscellany of pain, disappointment, joy and endowment that was theirs to carry. They hoped to learn again how to recognize and grasp opportunities, how to persist when difficulties are encountered and, above all, how to let go when necessary. This required the development of inner, active wisdom (Kurtz and Ketcham 1994). Such wisdom may be found in conscious, meditative isolation and in the hurly burly of life in the market place. Our group resembled more of a market place where it was possible to be alone in the presence of others in ways that felt supportive, intimate and strong. Each group member was carefully helped to clarify the particular wisdom which they hoped to harvest from their knowledge of life. How to hold fast to wisdom gained soon became the group's engaging task. They grew to value the careful visitation of dark corners of the soul, as well as the exploration of experiences that feel confused and to acknowledge feelings that were initially labelled as nasty, frightening, numb, or peculiar. In this process they grew to embrace the glorious mish-mash called life by means of systematic warm support for their quickening desire to tell about it. This meant allowing feelings to run freely through one's veins, as well as noticing that they were touched to the core by the others. This combination of factors facilitated the healing which emerged in this group for every person present: Tom, Laura, Pamela, Cathy, Jane, John, Susan and myself. Each of us discovered inner trouble spots we did not realize we had, and each of us was helped by others to become a bigger, more spacious human being. Much has been written about spirituality and healing, about the multiple connections between mind, body, beliefs and assumptions (Kunz 1985). I find such readings inspiring. Yet they rarely refer to the desperate wish of people who live in the grimmest of environments to plant a garden. I prefer a spirituality which is rooted in instrumentality; I like angels with sturdy shoes, a strong body, a warm heart, purposeful hands and a clear mind. In TSM groups I journey with my clients to facilitate their capacity to develop and maintain resilient vitality. In this process I use stories because they provide us with mediation when necessary, with inspiration when wanted and with examples to disagree with on all occasions. The story material is moulded, developed and played with, especially because a good story defies finite interpretation. It slips away from the aberration of fixed understanding and yet demands clarity of reflection. Once a group accepts the common denominator of our own humanity, the reality of perfect imperfection, and relishes both laughter and compassion, group work is relatively easy. We simply welcome lived experience into the circle of our shared existence; nothing more, but also nothing less.

'It is not right', said Crow,
'It is not right.
To have a world without real people.'
Crow Indian

8. Beyond the Story of One's Life

All of us have stories in the back of our minds which we use to interpret and convey events or ideas. The tales are emblematic containers that enable us to distill more or less significant experience from the ceaseless rhapsody of impressions. Whenever we feel unable to create a plausible story about something we are at best left with an exciting sense of puzzlement; at worst we feel ill at ease and rather lost. Our explanation of how the world works no longer suffices (Wells 1987, p.196). In the midst of a crisis we cannot connect how we feel and think now with how we had felt and thought until then. The inner mental model that had rendered life comprehensible until then has become inadequate. Shocking events disturb our self–world relationship. This makes us even more confused and frightened. The feelings we then experience are so contradictory and peculiar that we may surrender the attempt to make sense of it all to a numb silence. This alienated state of inexplicability must gradually be surmounted if we want to re-enter a shared social world in which we exchange feelings, stories and impressions with others (Linde 1993). Profound trauma wounds twice, first by causing pain and second by creating disorientation which sets us apart from others who often fail to comprehend what we are going through. In this sense the profound emotional pain of trauma makes a person doubly alone.

The fear of meeting misapprehension makes people who experience an intense life difficulty – such as serious illness, a painful divorce or having been made redundant – withdraw from companionship. They stop going out. Many explain that they prefer their own company to that of the acute discomfort felt in the company of non-comprehending others. Alternatively, a recently bereaved or traumatized person may still mix and mingle socially but refrain from ever talking about 'that'. Some typical undiscussed issues are the loss of a loved person, the specific way in which a job came to an end, sexual, financial or neglect-related difficulties in intimate relationships, physical or sexual abuse or a mental breakdown. Prolonged unwillingness or inability to speak about troubling events sooner or later results in a sorely felt diminishment of self. The future becomes a sombre pathway without end. Previously imagined options appear foreclosed. The lively inner world of tales and thoughts shrivels (Sarbin 1986). When the pain generated by the silence about what matters becomes too great, medical, spiritual or therapeutic help may be sought in the hope that in the healing space there will be an opportunity to speak one's truth, thereby to create a new tale of life. In spite of the preceding silence, and with possibly very little evidence to support the belief, the client trusts that in this environment they might be able to articulate their life experience, to make new sense. The search for healing is inspired by hope that the articulation of experiences contains the means to surmount their constraining effect (Schafer 1992).

Such unvoiced hope against hope was movingly exemplified by Frank, a bachelor in his mid-fifties, who joined a brief TSM group (10 sessions) which I offered in an adult education centre. The group focused on myths of death and dying. Early during the fifth session Frank contributed: 'Nobody wants to die, do they now?' His eyes drew away from even the briefest contact. 'I just want to live forever. That's all I want!' He laughed, a deep, uncomfortable laugh and sighed: 'This philosophical stuff is all nonsense. There's no rhyme or reason! I'm just bloody lost.' Frank had already told the group that he was, in professional terms, successful. But now his bewilderment drooped uncomfortably around his shoulders. His professional pursuit had carried him from one situation to another. An indescribable longing had made him journey from one love to another. None satisfied him. Changing countries more often than shoes, he found himself a stranger in an ever stranger world. He could entertain the group with anecdotes of whom he had met, whom he had outwitted and over whom he had triumphed. He also had a repertoire of merciless slagging tales. No institution, friendship or love had so far been able to elicit from him a sense of respectful mutuality. Laughing a disconcerting laugh, he would add after such a tale: 'I'm just the best. That's the tragedy really, isn't it?' Before even a ray of compassion could reach him he would entertain his wandering soul with yet another story that sought its own forgetfulness amidst its noisy telling. Had Frank designed this universe, the snow would never have occasion to melt on craggy hills; snow would never fall. He did not want the withered daffodil and the old or weary to deserve a hint of nature's pride, but clung ferociously to a fierce desire that one day he might long for nothing more. How he would arrive at such a place of dead expectation was a mystery to him. The last whispers of his hope were reluctant to surrender their tenuous hold to despair. Frank tried to organize his life story around one single thread: 'People are not to be trusted to stay around', and around one pivotal decision as to how to cope with this: 'I will go it alone.'

From his work with people under stress, Lahad (1992) identified several different coping strategies. These include a cognitive-behavioural approach, a primarily affective coping mode, social or belonging motivated ways of dealing with the effects of stress, imagining one's way through the situation and finally seeking sustenance and guidance from values and beliefs. Frank's habitual strategy of cognitive analysis of emotional situations had certainly done him proud professionally. However, it had left him out at sea in too small a boat in his intimate relationships. Over time he grew to trust the group sufficiently to share some of the more complex facts of his life. He was an only child who envied people with siblings. His father had died when he was nine years old. After his father's death he had tried hard to be a good son to his grief-stricken mother. His plight reminded me of the following Indian folktale:

> In a beautiful valley in a warm land there grew a great, wild fig tree. Whenever the long season came for bearing fruit, the tree was richly laden with figs. Parrots would come to that tree. They were there all day long, feeding to their hearts' delight. One particular parrot loved the tree so very much. The bird was born in that tree, and knew no other home. One day the tree was struck by lightning. It burnt and withered. Nothing but a broken stump remained. But this parrot did not leave the remains of the tree. Though the sun shone without mercy and harsh winds crashed against the ashen stump, the parrot did not go away to find a more fertile place. Without shelter or protection he quenched his thirst on the gray water that gathered in the stump's burnt wood. He did not leave his old, broken friend. One day a goose came and spoke to the parrot. Goose asked: 'How come you have not flown away. There is fruit on other trees. There too you may find shelter from the storms and shade from sun's harsh rays. Do you not want to live?' Parrot replied: 'My mother made a nest in this tree. I was born here. Here I found nourishment and care. How can I leave now that all this is gone. How can I abandon my tree of life?' Then Goose, who was no goose but a god, was touched by Parrot's faithful love. He granted him one wish. Without thought Parrot wished that his great wild fig tree would regain its fertile vigour. Goose who was god granted this wish. The tree's stump burst to life. Once more the faithful parrot was nourished by its sweet, wild figs.'[1]

---

1   Retold by the author. Contemporary version in Choksi (1980, pp.28–32).

Behind his cheerful front Frank had clung to his sorrow about his father's death like ivy to a wall. In his heart of hearts he was still the faithful boy who hoped to protect his mother from her suffering and thereby, paradoxically, his father from his death. Even in his mid-fifties, being a 'good' child took so much energy that there was no place for mourning. Yet his grief was vividly present, with all the rage, confusion and passion of an adult child. Decades after the actual event of his father's death he still abode at the lonesome gate of unacknowledged mourning, unable to hew a meaningful relationship with the events of his life. He could not say: 'Please listen to me, I have come to tell my tale.' He was so wholly *in* his story, that his relationship *with* the story inevitably surrendered its potential for perspective to his blind involvement with the immediate urgency of any given moment. Though he sensed that the story of his life unfolded without either his awareness or his consent, he presumed that this was how it had to be.

Dunne (1973) wrote that the blind search for everlasting life deprives a person of the sacrifice, the passion, the madness, the beauty and the love of mortal existence (p.7). These emotions were somehow always just beyond Frank's grasp. He had survived his young encounter with death but needed to learn to live again. More than forty years later he still felt very lost. The bursting into bloom that was potentially available to him required the claiming of the grief that was his to live through. His symbolic 'inner tree' could return to life again but in so far that his father's death had equalled the dying of the tree in the folktale, Frank had to come to grips with the fact that in this life mortality is inevitable, ubiquitous and real. He needed a reckoning with his relationship with the meaning of dying, death, living and birth. He was enabled to work through some of these issues in the TSM group. However, in his heart of hearts he wanted individual work. For him, as for some other clients, the TSM group primarily served as a jumping board to individual therapy. The initial validation and recognition of his emotional state provided him with sufficient belief that healing was within his reach. The group experience offered him a good enough gift of faith and hope so that he could embark on a further journey.

To use a different take

Research undertaken in Britain by Malan (1979) and others has established which factors contribute most to the successful outcome of psychotherapeutic interventions with individuals and groups. Their results indicate that people who report the greatest and longest lasting improvement and who attribute this betterment to a therapeutic process remember their therapy as having been

- helpful as well as gentle
- a process in which they (the clients) did most of the work
- an experience which was new, free and freeing.

Similar observations about the therapeutic efficacy of purposeful gentleness, involvement, activity and newness have been made by clients in other countries who participated in other forms of therapy (Leszcs, Yalom and Norden 1985). Positive therapeutic outcome of group work is also intimately linked with selecting members who can work together to form a coherent group, who can provide interpersonal learning and are able to develop altruistic behaviour towards one another. These factors are, of course, inter-dependent with the facilitator's skills in enabling a group of diverse people to develop a fruitful working relationship (Connelly, Piper and DeCarufel 1986). However, the wooing of distressed people into a renewed consent to life demands more than the instilation of hope and a growing awareness of connection with other lonely people (see Yalom 1975). It also requires some kind of corrective emotional experience.

Soon after World War II Alexander and French (1946) realized that a person's recovery from profound emotional distress depends, in substantial measure, on the client's ability to surmount the traumatic influence of earlier life events. Building on Freud's work, they suggested that problematic occurrences remained problematic because other people's specific responses to these events continued to exercise further traumatic influence. A therapist's way of responding to any retelling of painful experiences needed therefore to be such that re-traumatization was, at the very least, avoided. At best, the therapist's way of dealing with the vividly present past would allow troubling experiences and modes of relating to others to be reworked and integrated. They proposed that the corrective emotional experience has two essential components:

- the client's act of recounting and reliving problematic life events
- the client's experience of a vitally different emotional response to the retelling of a still vivid pain.

The telling about inner trouble in a new context (i.e. the therapy situation) and the receiving of a new response (from the therapist and/or from other group members) facilitated, in his view, the reparation of a troubling relationship with painful events. A person who is at the end of their tether needs access to a space and a relationship in which it will not be necessary to conceal their heart's multitudinous feelings behind a singular or a more abstract emotional façade. Often friends, strangers or relatives provide that space. Sometimes the therapy room becomes the first, but hopefully not the final, place where the story of a person's life is told, retold and reworked.

In order to render experience tellable the client needs to be or to become willing to tell their story within the limits imposed by narrative structure, for example beginning, closure and integrity of development. This involves engagement with the reality that so much can never be said. The willingness to narrate matters – particularly because breaks, gaps, and losses are as intrinsic to the rhythm of life as are presence, attachment and a sense of connection. Our capacity to tell about life's happenings or non-happenings provides the means by which separation from others can occur without the feltness of fantasized, irremediable loss. Narrative bridges the inevitable discontinuities in presence and shared experience, whilst the emotional capacity to integrate major losses in life relies on being able to overcome the minor fissures that appear in the course of everyday development (Holmes 1994).

The facilitation of a client's articulation of initially unspeakable experiences requires the establishment of an emotional space in which the inadequacy of words and sighs or groans is acknowledged and normalized (Leitch 1986). Meanwhile, attempts to try to convey what happened and what is happening are welcomed and supported. In the therapeutic environment stories may be told both in code (the symbolic aspect of each story) and in long hand (the reality-based aspects of a tale). No longer does the client have to make do with mere headline reportage about infinitely complex life events which distort and over-determine communications. There is encouragement to take one's space and to speak one's truth without danger of unhelpful recrimination but in an atmosphere of developing trust and reparation. It is not easy to tell, explore and rework complex life events. In therapeutic work around stories and storytelling this needs to be taken into account, whilst the practice systematically aims to facilitate, as Malan's research suggested, the clients' active engagement with their life story in order to develop fresh new ways of exploring, being and relating.

Listening to listening

My encounter with Frank made me ponder how little we often need to know in order to get a flavour of a person's primary relationship with the events of their life. As a result of story-work most TSM group members become reflectively aware that there is no such thing as a complete account of anyone's life (Freeman 1993). However many researchers may search through the available data of some one's existence, there will always be incomplete information. Quite apart from ethical limitations and the sheer economic cost of gathering minutiae, a selection must be made whenever a story is presented. The sifting of material for inclusion in a life account is informed by the following conscious or unconscious criteria:

- what is wanted in the situation
- what information is/could be significant or interesting to the listener
- what must be conveyed
- what might be of interest in the foreseeable future
- which conclusions might be drawn from what is said and desired.

Without our necessarily realizing it, these criteria also influence what we say to neighbours, colleagues, to acquaintances whom we meet in the street and to those whom we love most intimately. One group explored this issue of selectivity in communication in substantial depth after a group member, Christine, a depressed single woman in her thirties, wrote a fictional story about a young man whose two brothers had died in an accident years earlier.

> He sat and looked at the sky one day, wondering about his brothers and trying to get a message from the stars, a signal that they still existed, that they knew he existed. And one star shone back at him, winking at him, telling him that he too would know mysteries some day and that his brothers would be with him always. Just then there came a shooting star – like a flash – piercing him with energy and with hope. And he went to the dinner table, radiant, but said nothing to his parents.

Christine asked the group to reflect on what the young man in the story needed to learn most. The responses she received from the other group members focused on issues such as the 'timing' of the sharing of important life events, the story-man's need to pursue his own life and to stop gazing at the stars, his need for forgiveness, his need to create a monument for his siblings in order to move on, and ways to improve his relationship with his mourning parents. When Christine received these responses I encouraged her to witness what happened in her inner world as she reviewed each of these, such as any feelings, thoughts, or hunches she might feel about the suggestions. Then to explore the vistas created by some of the pertinent ones, and through this to find the point of view most relevant to her, either amongst the responses/suggestions themselves, or from her own responses, triggered by these. The process of 'relating to received responses' supports the emergence of a profoundly personal yet shared feeling for language which capably expresses both internal and interpersonal dynamics.

Pines (1989) describes this kind of therapeutic environment as a culture in which contributions are accepted, underlying themes unveiled and basic attitudes worked with. This is possible because the therapist brings to the situation a strong belief in the clients' maturational capacity, as well as a profound trust in their capacity to develop. In Christine's case the establishment of a habit of different ways of looking at a situation and of the need to select a personal direction from a profusion of possibilities were of paramount importance. Her story, her way of telling the story, and her way of relating to received responses confirmed to her that change is possible. The medium of creative expressive story-work and the repeated participation in the predictable sequence of telling–exploring–receiving–selecting–sharing exerts both a calming and a strengthening influence, if only because of the feeling that someone else has understood (Von Franz 1980, p.31).

In therapy groups which focus on story-work the participants learn to listen to stories, including life stories, in terms of:

- what is presented first
- how often it or someone is referred to
- what the character in the story believes to be a unique feature of his or her life
- which occurrences or relationships are considered important
- which people or events may have been implied by the narrative but are omitted from the narrative
- which sentences or reportages are unfinished
- which means–end relationships leave the listener ill at ease, in some sense without an explanation.

These modes of 'listening to one's listening' are not alien to people who join a therapy group. On the contrary. As noted before, many people with mental health difficulties have well developed capacities to observe, to question, and to analyze; however, their ability to express what sense is made of all this, in a manner and a way that works for them and their important others, is often depleted. In the therapeutic storymaking groups I aim to build on what clients can already do, such as 'noticing', and to create structured learning experiences for what they often need to develop further, such as 'communicating about what is noticed in a way that can be taken in by the recipient and vice versa'.

Whenever we tell a story, however brief a tale this might be, we convey how we thought, felt and saw our world; what we said or did or did not say and did not do; how we believe we were perceived by others and what we knew or imagined about our interaction with the environment. When a child or adult lives in an unsafe environment such telling may be dangerous; the telling will demonstrate this. Perceived mistrust or unkind scrutiny by others often results in the teller's adjustment of their tale – perhaps by giving it a density of detail which feels unreal, even suspect. Too much emphasis on minutiae and comprehensiveness generates unease in the listener. The story sounds too good to be true. Concern with giving the right information or a tight construction of episodity causes the listener to wonder why this story needs such fixed representation. What is hidden behind the smoke-screen of apparent clarity? Telling a life story is a complex affair. Too much clarity or emphasis and the story generates disbelief, too little clarity and the story is bewildering. No wonder many clients become anxious when first invited to tell a tale. They often have had ample exposure to non-constructive feedback to their stories from parents, teachers or friends. In the therapeutic space the client rightly hopes to gain access to a voice of authority, a willingness to truthfulness and a desire for communicative clarity. After that, practice is needed: solid, reinforcing practice.

Bless to me my body,
Bless to me my soul,
Bless to me my life,
Bless to me my belief.
Gaelic

To take the middle path

The creator of a bird's-eye view life story soon finds out that they need to decide whether to view life as a series of scenes which follow one after the other without necessary sequence, which was Frank's point of view, or as a predetermined path upon which episodes follow each other with predetermined inevitability, or as a mixture of both with possibly, but not necessarily, some kind of deeper pattern. This latter assumption was brought to our work by a man whom I shall call Cliff.

Cliff was a recently retired widower with three adult sons. He had struggled for some time with deep hopelessness.[2] His GP had told him how making a book or an audio tape about their childhood years had helped

---

2   For links between bereavement, disablement, redundancy and depression see Lin, Dean and Ensel (1986).

some of his other patients work through their depression. Cliff liked this suggestion but not the process of writing. Instead he embarked on the making of an audio tape. He was referred for individual brief therapy not long after he had told one of his sons about the taped memory project, as he called it. When his sons had not shown any interest in the project, Cliff had once more sunk into depression. During our first meeting he pondered: 'Maybe I had chosen the wrong moment. Do you think they might want to listen one day?' The profound hesitancy in his offering of self marked the story of his life as well as that of his family. Cliff reminded me of the reality that all of us need others to be affected by what we have to say. Shaking his head in a slow, mournful movement, he continued: 'It is not good to think of myself as a mere voice calling nobody nowhere.' With my encouragement Cliff continued the process of creating a reconstruction and a reinterpretation of his childhood days by expanding the available memory of this period. He chose his childhood rather than his adult life because this period was particularly important for him, especially because initially he could remember so little of that time. Like Frank, he too was an only child – though in his case a first-born sister had died, aged three, before he was conceived. Cliff had married in his early twenties. His mother had died shortly after the birth of his first son. His father had died a couple of years later, when they were expecting their second child.

Whilst Cliff focused on elaborating his knowledge of the years of his youth during the rest of the week, during our sessions we worked together to enliven his perspective on the impact of this era on his present situation. This involved working through his grief about his unknown sister's death, his parents' death, his wife's death, his retirement and the many unforgivens of his life (Priefer and Gambert 1984). By daring to create his tape-recorded telling, he gradually learned to convey how he thought and felt, clarify how he believed he was perceived by others and discover what he knew about the world and his place within it. Cliff's pursuit of his half-forgotten childhood memories made him deal with real problems in the present. Most urgent of these were his depression, which tired him easily, and the uncomfortable emotional distance between himself and his children. His exploration of his childhood days was initially guided by his search for a relief from pain and isolation. He hoped to create a sufficiently cohesive theory which might explain how come he could not really talk about important issues with his sons and their families, let alone with his few friends. He felt that the main issues that had made his childhood and his adulthood complex needed clarification. He began with an attempt to reconstruct the story of his boyhood days. He gathered and studied old photos for clues about his forgotten past, travelled to interview some distant, elderly relatives and traced a few people who had known the family at that time. He also read books about the years of the great depression which had affected his childhood. He searched through old newspapers for information about companies in trouble, and particularly the bankruptcy of his father's company. Gradually he came to appreciate the profound sense of imperiled continuity that had pervaded his childhood days. Thus he deepened his knowledge of himself and his circumstances.

Having created a safer refuge for his memories, he began to surrender his hope that one day his sons would understand him. Though he still wanted greater intimacy, he no longer required it. This freed his children to pursue their own journey towards him. Their father had become a better listener. For a while he aimed only for his own recognition of the fitfulness and foibles of his young life, as well as the creation of sufficient hope to move forward with greater ease into his remaining years. The surface story of his childhood could easily have read like a litany of unrelieved misery, but ultimately Cliff did not create a pathography. 'It would have been all too easy', he later said, 'to tell a one-theme story of abandonment and neglect. But that's not only how it was and it is not how I want to remember.' Ultimately he did not want to tell a tragic tale. As the weeks passed he taped and re-taped, told and retold his childhood story until he arrived at an interpretation that felt comfortable for now. He proudly grew to recognize the importance of people, events, animals and objects in the developing account of his life. His growing ability to give credit to formative influences and processes convinced him that he wasn't a 'bad' person after all. One day he shared with me the following story, which he had come across in one of his school books. It had profound meaning for him:

> Whenever misfortune came to a certain people, one in their midst would go out and retreat into the forest, light a fire, say a prayer and the misfortune would not happen. Time passed. After a while another misfortune came and a new person was chosen to go out into the forest. This one knew the place and the prayer but not how to light a fire. None the less, misfortune was avoided. Again time passed. Another person was chosen to go into the forest. This one knew only the place, the prayer and the fire had been forgotten. But still misfortune was avoided. Then, much, much later, a new misfortune threatened the people. Now the task fell to someone who knew nothing about lighting a fire, nothing at all about prayer and who did not even know the place. All this person could do was to tell this story. It sufficed.

Towards the end of our twelve sessions he told me that he was no longer a disappointed man. He now felt that his life had been, by and large, a good life. The tape-recording of a story of his childhood had helped him to pay careful scrutiny to his important relationships. The limits set by the finiteness of the recording process made him identify, amongst the miscellany of influences and events, those that had mattered enough to be spoken about on tape. In the process of recording, and during our work together, he learned to attend to the meaning he was able to call forth from his memories and, above all, to the consequences he attributed to this in his world now. Where necessary he began to attempt to make reparation. His introspective narrative process enabled him to study his life's history. In this sense he followed in the footsteps of all other authors who aim to represent an individual in his or her environment (Runyan 1984). Cliff created a meaningful condensation of his perspective on his experiences on two 90-minute tapes. One tape did not suffice. The creation of the material, the trying out of ideas and the editing process made him less of a stranger to himself. His first realization that the life story is not a constant given had been more than a little perturbing. The sense of developing perspective and of the reality of the re-interpretability of events made him feel uneasy. But as he became more familiar with the fact that our story of life is changed, developed and reorganized in the process of living, depending on further events, other contacts, age itself and above all on who is listening, he relaxed. His tapes no longer needed to be once-and-forever statements. He seriously contemplated the possibility that in a few years time he might review and re-edit them.

Cliff, Christine, and Frank achieved different levels of fruitful change. This change was vitally linked with the quality of the conversation between us, which provided, at the very least, a corrective emotional experience as far as the potential of self-expression and the quality of relationships was concerned. Frank and Christine were members of a group. Their change was also promoted thanks to the developing quality of their relationships with the other clients. As discussed, the members of a storymaking group learn to function with and towards one another in a healing mode. Their working alliances offer articulated experience of relationships and conversations which are based on mutuality. Together these promote the clients' capacity for negotiation and a growing willingness to work through misunderstanding. In this process it is the therapist's paramount task to establish and to tolerate an attitude of warm, involved detachment (Hobson 1985).

When the poet Wordsworth wrote about our need to develop the capacity to think and feel without immediate external excitement and to acquire greater power in expressing such thoughts and feelings, he did not write about group-therapy practice, though his words well convey some of its aims (see Abrams 1974). In my experience the internalization of the capacity for greater, yet more contained, expression helps group members to deal more effectively with life's challenges – particularly because they have felt understood (Gustafson 1986).

From rumination to contemplation

At some point in our lives the stories we tell ourselves need to become close relatives so that inner coherence and a meaning of kinds can emerge. Victor Frankl, who spent three years in Nazi concentration camps, observed that death came quickly to those for whom life had lost its coherency and meaning. Amidst utter suffering people need to find a 'why' of kinds. He writes: 'Life ultimately means taking the responsibility...to fulfill the tasks which it constantly sets for each individual...sometimes the situation in which a man finds himself may require him to shape his own fate by action. At other times it is more advantageous for him to make use of an opportunity for contemplation...' (1963, pp.121–4). Frankl's words also suggest that in order for therapy to be successful the question: 'what meaning or purpose can I distill from the miscellany of my experiences' must be addressed. In this context, therapy groups offer more than mere cost effectiveness; they also grant group members the opportunity to explore such meanings with each other. Not only does the sharing of sorrow with others like oneself potentially remedy a deeply felt sense of isolation, it also enables participants to attune their reflectivity to one another, and to become active participants in the creation of a shared perspective on life experiences. In a therapy group people can check perceptions, modify responses and connect present ways of being with others with former ways of behaving – thereby learning about themselves in relation to others, about their place in the microcosm of the group and, by inference, within the macrocosm of the world beyond the group (Turner 1983).

The longing for a quieting unity of life pattern brings many people to the therapeutic situation. Here they hope to gain access to an explanatory frame-story in which aspects of their life experience will become so integrated that if any one scene were to have been displaced, absent or perturbed, the whole would no longer have fitted. It would have become disjointed. The process and procedures of therapy are initially seen as a vehicle to change a rambling, contradictory story of life into a more causal plot in which the influencing powers of actions performed by others will be balanced with actions exercised by oneself. In the course of the therapeutic process this longing for a hyper-coherent life story often changes into acceptance of the realization that incidents are, in storied terms, more the illustration of character than determinators of direction. However, behind this search for meaningful episodity lurks the wish to establish oneself as a good enough character who has acted in a complete enough life story. To reach this conclusion the client in therapy needs to evaluate their moral deeds, to formulate an understanding of the nature of the events which befell them and of their consequences, and to explore the degree and the kind of responsibility which may be attributed to themselves as well as to others.

Meanwhile, both they and the therapist need to bear in mind that at different historical moments and in different cultural contexts alternative demands were or are placed upon the life story. Commitment to piety or achievements in warfare may have been emphasized over interpersonal claims, such as 'I have a sense of humour', or 'I was always there when I was needed'. Presently the life story is primarily expected to have and to create coherency. Such coherency is meant to provide the teller with a sense of continuity, steady traits and lasting influences. Such a comprehensive story of life might even be reduced to a catchword or dominant role, such as: The Wanderer, The Friend, The Reconciler, The Fighter (Landy 1994). Through the establishment of such a working title, present-day life-tale tellers aim to convey a good enough explanation of who they are and how things came to be. The Bushmen of the Kalahari desert say that without a story of one's own, we do not have a life of our own (Van der Post 1971). Many people who experience emotional difficulties, such as Frank, Christine or Cliff, feel that they have a story, but that the story makes for an uncomfortable fit. Furthermore, the story's plot seems to compel them to an uneasy existence – in their case a felt sense of dissatisfaction with their story motivated the search for retelling. Such dissatisfaction is felt and constructed by an individual and between individuals.

I vividly remember how Cliff's telling of his childhood memories into the plastic indifference of a tape-recorder had seemed to contrast sharply with the reported experience of another old person. Athia, a female client in her middle thirties from a Mediterranean country of origin, told me how towards the end of his life one of her uncles had employed a young man to talk to him about events, gossip and ideas. He had wanted to fill his dying life with stories. When friends and relatives came to visit the sick old man, they had told him their memory-tales of him and of people he also knew, as well as other stories. Their shared reminiscing had been a central social practice. The telling of memories allowed for testimony and the emergence of a possibly somewhat wistful solidarity. Above all, the fact that in the face of death stories were not evicted from daily life permitted a continuing claim on the present. This offered more than comfort and assurance, it generated a vibrant sense of aliveness. My client said:

> 'We told him about things we had done together with him, or about memories we cherished of him. Some of these memories involved us, but not necessarily so. We also talked about things that reminded us of him. We would talk and talk. We returned his life to him as abundantly as we could.'

Holding me with her eyes, she added: 'That's what I want when I die. But I'm afraid the people I know will be in too many different places to give me my stories back.'

Whilst I absorbed her words, and the meaning they had for her, my inner eye witnessed the urgent silence which emanates from the profoundly unhappy people who have crossed my path. In their depressed inner world imaginal activity is rarely directed towards anticipated action. Athia was beginning to recognize and to exercise influence on her life's events. During the early stage of our work together she had needed access to safe, yet surprising, forays to lead her beyond the self-enclosing pain of her sadness-saturated illness. From the moment she acknowledged that she longed to be given back her stories, she made great progress. Until she became depressed she had not realized the loss entailed in her restless wandering. The memory of her uncle's death constituted a vital recollection because it also reminded her of what she so wanted for herself.

Embedded in people's narratives are the practical, ethical and philosophical underpinnings upon which they habitually draw to make sense of life. These too are subject to age, experience and circumstance. The way Myra, a single unemployed young woman in her mid-twenties, now reflects on her turbulent adolescence will differ from how she will see this period some years later when she may have a paid job in which she is respected, or how she will understand what happened in her teens if she were to be in a steady relationship in her mid-forties. The significance which we attribute to facts or to relationships depends primarily on how we understand these factors to have contributed to who we believe ourselves to be *now*, to the *current* felt sense of personal integrity and to our *current* life philosophy (Gergen 1977, p.142). In addition, the manner, form and content of how we talk about our life is profoundly influenced by how we believe ourselves to be perceived by others, particularly by the person who is listening to us, and by how we perceive ourselves in this relationship. In this sense the recounted past is never more than a reflective construction of present understanding and present circumstance, both in terms of the social, historical and personal environment and in terms of to whom the story is told. Each life story is a temporary tale saturated with verisimilitude which searches for veracity, especially because the story is invested with the full weight of belief that it is a reliable representation of lived events (Cohler 1990).

This narrative flexibility opens up a unique opportunity. It allows for the changing of the past in the present. It also generates a profound insecurity, for if we fully realize that the life story reflects the larger socio-political context, and is linked with how we are listened to in terms of what can be articulated as well as informed by changing ideas about what befell us, then we become aware that the very act of telling is in and of itself a consent to change – change which is not solely located in the outcome of the telling, nor merely in the content of the told, but which is – as process – situated in both the act of telling and the interactive dynamics between storyteller and listener (Rosenwald and Ochberg 1992). Furthermore, the act of having told may exercise a continuing influence. Though part of a real past (real because the telling did happen), it will continue to redirect the remembered shape of this past, influence further present situations and affect the shape of the imagined future in essentially unpredictable ways. These multiple possible effects of storytelling are actual givens the moment we open our mouths to speak.

Our life story is composed of lightly remembered incidents, of passionate themes, of unvoiced threshold tales and notorious (in family circles) refrain tales. In TSM groups this miscellany of stories emerges because its members become skilled listeners. They learn to sense changes in voice and posture, to notice an unusual choice of words, the way a sentence is constructed, the fluctuations in enthusiasm, the sequence and acceleration of the recounted events, as well as a story's aftertaste. Though initially these data provide little more than information, after several stories have been told the information accumulates. This bundle of knowledge leads the listener to construe understanding hypotheses of possible connective threads which seem to run through the stories a person tells. They also learn to translate such understandings into workable communications. Together the group members create the meanings they discover (Schieffelin 1993) – thereby to weave and to mend.

ᢌᡪᢌᡪᢌ

It starts when two people see each other.
They greet each other.
Now we greet each other.
Seneca

The maintenance of optimal telling conditions

Exploratory retelling may be especially pertinent with our familiar repertoire of well-tried life stories. Such stories are often greeted by family members or close friends with words like: 'Oh, not again…' However, when someone listens attentively to what we have to say and to how we say what we say, other linked tales may be drawn out of us which we did not even realize lingered in the shadow of the oft-told story. Such further stories may have sojourned for years on the edge of awareness but failed to make the crucial transition to articulation, amongst other reasons because such articulation also depends on the presence of others who listen well enough. Good enough listening relies on empathy, interest, a willingness to discover and a capacity to respond meaningfully.

In therapeutic work with stories there is, however, more at stake than the mere facilitating of storytelling in an atmosphere of careful listening. The storytellers may also be helped to shape their tales in alternative ways. Aristotle demanded that a plot, which is a coherent sequence of action, have a beginning, a middle and an end

- ○ A beginning is something that does not follow anything by causal necessity but after which something naturally occurs.

- ○ A middle is something which is assumed to be preceded by something else and succeeded by something else.

- ○ An end has something that happens before it, and is not followed by something else.

When a person tells a life story they do not necessarily follow this kind of basic plot structure. They may not yet have a beginning, middle or end to their fragment of experience. Particularly when the specific scene is traumatically coloured, the memory is more likely to resemble a set of frozen images with large gaps missing in between – like a movie with big, blank spaces. These gaps can be profoundly disconcerting and become critical scenes or themes which create a shackling past. Claire, a depressed woman in her late thirties, described how in the early hours of the morning, when memories came to haunt her, she returned again and again to a time several years earlier when she had decided to leave her boyfriend for her lover. In the memory she saw herself crying on the staircase, knowing only that she wanted to leave. Not why, or what next, or how come, only *that* she had to go. She identified the crying-on-the-staircase memory as the beginning of a period of destructive change. It was her prime 'if only'.

Jennifer, a young woman who suffered from bulimia, described:

> I still see myself on a road. My mother is telling me that she's leaving daddy that night. I am five years old. Wherever I am, I am only ever in one place. It is raining and I am on that road.

Although it is important not to idealize such frozen moments into 'forever in their clutch' statements, it is also important to work out with the individual which hoped-for life-scenarios are entailed in their memory of these events – to ascertain, for example, what homecoming would mean to Jennifer, who still sees herself as a young girl on that road, or which other staircase memories are important to Claire, who chose the lover over the boyfriend.

In group work around stories clients become both chroniclers, in the sequenced incidents sense, and storytellers, in the meaning sense, of their lives. This includes:

- the description in expressive media of various life-facts/events
- the practice of memory recall in relation to these facts/events
- developing the capacity to stay emotionally active and present
- learning to give form to what is felt, thought and recalled in relation to other people's experiences and to the impact these have upon oneself
- recognizing and managing tension, conflict and affection.

Through storytelling we consent to an emerging future. During any process of retelling the client is confronted with the reality that the uncovering of painful memories takes time. Such telling also hurts initially. It is an unfamiliar, grateful pain – grateful for having been allowed to be expressed at last. Each telling of previously under-emphasized painful events revivifies the helplessness the client and their important others felt in the traumatic situation. During the renarration of traumatic memories we may stumble across a sudden awareness that the apparent emotional clarity of a particular scene can be accompanied by an equally rawly felt emotional ambiguity; one shift of the lens of perspective upon a poignant occasion and different considerations, feelings and judgments may emerge. The telling is but a starting place for new ways of relating to the impact of an event. Through engagement with other group members' creatively expressed understanding and compassion, a shackling memory's hold can be released. Over time, participants in TSM develop exercised awareness of how much or how little they can use of another person's contribution. They become discerning listeners and givers. This promotes a sense of their own and each other's therapeutic pace. The in-depth exploration of a painful, storied memory and its associated consequences requires evidence of the clients' capacity for containment. Following the sharing and containing of the remembered experience *per se*, the interactive generation of different ways of dealing with memories is used in order gradually to release the teller from a flash-bulb-memory's curtailing grip. The surmounting of a grief-memory's constraining effects can only be achieved if the timing, pacing and ways of being with the client concerned respect the client's inner awareness of the rightness of the moment.

When Jennifer was about to tell her 'if only' memory to the group, I invited her not merely to tell her specific memory but also to instruct the other group members, before her telling, how she wanted them to respond to her story. She informed the group that she intended to share a memory of herself as a little girl, which involved a particularly important scene. After they had heard her story, she wanted each group member to write about a different way in which the girl might have reacted in the situation. Only then did she tell her memory story. The group embarked on its work on her behalf. When the responses had been created Jennifer received many ideas about different, possible reactions. One of these read: 'I wish she had shouted: NO...' Jennifer became tearful when she later read this suggested response to the group. I quietly asked: 'Is the girl's unshouted "No" an already familiar friend?' She responded: 'My mother took me for that walk just after lunch.' Then the sobs came. The group sustained her through the momentary fear excited by the reconnection with a potent memory (Brown and Kulik 1977). It was but one of the numerous reconnections that needed to be made, but it was a crucial one.

I also remember Janet who in her mind's eye returned again and again to the moment her husband told her he was having an affair with her best friend and intended to seek a divorce. They had been in the kitchen. She was stirring vegetables in the frying pan. She remembered exactly which vegetables, their smell, the heat. Not long after her husband's declaration she had become frightened to leave her home, obsessed with thoughts of the house burning down, as if by the very act of movement away from the stove she would commit a gruesome act. These frozen memories signal and evoke distress. This is a survival necessity. When we are young our survival depends on the distress signals being both sent and picked up, so that relief can be initiated. However, many people who experience long-term emotional illness have found that their distress was insufficiently alleviated. Over time their willingness and their ability to seek and to use help-offering responses has decreased. In turn this has frequently led to diminished interpersonal efficacy, which increased a downward spiral of felt isolation. Group work with a person's frozen memory and its impact on their life story is most effective when three issues are born in mind:

- Each person's willingness to narrate has to be supported.

- Fluent access has to be created to those stories which are most relevant to the process of bringing about betterment in this person's daily life.

- The capacity of other group members to listen responsively has to be purposefully engaged.

Members of TSM groups have described the effect of this kind of work with key memories in terms of a stronger ability to cope with life events, with intimate relationships and thereby with life's challenges. They note that as a result of working with their stories, a more developed resilience emerged. In such story work I assume that each of us comes together with a historical moment and that this affects our story profoundly. I accept that any story told, whether fictional or based on memory, is intimately linked with both the teller's and the listener's intrapsychic world, with what they know or sense about their interpersonal world, with the fluctuating dynamics between these and with the larger socio-economic context in which the storymakers find themselves. The purposeful exploration of these dynamics of influence supports TSM participants in their effort to wrestle some kind of meaning from the events of their life.

During a later storymaking session Janet described a felt sense of distance in all her relationships. One evening she wrote the following story:

> On a high mountain, where there was a beautiful deep green forest, lived a little goblin whose name was Nobby. Nobby lived in a dark cave and was very lonely. It was by some magic power that he came to that cold and dark cave and he could not find his way out. One day he was sitting by the cave when a beautiful white stag came up to him. 'You look very sad little man', said the stag. 'I am cold and all alone', said Nobby. 'There is a pile of logs not far away, why don't you bring them to the cave and make a fire?' So Nobby did. He thanked the Stag. He sat by his fire and all of a sudden a little bear came limping along. 'Please help me', said the bear, 'I have hurt my foot.' Nobby helped.

Her tale contains an ample dose of wishful thinking as well as some signs of her emerging capacity to conceive of the possibility of unexpected help, albeit in stories. The deer magically appears. It happens to amble by and offers Nobby some rather obvious advice: fetch some wood and make a fire. The emergence of the helpful deer was a great comfort to Janet but she most liked the story's statement that 'Nobby helped the bear'. Thinking about this aspect of her story she said: 'I need people to need me. But I'll never let them know that. I need everyone so much, it terrifies me.' She then connected this story with her childhood during World War II. She had been sent from a large city to the country as her parents, as well as the government, believed she would be safer there. Initially she had been very unhappy but gradually she had learned to make do. This is what she still did most of her life: make do. Once both these stories had been told, the group was able to tackle, in a much more explicit manner, her various complex ways of managing the dread of intimacy. Years later she wrote to me, saying how the recognition of her deeply ambivalent feelings about intimacy had enabled her to rebuild her relationships in stronger ways.

Janet's deep sense of alienation, the result of the felt emotional coldness between herself and important others, had gradually been surmounted. Participants in TSM often voice this process of making and sharing stories in a structured responsive climate as 'permission to be, being heard and being expected to respond'. After a few such sessions group members also acquire a growing awareness of some inherent story characteristics, such as those mentioned above. The repeated use of these characteristics to create numerous stories at will supplies group members with actual tools that create awareness of the uses of story, for example

- as a mediating form between the interpersonal world of culture and the intimate world of desires and belief
- to conserve and to reconstrue memories
- to alter the past (through retelling and reinterpretation)
- to state a point of view without confrontation and which nonetheless provides a basis for discussion.

Because language has an inescapable imprecision, stories which use words permit a sensing of the logic of the storied events. Through asking informed questions about the story 'within the story frame', the teller can develop their story.

An example of such an investigation is encapsulated in the following vignette from practice. Rosemary, a single childless woman in her late forties who felt very ill at ease with conflicting feelings, once wrote the following story outline:

> A girl walks along on the road. She is three years old. It is a sunny day. She meanders along quite happily. She comes to some houses and wanders into one of the gardens. A lady comes out of the house, says hello to the child and talks with her for a while. She invites the child inside, gives her something to drink and then the girl continues her journey. She is very happy.

In the ensuing work with the story various group members asked Rosemary questions which aimed to clarify a number of puzzling story aspects. Such engagement of the client in a conservation about their story needs to take into account that questions are culturally situated and socially constructed (Madigon 1993). The group member is the ultimate source of knowledge. I believe that, where possible, participants in the therapeutic process need to become aware of the extent to which they grant others levels of authority and spheres of influence. Such awareness-raising about the granting of influence relies on a group culture in which ideas are offered as true contributions, no more but also no less, and perceptions become possible avenues for exploration (Anderson and Goolishian 1988). Rosemary tried to formulate an answer to various questions, as best she knew how, within the story-frame:

SANDRA: Where did the girl live?
ROSEMARY: I don't know, not near there.
JACK: If she didn't live near there, how come she was alone on that road?
ROSEMARY: I don't know. She was happy.
SANDRA: Did that woman recognize the little girl?
ROSEMARY: I told you, she didn't know her.
JULIA: Wasn't anybody worried about the girl being quite a way away from where she lived?
ROSEMARY: No one has noticed she was gone.
HARRY: Who could have noticed?
ROSEMARY: Her mother I suppose.
JACK: How come her mother hadn't noticed?
ROSEMARY: Her mother was ill.

Breaking the story frame, she added: 'Oh stop it.'

At this point Rosemary became quite tearful. After a sad silence, she sighed: 'My mother was very ill when I was three. But that story wasn't about me. It was about a happy, little girl. I wasn't happy then. Oh, I'm so confused.' Again she was silent for a while. The group waited quietly. Looking up, she continued: 'I so wanted my childhood to have been happy. But it wasn't. It just wasn't. That's the first time I've ever said that. You might as well know it now: I wasn't a happy child.' She looked a little dazed when it came home to her that she had publicly acknowledged at last that she had been an unhappy child. She also seemed surprised that it had not been too difficult to say so. The group was easily capable of holding the awareness that she had been an unhappy little girl, in fact it was a relief as most group members had sensed this about her from the word go.

Rosemary's story about the little girl on the road can be thought of as both a reflection of her lived life-experience, as something of the past and as an encapsulation of her possible self – like a reference to something not quite realized yet but something still to come. She both was and was not a happy little girl on the road. This dual reality was encapsulated in her story. The act of telling it to truly attentive others allowed her to experience that the past wasn't quite so far past and that the future wasn't quite so distant. By means of telling she was able

- to describe her self-belief in relation to certain experiences in her life and thereby to make this accessible to others
- to develop her explanations and interpretations of these experiences
- to learn to develop a new course of action based on insight gained from new, different interpretations.

A steady inner point of view

Her very brief story about a little girl, and the group's curiosity about her story, contributed to Rosemary's process of creating a reconstruction and a re-interpretation of an important period in her life. Through such systematic story-work both she and the group learned to become more aware of the influence exercised by various aspects on the formulation of our psycho-social self-stories. These are:

- the level and effect of a person's or a story-character's constitutional givens, such as the kind of body they were endowed with. Their size, appearance and general physical health

- the specific ways in which a person or a story character synthesizes experience in order to make sense of their world, to create meaning and to cope with anxiety or conflict

- the major characteristics of the person's or the story character's family and of the social/historical structure into which they were born

- the conditions of the telling situation, including the quality of listening offered.

In the course of TSM group work the participants are helped to clarify key habits which guide their way of being in the world (such as running away and pretending nothing was the matter), as well as some basic assumptions which inform their decisions (such as nobody really wants to know how I feel). As the group progresses most participants extend their knowledge base by asking relatives and friends for further information and feedback. A lot of talking happens back home, at work, with friends, at clubs. Sociality is sought out, contacts are remade. The clients are encouraged to weave a developed understanding of their individual life into the relationships within the wider web of their community of emotional kin (Bromley 1977, p.163). As this process progresses, many clients, like Rosemary, realize how dearly they want the story of their life to fit the neat confines of a unified story plot. Such a plot is understood to consist of a series of interrelated actions which progress, because of the interplay of one force upon another, through a struggle of opposing forces to a climax and denouement. The struggles are against the ways of the world, the forces of nature or destiny and, above all, against other human beings. The clients long to be able to separate distinctly those events that advanced the conflicts they lived through to a crisis point from those that were, with the benefit of hindsight, far less important. They would not mind knowing beyond doubt which action or inaction set the sails irrevocably towards which events, to discover, beyond all reasonable doubt, upon which decision which action had hinged, how a crisis was evoked, constituted and made inevitable – if only to determine what their share was in such seemingly unavoidable developments.

But here the parallel between story-plot and life-plot abruptly ceases. When Rosemary reflected in greater depth on the story of her life she realized that she could no longer say with absolute certainty that the events of her childhood had called forth particular events which were irremediably resolved in prescribed ways. No such chance. Amidst the complexity and turmoil of human life the concept of unified plot breaks down. Life experience is, by its very nature, episodic. Bruised and confused, we may attempt to construct a tale of inevitable coherence upon the basis of the lived bewilderment, but, let us hope, we won't quite succeed. For we are moved forward by necessary reconciliation with choice, ultimate confusion and wonder. A position of secure inner wonder gives birth to fruitful doubt and creative uncertainty. Both of these are fundamental to flexible, resilient living. All of us need to travel beyond the creation of ever-seductive inevitable life-plots towards a much more complex acceptance of the reality that none of us will ever know whether the spiral of change is moving backwards or upwards or momentarily not moving at all. The story of life does change in unpredictable ways (Frosh 1991). Such is the way of things.

Whenever we are without a vision of a possible future we are reluctant to tell a story, ashamed of what the tale might unveil. And yet, precisely because we feel troubled or lonesome, we need to tell about our plight because this is how we survive. Singing-bones and story-cloaks enable a group member to tell of the life that can be found beyond the current situation. This reaching for balance beyond certainty was aptly demonstrated by Sofia, a depressed young woman in her early thirties who had some years earlier given up a successful career as a scientist to retrain as a carpenter in the hope that this would resolve her heart's lament. It had not. She remained depressed. In this condition she asked herself very few questions about herself. Shortly after joining a storymaking group, she wrote the following brief story:

> A young woman has left her home. It is a misty Autumn morning. There's a thick fog. She walks towards the fence that surrounds her home. She has taken a sword with her. She leans against the high picket fence, sword in hand, and tries to peek over it. The fog is less thick now.

In the reflection phase of the work, Sofia said: 'That story is really also about me. I'm ambivalent about going out into the world. I really am. I remain peeking over that fence. I wonder why?' She had been unable to ask herself this kind of question in relation to her depressive illness. The subject matter of her story was presented in both a particular way, this woman in this fog, and on the general plane, people sometimes feel in a fog (Raphael 1959). This duality was exploited during the exploration of the storied event (the peeping over a fence). Other group members were invited to speak about their experience of feeling in a fog. Sofia was asked to clarify what was specific about her fog (which will be like and yet unlike others) and about the act of peeping over a fence (e.g. what kind of fence, for her fence isn't mine or yours). The story contained thought in the process of being thought.

It provided the kind of self-reflective leverage this client needed to begin to have interest in herself again.

By means of such group work participants hope to develop or to rediscover a steady inner viewpoint from which to get a self-reflective leverage on their life. They search for relationships with people who are unbound to the same automatic assumptions about the world, and for relationships which might grant them the opportunity to be self-oriented and to concentrate upon something or someone other than themselves (Frattaroli 199). As a result of this they hope to regain the ability to move beyond the paralysis of 'for ever' to the time-boundness of life. This involves developing and using the capacity to anticipate events, such as interpersonal responses and through this to strengthen the willingness to communicate about those life experiences that were previously considered unmentionable.

However episodic life's stories might be, at some point the tales which matter need to become more intimate relatives. An inkling of a purposive course of life sustains people through even the direst of circumstances. Athia, the Mediterranean woman referred to earlier, emphasized that this is what her uncle searched for. He wanted some kind of thread that might bind the miscellaneous bundle of experiences that made up his life into a more or less coherent whole. Weak and unable to talk much himself, he invited other people to help him to gather his life story, especially because he was dying. In the course of a TSM group the participants learn to become storytellers: chroniclers (by linking incidents or events) and meaning makers (in the interpretative, evaluatory sense). Thereby they rediscover that whenever a story is told, the past becomes the present. The telling is an affirmation and an exploration, a starting point for change. In therapeutic storymaking stories are created in the 'near experience' understanding which both teller and listener bring to their encounter. Once told, the stories are open to reinterpretation and evaluation of content. Thus to become clearer or more comprehensive accounts of experiences (Cohler 1994). In TSM the constraint of the telling situation is knowingly used to become the container which facilitates the retelling, a retelling which continues until both the story and the experience of telling exercise not a life-limiting but a life-enhancing role.

I have made a footprint,
there is cheer in my dwelling.
I have made a footprint,
I live in the light of day.
Osage

9. Completed for Now

Towards the end of a TSM group its members have, one hopes, gained an aware, felt sense that

- the help they offer each other is important and valued
- their ability to recollect events or to observe new or different behaviour in a person or in the group matters
- their physical and emotional presence counts
- conflict and conflict resolution are vital aspects of interpersonal learning (Fuhriman and Butler 1983)

Such awareness in itself exercises a persistent, healing influence. It is transferable to other situations and becomes an inner point of reference that informs emotional resilience. How best to facilitate its early functional presence in people who join a group because they are emotionally unwell is a crucial issue for practice. In addition to having the skills of a good group worker and bringing to the work relevant life-experience, curiosity and warmth, the TSM facilitator needs to be able to teach participants both how they can create relevant stories at will and how to use processes of story elaboration and story reconstruction to review and to reinterpret life events. We always both create our story *and* embody it. The transcendence of unwelcome limits that some stories impose remains within reach. In this book I have explored how in TSM this transcendence is aimed for by means of interactive storytelling and storymaking.

In my experience most people who join a storymaking group seek to re-tell their lives. They come to tell their stories in the hope that this time they will be able to tell them well enough so that they will feel heard, whilst most also want to discover how to deal more effectively with the impact of those life stories that are a felt hindrance. In each group I nurture an atmosphere in which the theories and stories that participants use to explain why they behave as they do can be explored. The creative–expressive procedures of storymaking, movement, painting, dramatization and writing – as well as response (feed-back) and interpretative processes – offer group members access to alternative versions of their initially rather fixed accounts of events. The early stories tend to have a 'because of this – therefore I...' tenor. Through different ways of telling a story an alternative light is cast on events. These differences promote the kind of play with possibilities that eases life-limiting cause and effect understanding.

In the process of such supported re-storying the teller gradually grows to differentiate storied themes of passive, wishful thinking from those which contain ideas that can actually be realized if wanted and worked for. The response task procedures further invite group members to formulate and to consider alternative understanding hypotheses. Within the groups due weight is given to concepts such as circumstantial necessity, urgency and normality, however culture-based these concepts may be. This includes emphasis on the fact that all of us use survival strategies in stressful circumstances. The energy and creativity a group member demonstrated in having been able to deal with a difficult or overwhelming situation at all deserves to be recognized.

I believe that the problem a client presently experiences rarely resides in their original coping solution, which was more often than not relevant to their situation. The trouble frequently rests in their persistence in solution behaviour long after the problem has gone away. Ryle (1992) proposes that 'a useful description of a neurotic is that he is someone who continues to act in ways that work badly for him, but is unable to revise his ideas or behaviour in the light of adverse outcomes' (p.2). In TSM the suggested connection between a weak, adjustment-creating interpersonal feedback loop and emotional illness is made therapeutically useful through a combination of facilitator style, the establishment of a specific, reciprocal group culture and story-based procedural as well as interpretative interventions. Combined, these nurture the participant-storymaker's facility to establish and to manage a more fruitful relationship with others. The strengthening of interpersonal bonds and intrapsychic resilience is worked for through the provision of steady support for the client's involvement in the process.

People who experience mental ill health often need to become more able to recognize and to name feelings. The telling about the there and then of their situation and their experience of the here and now in literal and metaphoric form provides the training ground where this is practised. In my experience this kind of emotional learning can only happen when the group member feels safe enough to express what is going on for them. Containment, appreciation of effort and congruent understanding are the interpersonal and therapeutic processes which facilitate such expression. TSM participants practise the use of memory or fictional stories for purposes such as:

- illustration, e.g. to make a point or to expand an example
- identification, e.g. to create alignment with a significant character by means of emotional investment
- projection, e.g. to interpret character motives, to analyze relationships, to develop meanings, or to draw a moral or a lesson
- insight, e.g. to recognize and to explore links between self and story character
- integration, i.e. knowingly to draw aspects of a story's explored meaning into one's life.

Narrative allows us to attend and to re-attend to particularities of thought, conversation, actions, subjective meaning and social contexts. It represents us in our environment.[1]

A mutual, sincere interest – more often than not

In TSM many stories are told – some long, some short, some fictional, some memory-based. Marion, a woman in her mid-fifties who was recovering from physical and emotional illness, wrote:

> The mutual sincere interest in the small things of life is something that is so readily lost when life is really tough. I believe that building mutual respect begins with a tender attention for our little stories.

Aware interactivity with their own and other people's stories is especially promoted by means of the response task procedure. This aspect of the work encourages participants to develop self-directed tenderness, emotional mastery, the capacity to tolerate spontaneity and experience of the kind of joy which accompanies necessary doubt. In between, steps on the way to problem resolution become more readily accepted as normal facets of making progress. These are substantial skills for clients who initially bring to the therapeutic situation a firm wall between what they feel, what they think

---

1   See also Runyan (1984) The author discusses how introspective, narrative processes can be used to study individual life histories and particularly how both insight and rigour may be brought to this practice. The chapter on the Case Study Method, pages 121–153 is particularly relevant to therapists who use narrative structures in their work.

they communicate and how they interpret the communications that come back to them. When they first join a group most clients hold firm to a self-limiting structure of ideas about how the world operates whilst they oscillate between will and counterwill. The warm-ups, the stories, the response tasks and leadership style aim to bring within reach a platform in the self from which the client can more flexibly respond to others and to their life's events.

During my own practice, a story which I first heard Ashley Ramsden, a British storyteller, tell is never far from consciousness. It says:

> Rabbi Zoshia was a wise man. Once, while speaking about God, Rabbi Zoshia said: 'Remember, when I die God will not say to me, Rabbi Zoshia, why weren't you more like Father Abraham? No, he will say, why weren't you more like Rabbi Zoshia?'

A similar longing to become more like oneself inspires many people who seek and need the kind of healing offered through storytelling and story-making. Stories stimulate the analogizing process in which we think our-selves to be like and yet unlike Rabbi Zoshia. By means of analogy we create parallel interwoven stories about ourselves into any tale, whether this is a memory-based or fictional story (Nichols and Balch 1995). Analogizing is fundamental to the very act of seeing, reading about, hearing or playing a fictional or historical character. When the analogizing process is knowingly used to promote healing development, the main issues that are at stake for the participant need careful stating, whilst person-specific ways need to be found to help each client to surmount their life-restricting explanatory claims. I believe that whilst early psychic structures are probably enduring and resistant to reorganization, therapeutic work can change the solutions a person uses to deal with internal and external problems – particularly when those solutions have themselves become problems. In therapeutic storymak-ing the client is encouraged to shift their relationship with their difficulties (Watzlawick, Weakland and Fisch 1974). Quite often this means changing a symptom by keeping it differently.

A person's problematic relationship with life's complexities is likely to be manifested in behaviour in the group (including ways of relating to the facilitator), in talk about reported events outside the group and exemplified in a character's pattern of coping with problems or potentialities in either a fictional story or a memory story. The procedures utilized in therapeutic storymaking aim to weave links between these realms of being to establish with the client which inconsistencies, paradoxes and continuities are part and parcel of their preferred life story. Steady support is offered for the development of a productive will to doubt. Established certainties are also relative. In my experience the creation of an intimate relationship between relative clarity of understanding or intention and useful doubt nurtures a vividly felt sense of being alive, of joyous laughter. Meanwhile, the facilitator aims systematically to nurture a person's use of those intrapsychic and interpersonal resources that help the self to tackle, process and work through complexities. The facilitation of this process of reflection and more adaptive integration begins at the moment of encounter between the facilitator and the participants. It continues until their roads part. During the ending process, Sandra, a woman who had flourished in the group, wrote:

> 'Going to new places, to new faces, moving, open, no fear and fear, great excitement. Maybe sorrow, there is always a little bit of sorrow. The unknowing means also leaving behind part of yourself you know, but expanding. Learning new things. Feeling refreshed.'

When our roads part, the memories and the stories remain. I treasure the case notes, the drawings or poems I have been given, the letters I receive and my own recollections of the intense, brief work with a group or an individual. In each group the group members and I interact with one another's purpose, memories and hope. Together we try to make sense through thick and thin of confusing, painful and curious experience. This commitment lasts for the duration of the therapeutic work. Over time the storied events have settled into memory. I sincerely hope that I have fairly represented the experiences of the people whose presence in my life inspired the preceding pages. Together we learned that feelings, if acknowledged rather than disowned, if contended with rather than evaded, soften the heart and strengthen our being. Stories and storytelling are quiet means to inspiring ends.

References

Abrahams, R.D. (1983) *African Folktales.* New York: Pantheon Books.

Abrams, M.H. (ed) (1974) *The Norton Anthology of English Literature.* New York: W.W. Norton and Company.

Achterberg, J. and Frank Lawlis, G. (1978) *Imagery of Disease.* Champaign, Ill: Institute of Personality and Ability Testing.

Ackerly, W.C. (1967) 'Latency age children who threaten to kill themselves,' *Journal of American Child Psychiatry 2,* 242.

Admad, C. and Will, A. (eds) (1993) *'Race' and Health in Contemporary Britain.* Stony Stratford: Open University Press.

Alexander, F. and French, T.M. (1946) *Psychoanalytic Therapy: Principles and Applications.* New York: Ronald Press.

Altieri, C. (in Tyrrell, L. (1990)) 'Storytelling and moral agency.' *The Journal of Aesthetics and Art Criticism 48,* 2, 124.

Anderson. W. (ed) (1977) *Therapy and the Arts.* New York: Harper Colophon Books

Anderson, H. and Goolishian, H. (1988) 'Human systems as linguistic systems: preliminary and evolving ideas about implications for clinical theory.' *Family Process 27,* 371–393.

Anderson, H. and Goolishian, H. (1992) 'The client is the expert. A not knowing approach to therapy.' In S. McNamee and K. Gergen (eds) *Therapy as Social Construction.* Newbury Park: Sage.

Argyle, M. (1972, Second Ed.) *The Psychology of Interpersonal Behaviour.* Harmondsworth: Penguin Books.

Atkin, K. and Rollings, J. (1993) *Community Care in Multi-Racial Britain.* Social Policy Research Unit, London: HMSO.

Austin, J.L. (1962) *How to Do Things with Words.* Cambridge, Mass: Harvard University Press.

Aylwin, T. (1989) *Storytelling and Education.* London: School of Primary Education, Thames Polytechnic.

Aziz R. (1990) *C.G. Jung's Psychology of Religion and Synchronicity.* Albany: State University of New York Press.

Baldwin, J. (1966) 'Unnameable objects, unspeakable crimes.' In T. Ebony (ed) *The White Problem in America.* Hartford, WI: Lancer Books.

Bang, I. and Ryuk, Y. (1962) (Trans. J.S. Gale) *Korean Folktales.* London: Charles E. Tuttle Company.

Barker, P. (1985) *Using Metaphors in Psychotherapy.* New York: Brunner/Mazel.

Barnitt, R. and Fulton, C. (1994) 'Patient agreement to treatment: a framework for therapists.' *British Journal of Therapy and Rehabilitation 1,* 3–7.

Bartlet., F.C. (1932) *Remembering: A Study in Experimental and Social Psychology*. New York: Macmillan.

Barton, D. and Ivanic, R. (1991) *Writing in the Community*. London: Sage.

Bates, B. (1986) *The Way of the Actor*. London: Century.

Bateson, G. (1972) *Steps to an Ecology of Mind*. New York: Ballantine Books.

Bauman, R. (1986) *Story, Performance, and Event: Contextual Studies of Oral Narrative*. Cambridge: Cambridge University Press.

Baumann, H. (1975) *Hero Legends of the World*. London: Dent and Sons.

Baumeister, R.F. and Newman, L.S. (1994) 'How stories make sense of personal experiences: motives that shape autobiographical stories.' *Personality and Social Psychology Bulletin 20*, 6, 676–690.

Beck, A.P. and Peters, L. (1981) 'The research evidence for distributed leadership in therapy groups.' *International Journal of Group Psychotherapy 31*, 1, 43–71.

Beier, U. (1970) *The Origin of Life and Death*. London: Heinemann.

Belk, R.W. (1991) 'The ineluctable mysteries of possessions.' In F.M. Rudmin (ed) 'To have possessions: a handbook of ownership and property.' (Special Issue). *Journal of Social Behavior and Personality 6*, 6, 479–481.

Berger, D. (1989) 'Developing the story in psychotherapy.' *American Journal of Psychotherapy 43*, 1, 248–259.

Berne, E. (1966) *Principles of Group Treatment*. New York: Grove Press.

Berne, E. (1970) *Group Treatment*. New York: Grove Press.

Berry, C. (1973) *Voice and the Actor*. London: Harrap.

Bettelheim, B. (1975) *The Uses of Enchantment*. New York: Knopff.

Bion, W.R. cited in P. Casement (1985) *On Learning From the Patient*. London: Tavistock Publications.

Boal, A. (Trans. A. Jackson) (1992) *Games for Actors and Non-actors*. London: Routledge.

Boas, F. (1940, Repr. 1982) *Race, Language and Culture*. Chicago: University of Chicago Press.

Borden, R.J. (1980) 'Audience influence.' In P.B. Paulus (ed) *Psychology of Group Influence*. Hills Dale, NJ: Erlbaum.

Bower, G.H. and Morrow D.G. (1990) 'Mental models in narrative comprehension.' *Science 247*, 44–48.

Bowers, P.F., Banquer, M. and Bloomfield, H.H. (1974) 'Utilization of non-verbal exercises in the group therapy of outpatient chronic schizophrenics.' *The International Journal of Group Psychotherapy 1*, 13–24.

Bowlby, J. (1988) *A Secure Base: Clinical Applications of Attachment Theory*. London: Routledge.

Brinton, D.G. (1868) *Myths of the New World*, repr. as Brinton, D.G. (1976) *Myths of the Americas*. New York: Rudolf Steiner Publications.

Bromley, D.B. (1977) *Personality Description in Ordinary Language*. London: Wiley & Sons.

Bronfenbrenner, U. (1979) *The Ecology of Human Development*. Cambridge, MA: Harvard University Press.

Brook, P. (1988) *The Shifting Point*. London: Methuen.

Brown, R. and Kulik, J. (1977) 'Flashbulb memories.' *Cognition 5*, 73–99.

Bruner, E.M. (1993) 'Epilogue: creative persona and the problem of authenticity.' In S. Lavie, K. Naryan and R. Rosaldo (eds) *Creativity/Anthropology*. Ithaca: Cornell University Press.

Bruner, J. (1986) *Actual Minds, Possible Worlds*. Cambridge, MA: Harvard University Press.

Bruner, J. (1990) *Acts of Meaning*. Cambridge, Mass: Harvard University Press.

Bruner, J. (1991) 'The narrative construction of reality.', *Critical Enquiry*, 18, 1–21.

Buie, D. (1981) 'Empathy: its nature and limitations.' *Journal of the American Psychoanalytic Association 29*, 281–307.

Burland, C.A. (1974) *Myths of Life and Death*. London: Macmillan.

Butkovich, P., Carlisle, J., Duncan, R. and Moss, M. (1975) 'Social system and psychoanalytic approaches to group dynamics: complementary or contradictory.' *The International Journal of Group Psychotherapy*, January, 3–31.

Butler, R.N. (1964) 'The life review: an interpretation of reminiscence in the aged.' In R. Kastenbaum (ed) *New Thoughts on Old Age*. New York: Springer.

Bygrave, P.L. (1994) 'Development of listening skills in students in special education settings.' *International Journal of Disability, Development and Education 41*, 1, 51–60.

Cage, J. (1968) *Silence, Lectures and Writings*. London: Marion Boyars.

Calvino, I. (1992) (Trans. P. Creagh) *Six Memos for the Next Millenimum*. London: Jonathan Cape.

Cameron, A. (1984) *Daughters of Copperwoman*. London: The Woman's Press Ltd.

Campbell, J. (1959, repr. 1969) *The Masks of God: Primitive Mythology*. London: Souvenir Press.

Campbell, J. (1975) *The Hero with a Thousand Faces*. London: Abacus.

Case, C. and Daley, T. (1992) *The Handbook of Art Therapy*. London: Tavistock.

Cassirer, E. (1946) (Trans. S.E. Langer) *Language and Myth*. New York: Dover Publications.

Cattanach, A. (1992) *Play Therapy with Abused Children*. London: Jessica Kingsley Publishers.

Choksi, M. (1980) *Bird Legends of India*. Bombay: Orient Longman.

Chomsky, N. (1971, repr. 1975) *Problems of Knowledge and Freedom*. London: Fontana.

Cohler, J. (1990) 'The life-story and the study of resilience and response to adversity.' *Journal of Narrative and Life History I*, 169–200.

Cohler, J. (1994) 'The life-story perspective within the human sciences.' *Contemporary Psychology 39*, 2.

Cole, C. (1995) 'No story, no analysis? The role of narrative in interpretation.' *Journal of Analytical Psychology 40*, 3, 405–416.

Coles, R. (1989) *The Call of Stories*. Boston: Houghton Mifflin.

Collins, J.L., Rickman, L.E. and Mathura, C.B. (1980) 'Frequency of schizophrenia and depression in a black inpatient population.' *Journal of the National Medical Association 72*, 9, 851–856.

Colwell, E. (ed) (1991) *Storytelling*. Woodchester: Thimble Press.

Connelly, J.L., Piper, W.E. and DeCarufel, Fl. (1986) 'Premature termination in group psychotherapy: pretreatment and early treatment predictors.' *International Journal of Group Psychotherapy 36*, 145–152.

Cooper, J.C. (1983) *Fairy Tales: Allegories of the Inner Life*. Wellingborough: The Aquarian Press.

Coyne, J.C. and Downey, G. (1991) 'Social factors and psychopathology: stress, social support and coping process.' *Annual Review of Psychology 42*, 401–425.

Crew, F. (1975) *Out of my System: Psychoanalysis, Ideology, and Critical Method*. Oxford: Oxford University Press.

Cunningham, A. (ed) (1973) *The Theory of Myth*. London: Sheed and Ward.

Cyrulnik, B. (1993) (Trans. I.S. Leonard) *The Dawn of Meaning*. New York: McGraw-Hill.

Daldin, H. (1994) 'Expanding the clinical utility of the concept of developmental help to engage the severely disturbed adult patient in a psychoanalytic process.' *British Journal of Psychotherapy 10*, 4, 521–533.

Daniel, S. and McGuire, P. (eds) (1972) *The Paint House: Words from an East End Gang*. Harmondsworth: Penguin Books.

Davis, P. (1995) *If You Came This Way: A Journey Through the Lives of the Underclass*. New York: John Wiley and Sons.

de Campos, A. (1993) 'Schizophrenic behaviour and social psychiatry research.' In F.A. Jenner, A.C.D. Monteiro, J.A. Zagalo-Cardoso and J.A. Cunhan-Oliveira (1993) *Schizophrenia, a Disease or Some Ways of Being Human?* Sheffield: Sheffield Academic Press.

De Lauretis, T. (1982) *'Alice Doesn't': Feminism, Semiotics, Cinema*. Bloomington: Indiana University Press.

De Waele, J.P. and Harre, R. (1979) 'Autobiography as a psychological method.' In G.P. Ginsburg (ed) *Emerging Strategies in Social Psychological Research*. New York: John Wiley and Sons.

Dewald, P.A. (1994) 'Principles of supportive psychotherapy.' *American Journal of Psychotherapy 487*, 4, 505–518.

Dimino, J., Gersten, R., Carnine, D. and Blake, G. (1990) 'Story-grammar: an approach for promoting at-risk secondary students' comprehension of literature.' *Elementary School Journal 91*, 1, 19–32.

Donovan, J. (1996) 'Exploratory-level dramatherapy within a psychotherapy setting.' In S. Mitchell (ed) *Dramatherapy Clinical Studies*. London: Jessica Kingsley Publishers.

Dossey, L. (1982) *Space, Time and Medicine*. Boulder: Shambala Publications.

Douglas, M. (1993) 'The idea of home; a kind of space.' In A. Mack (ed) *Home: A Place in the World*. New York: New York University Press, 261–281.

Dunne, J.S. (1973) *Time and Myth*. London: SCM Press.

Durrell, A. and Sachs, M. (ed) (1990) *The Big Book of Peace*. New York: Dutton.

Duryea, M.L. and Potts, J. (1993) 'Story and legend; powerful tools for conflict resolution. Special issue: Native American perspectives on peacemaking.' *Mediation Quarterly 10*, 4, 387–395.

Efran, S. and Schenker, M.D. (1993) 'A potpourri of solutions, reviewing Steve de Shazers's solution focused therapies.' *The Family Therapy Networker*, May/June, 71–74.

Eliade, M. (1957) *Mythes, Rêves et Mysteres.* Paris: Gallimard.

Emunah, R. (1994) *Acting for Real: Drama Therapy Process, Technique and Performance.* New York: Brunner\Mazel.

Ferron, E.G. (1991) 'The black and white group.' *Group Analysis*, Sage, Vol. 24, 201.

Festinger, L. (1957) *Theory of Cognitive Dissonance.* Evanston, Ill: Row and Peterson.

Finkelstein, V. (1993) 'The commonality of disability.' In J. Swain, V. Finkelstein, S. French and M. Olivers (eds) *Disabling Barriers – Enabling Environments.* London: Sage.

Fonagy, P. (1989) 'On tolerating mental states: theory of mind in borderline personality.' *The Bulletin of the Anna Freud Centre 12*, 2, 91–115.

Foulkes, S.H. (1964) *Therapeutic Group Analysis.* London: Allen and Unwin.

Foulkes, S.H. and Anthony, E.J. (1957) *Group Psychotherapy, The Psycho-analytic Approach.* Harmondsworth: Penguin Books.

Frankel P.E., Miller, F.D. and Paul, J. (1992) *The Good Life and the Human Good.* Cambridge: Press Syndicate of the University of Cambridge.

Frankl, V.E. (1963) *Man's Search for Meaning.* Boston: Beacon Press.

Frattaroli, E.J. (1990) 'A new look at Hamlet.' *International Review of Psycho Analysis 17*, 269.

Freeman, M. (1993) *Rewriting the Self: History, Memory, Narrative.* New York: Routledge, Chapman & Hall.

Freire, P. (1972) *Pedagogy of the Oppressed.* Harmondsworth: Penguin.

French, M. (1985) *Beyond Power.* London: Cape.

Fromm, E. (1951) *The Forgotten Language.* New York: Grove Press.

Frosh, S. (1991) 'The semantics of therapeutic change.' *Journal of Family Therapy 13*, 171–186.

Fuhriman, A. and Butler, T. (1983) 'Curative factors in group therapy: a review of the recent literature.' *Small Group Behavior*, 131–143.

Gambrell, L.B. and Chasen, S.P. (1991) 'Explicit story structure instruction and the narrative writing of fourth- and fifth-grade below-average readers.' *Reading Research and Instruction 31*, 1, 54–62.

Ganster, D.V. and Victor, B. (1988) 'The impact of social support on mental and physical health.' *British Journal of Medical Psychology 61*, 17–36.

Gardner, R.A. (1971) *Therapeutic Communication with Children: The Mutual Storytelling Technique.* New York: Jason Aronson.

Garnett, L.R. (1996) 'Taking emotions to heart.' *Harvard Health Letter 21*, 11, 1–3.

Gaster, Dr. T.H. (ed) (1959) *The New Golden Bough by Sir James George Frazer.* New York: Mentor Book.

Georges, A. (1968) *Studies on Mythology.* Homewood, Ill: The Dorsey Press.

Gergen, K. and McNamee, S. (eds) (1991) *Social Constructionism in Therapeutic Process.* London: Sage.

Gergen, K.J. (1977) 'Stability, change and chance in understanding human development.' In N. Datan and H. Reese (eds) *Life-Span Developmental Psychology: Dialectical Perspectives on Experimental Research.* New York: Academic Press.

Gergen, K.J. and Gergen, M.M. (1983) 'The social construction of narrative accounts.' In K.J. Gergen and M.M. Gergen *Historical Social Psychology.* Hillsdale NJ: Erlbaum Associates.

Gergen, M. (1992) 'Life stories: pieces of a dream.' In G.C. Rosenwald and R.L. Ochberg (eds) *Storied Lives.* New Haven: Yale University Press, 127–144.

Gersie, A. (1991) *Storymaking in Bereavement.* London: Jessica Kingsley Publishers.

Gersie, A. (1992) *Earthtales.* London: Merlin Press.

Gersie, A. and King, N. (1990) *Storymaking in Education and Therapy.* London: Jessica Kingsley Publishers.

Gescan, R. (1970) *Kikuyu Folktales.* Nairobi: East African Literary Bureau.

Gillis, J.R. (1996) *A World of Their Own Making. Myth, Ritual, and the Quest for Family Values.* New York: Basic Books.

Gofman, E. (1978) 'Response cries.' *Language 54,* 787–815.

Goforth, F. and Spillmann, C. (1994) *Using Folk Literature in the Classroom.* Phoenix: Oryx Press.

Goldberg, A. (1988) 'Changing psychic structure through treatment.' *Journal of American Psychoanalytic Association 36,* Suppl. 211–224.

Gotterer, S.M. (1989) 'Storytelling: a valuable supplement to poetry writing with the elderly.' *The Arts in Psychotherapy 16,* 127–131.

Grainger, R. (1990) *Dramatherapy and Healing.* London: Jessica Kingsley Publishers.

Grainger, R. (1995) *The Glass of Heaven: the Faith of the Dramatherapist.* London: Jessica Kingsley Publishers.

Greenberg, I.A. (ed) (1974) *Psychodrama, Theory and Therapy.* New York: Souvenir Press, Behavioral Publications.

Greenberg, L.A. and Stone, A.A. (1992) 'Writing about disclosed versus undisclosed traumas: immediate and long-term effects on mood and health.' *Journal of Personality and Social Psychology 63,* 75–84.

Griaule, M. (1965) *Conversations with Ogotomêlli,* Oxford: Oxford University Press.

Grinberg, L. and Grinberg, R. (1984) 'A psychoanalytic study of migration: Its normal and pathological aspects.' *Journal of the American Psychoanalytic Association 32,* 13–38.

Gustafson, J.P. (1986) *The Complex Secret of Brief Psychotherapy.* New York: W.W. Norton and Co.

Haggarty, B. (1989) Interview with Peter Brook in *Souvenir Programme.* International Storytelling Festival, The South Bank Centre, London.

Haley, J. (1976) *Problem-Solving Therapy.* New York: Harper and Row.

Halifax, J. (1979) *Shamanic Voices.* Harmondsworth: Penguin.

Haring-Hidore, M., Stock, W.A., Okun, M.A. and Witter, R.A. (1985) 'Marital status and subjective well-being: a research synthesis.' *Journal of Marriage and the Family* *47*, 947–953.

Harris, P. (1995) '"Who am I?" Concepts of disability and their implications for people with learning difficulties.' *Disability and Society 10*, 3, 341–351.

Hawkins, P. and Shohet, R. (1989) *Supervision in the Helping Professions.* Stony Stratford: Open University Press.

Henderson, J.L. and Oakes, M. (1963) *The Wisdom of the Serpent.* New York: Collier Books.

Heron, J. (1977) *Dimensions of Facilitator Style.* London: British Postgraduate Medical Foundation.

Heuscher, J.E. (1974) *A Psychiatric Study of Myths and Fairy Tales,* 2nd Edition. Springfield: Charles E. Thomas Publ.

Higgins, R. (1993) *Approaches to Case-Study.* London: Jessica Kingsley Publishers.

Hilton, R.W. (1995) 'Fragmentation within interprofessional work.' *Journal of Interprofessional Care 9*, 1, 33–40.

Hobson, R.F. (1985) *Forms of Feeling: the Heart of Psychotherapy.* London: Tavistock Press.

Hofling, C.K. (1976) 'Current problems in psychohistory.' *Comprehensive Psychiatry 17*, 1, 227–239.

Hoglend, P. (1993) 'Transference interpretations and long-term change after dynamic psychotherapy of brief to moderate length.' *American Journal of Psychotherapy 47*, 494–505.

Holmes, J. (1994) 'The clinical implications of attachment theory.' *British Journal of Psychotherapy 11*, 1, 62–76.

Holt, D. (1987) *Theatre and Behaviour.* Oxford: Holt.

Hugman, R. (1991) *Power in the Caring Professions.* Basingstoke: Macmillan.

Jackson, S.W. (1992) 'The listening healer in the history of psychological healing.' *American Journal of Psychiatry 149*, 12, 1623–1632.

Jacobs, M. (1971) *The Content and Style of an Oral Literature.* Chicago: University of Chicago Press.

James, J. (1996) 'Dramatherapy with people with learning difficulties.' In S. Mitchell *Dramatherapy Clinical Studies.* London: Jessica Kingsley Publishers.

Jennings, S. and Gersie, A. (1987) 'Dramatherapy with disturbed adolescents.' In S. Jennings (ed) *Dramatherapy.* London: Croom Helm.

Jennings, S. and Minde, A. (1993) *Art Therapy and Dramatherapy: Masks of the Soul.* London: Jessica Kingsley Publishers.

Johnson, D.W. and Johnson, R.T. (1993) 'Creative and critical thinking through academic controversy.' *Amercan Behavioral Scientist 37*, 1, 49.

Jones, P. (1995) *Drama as Therapy, Theatre as Living.* London: Routledge.

Jourard, S.M. (1964) *The Transparent Self.* Princeton: D.v.Nostrand Company.

Jung, C.G. (Repr. 1978) (Trans. R.F.C. Hull) *Psychology and Religion, Collected Works, Vol II.* Princeton: Princeton University Press.

Karau, S.J. and Williams, K.D. (1993) 'Social loafing; a meta-analytic review and theoretical integration.' *Journal of Personality and Social Psychology* 65, 4, 681–706.

Kellerman, P.F. (1992) *Focus on Psychodrama.* London: Jessica Kingsley Publishers.

Kirk, S. (1970) *Myth. Its Meaning and Functons in Ancient and Other Cultures.* Berkeley: University of California Press.

Klecan-Aker, J.S. (1993) 'A treatment programme for improving story-telling ability.' *Child Language Teaching and Therapy* 9, 2, 105–115.

Klein, E.B. and Astrachan, B.M. (1971) 'Learning in groups: a comparison of study groups and T-groups.' *Journal of Applied Behavioral Science* 7, 659–693.

Kleinman, A. (1988) *The Illness Narratives.* New York: Basic Books.

Kluckhohn, C. (1942) 'Myths and rituals: a general theory.' *Harvard Theological Review* 35, 45–79.

Koestler, A. (1952) *Arrow in the Blue.* London: Macmillan.

Kohut, H. (1959) 'Introspection, empathy and psychoanalysis.' *Journal of the American Psychoanalytic Association* 7, 459–483.

Konopka, G. (1963) *Social Group Work.* New York: Prentice Hall.

Kroeber, T. (1959) *The Inland Whale: Nine Stories Retold from California Indian Legends.* Berkeley: University of California Press.

Kunz, D. (ed) (1985) *Spiritual Aspects of the Healing Arts.* Wheaton, Ill: The Theosophical Publishing House.

Kurtz, E. and Ketcham, K. (1994) *The Spirituality of Imperfection.* New York: Bantam Books.

Kushner, H.S. (1981) *When Bad Things Happen to Good People.* New York: Schocken.

Lacan, J. (1979) *The Four Fundamental Concepts of Psycho-analysis.* Harmondsworth: Penguin.

Lahad, M. (1992) 'Story-making in assessment method for coping with stress.' In S. Jennings. *Dramatherapy.* London: Routledge.

Landreth, G.L. (1993) 'Self-expressive communication.' In C.E. Schaefer (ed) *The Therapeutic Powers of Play.* Northvale, NJ: Jason Aronson.

Landy, R.J. (1994) *Persona and Performance.* London: Jessica Kingsley Publishers.

Lang, A. (1885, repr. 1974) *Custom and Myth.* Wakefield: EP Publishing Limited.

Laube, J. and Trefz, S. (1993) 'Group therapy using a narrative theory framework: application to treatment of depression.' *Journal of Systemic Therapies* 13, 2, 29–37.

Leitch, T. (1986) *What Stories Are: Narrative Theory and Interpretation.* State College: Pennsylvania State University Press.

Lerner, A. (ed) (1978) *Poetry in the Therapeutic Experience.* New York: Pergamon Press.

Leszcs, M., Yalom, I.D. and Norden, M. (1985) 'The value of inpatient group psychotherapy and therapeutic process: patients' perceptions.' *International Journal of Group Psychotherapy* 35, 177–196.

Levontin, R.C., Rose, S. and Kamin, L.J. (1984) *Not in our Genes: Biology, Ideology and Human Nature.* New York: Pantheon Books.

Lin, N., Dean, A. and Ensel, W. (1986) *Social Support, Life Events and Depression.* Orlando, Fl: Academic Press.

Linde, C. (1993) *Life-Stories: the Creation of Coherence*. Oxford: Oxford University Press.

Locke, S. and Hornig-Rohan, M. (1983) *Mind and Immunity*. New York: Institute for the Advancement of Health.

Long, C.H. (1969) 'Silence and signification.' In J.M. Kitagawa and C.H. Long (eds) *Myths and Symbols*. Chicago: The University of Chicago Press.

Lowe, J.L. and Herranen, M. (1978) 'Conflict in teamwork: understanding roles and relationships.' *Social Work in Health Care 3*, 3, 323–333.

Lowie, R.H. (1935) *The Crow Indians*. New York: Holt, Rinehart & Winston.

Luria, A.R. (Repr. 1987) (Trans. L. Solo Taroff) *The Life of a Mnemonist*. Cambridge, MA: Harvard University Press.

Luthi, M. (1975) *Das Volksmärchen als Dichtung, Aesthetik und Anthropologie*. Frankfurt: Eugen Diederichs Verlag.

Lynch, J.J. (1977) *The Broken Heart: The Medical Consequences of Loneliness*. New York: Basic Books.

Mack, J.E. (1971) 'Psychoanalysis and historical biography.' *Journal of the American Psychoanalytic Association 19*, 143–179.

MacKinnon, J.R. (1984) 'Health professionals' patterns of communication: cross purpose or problem solving?' *Journal of Applied Health*, February, 3–13.

Maclagan, D. (1977) *Creation Myths*. London: Thames and Hudson.

Madigon, S.P. (1993) 'Questions about questions: situating the therapist's curiosity in front of the family.' In S. Giligan and R. Price (eds) *Therapeutic Conversations*. New York: W.W. and Norton Co.

Mair, M. (1989) *Between Psychology and Psychotherapy: a Poetics of Experience*. London: Routledge.

Makari, G. and Shapiro, T. (1993) 'On psychoanalytic listening.' *Journal of American Psychoanalytic Association 41*, 4, 991–1020.

Malan, D.H. (1979) *Individual Psychotherapy and the Science of Psychodynamics*. Oxford: Butterworth, Heinemann.

Malinovski, B. (1922) *Argonauts of the Western Pacific*. London: Routledge.

Marriott, A. (repr. 1963) *Saynday's People*. Lincoln: University of Nebraska Press.

Marriott, A. and Rachlin, C.K. (1968) *American Indian Mythology*. New York: Mentor Books.

Marzillier, J. (1993) 'Ethical issues in psychotherapy: the importance of informed consent.' *Clinical Psychology Forum*, April, 33–37.

Maslow, A. (1977) 'The creative attitude', In W. Anderson (ed) *Therapy and the Arts*, New York: Harper Colophon Books.

Maslow, A.H. (1962) *Toward a Psychology of Being*. Princeton, NJ: van Nostrand.

May, R. (ed) (1969) *Existential Psychology*. New York: McGraw-Hill.

May, R. (1977) 'Creativity and encounter.' In W. Anderson (ed) *Therapy and the Arts*. New York: Harper Colophon Books.

McGoldrick, M., Anderson, C. and Walsh, F. (1989) *Women in Families: a Framework for Family Therapy*. New York: W.W. Norton and Co.

Medical Ethics Committee and Mental Health Committee (1990) *Proposals for the Establishment of a Decision Making procedure on behalf of the Mentally Incapable.* London: British Medical Association.

Mellon, N. (1992) *Storytelling and the Art of Imagination.* Shaftesbury: Element.

Menninger, K. (1963) *The Vital Balance.* New York: The Viking Press.

Mensen, S. (1993) 'Critical thinking and the construction of knowledge.' *American Behavioral Scientist, Sept. 37,* 1, 85–93.

Miller, A. (1988) *Plays: TWO, After the Fall.* London: Methuen.

Moloney, F. (1995) 'A Heideggerian hermeneutical analysis of older women's stories of being strong.' *Journal of Nursing Scholarship,* Summer, 2, 2, 104–109.

Moloney, M.F. (1995) 'A Heideggerian hermeneutical analysis of older women's stories of being strong.' *IMAGE – Journal of Nursing Scholarship 2,* 2, 104–109.

Moody, H.R. (1992) *Ethics in an Ageing Society.* Baltimore, MD: John Hopkins University Press.

Morley, S. (1993) 'Vivid memory for "everyday" pains.' *Pain 55,* 55–62.

Morrison, M.R. (1986) 'Poetry as therapy.' *Current Psychiatric Therapies 23,* 59–63.

Nichols, W.C. and Balch, W.H. (1995) 'The story and storytelling: an introduction.' *Family Therapy (Special Issue) 17,* 1, 3–15.

Nisbett, R.E. and Ross, L. (1980) *Human Inference: Strategies and Shortcomings of Social Judgement.* New York: Prentice Hall.

Nitsun, M. (1989) 'Early development, linking the individual and the group.' *Group Analysis 22,* 249–260.

Oaklander, V. (1988) *Windows to Our Children.* Moab, Utah: Real People Press.

Oksenberg Rorty, A. (1988) *Mind in Action.* Boston: Beacon Press.

Oster, G.D. and Gould, P. (1987) *Using Drawing in Assessment and Therapy: a Guide for Mental Health Professionals.* New York: Brunner/Mazel.

Page, S. and Wosket, V. (1994) *Supervising the Counsellor: a Cyclical Model.* London: Routledge.

Palmer, G.B. and Jankowiak, G.B. (1996) 'Performance and imagination: toward an anthropology of the spectactualar and the mundane.' *Cultural Anthropology 11,* 2, 225–258.

Pascal, R. (1960) *Design and Truth in Autobiography.* Cambridge, MA: Harvard University Press.

Paul, R.W. (1993) 'The logic of creative and critical thinking.' *American Behavioral Scientist 37,* 1–27.

Peirce, C.S. (1960) *Collected Papers, Vol. 2.* Cambridge, MA: Harvard University Press.

Pellowski, A. (1987) *The Family Storytelling Handbook.* New York: Macmillan.

Pennebaker, J.W. (1993) 'Putting stress into words: health, linguistic and therapeutic implications.' *Behavioral Research Therapy 31,* 6, 539–548.

Piaget, J. (1952) *The Origins of Intelligence in Children.* New York: International University Press.

Pines, M. (1989) 'Group analysis and healing.' *Group Analysis 22,* 4, 417–429.

Priefer, B.A. and Gambert, S.R. (1984) 'Reminiscence and life review in the elderly.' *Psychiatric Medicine 2*, 1, 91–100.

Propp, V. (1984) (Trans. L. Scott) *The Morphology of the Folktale.* Austin: University of Texas Press.

Proshansky, H.M., Fabian, A.K. and Kaminoff, R. (1983) 'Place-identity: physical world socialization of the self.' *Journal of Environmental Psychology 3*, 57–83.

Radin, P. (Repr. 1957) *Primitive Man as Philosopher.* New York: Dover Publications.

Raphael, D.D. (1959) *The Paradox of Tragedy.* Bloomington: Indiana University Press.

Redl, F. and Wineman, D. (1951) *Children Who Hate.* New York: The Free Press.

Reid, A.L. (1971) *Philosophy and Education.* London: Heinemann.

Rennie, D.L. (1994) 'Storytelling in psychotherapy. The client's subjective experience.' *Psychotherapy 31*, 2, 234–243.

Richards, I.A. (1960) *Principles of Literary Criticism, 2nd edition.* London: Routledge.

Ricoeur, P. (1984) *Time and Narrative.* Chicago: University of Chicago Press.

Rivers, W.H.R. (1912) 'The sociological significance of myth.' *Folk-lore 23*, 307–331.

Rogers, C. (Repr. 1974) *Encounter Groups.* Harmondsworth: Penguin.

Rosaldo, M. (1984) 'Toward an anthropology of self and feeling,' In R.A. Schweder and R.A. Levine (eds) *Culture Theory, Essays on Mind, Self and Emotion.* Cambridge: Cambridge University Press.

Rosen, B. (1988) *And None of It Was Nonsense: The Power of Storytelling in School.* London: Mary Glasgow.

Rosen, H. (1993) *Shapers and Polishers: Teachers as Storytellers.* London: Harper Collins.

Rosenwald, G.C. and Ochberg, R.L. (eds) (1992) *Storied Lives: The Cultural Politics of Self-Understanding.* New Haven, CT: Yale University Press.

Rothenburg, J. (ed) (1972) *Shaking the Pumpkin.* New York: Doubleday and Company.

Rubin, D.C. (ed) (1989) *Autobiographical Memory.* Cambridge: Cambridge University Press.

Rubin, D.C. (1995) *Memory in Oral Tradition.* Oxford: Oxford University Press.

Rugoff, M. (1977) *The Penguin Book of World Folktales.* Harmondsworth: Penguin Books.

Runyan, W.M. (1984) *Life Histories and Psychobiography.* Oxford: Oxford University Press.

Russell, B. (1958) *The Will to Doubt.* New York: Philosophical Library.

Ruthrof, H. (1981) *The Reader's Construction of Narrative.* London: Routledge and Kegan Paul.

Ryle, A. (Repr. 1992) *Cognitive-Analytic Therapy: Active Participation in Change.* Chichester: John Wiley and Sons.

Sabat, S. and Harre, R. (1992) 'The construction and deconstruction of self in Alzheimer's disease.' *Ageing and Society 12*, 4, 443–461.

Sarbin, A. (1986) *Narrative Psychology, the Storied Nature of Human Conduct.* New York: Praeger.

Sartre, J.P. (1965) *Nausea.* New York: Penguin.

Sawyer, S. (1942) *The Way of the Storyteller.* New York: Viking.

Scarry, E. (1985) *The Body in Pain*. New York: Oxford University Press.

Schafer, R. (1992) *Retelling a Life: Narration and Dialogue in Psychoanalysis*. New York: Basic Books.

Schieffelin, E.L. (1993) 'Performance and the cultural construction of reality; a New Guinea example.' In S. Lavie, K. Narayan and R. Rosaldo (eds) *Creativity/Anthropology*. Ithaca: Cornell University Press.

Schieffelin, E.L. and Crittenden, R. (eds) (1991) *Like People You See in a Dream*. Palo Alto: Stanford University Press.

Schrodinger, E. (Trans. C. Hastings) (1983) *My View of the World*. Woodbridge, CO: Oxbow Books.

Schuurman, C.J. (1963) *Mythe en Realiteit*. Amsterdam: Wereldbibliotheek, n.v.

Scofield, G.R. (1993) 'Ethical considerations in rehabilitation medicine.' *Archives of Physical Medicine and Rehabilitation, 74*, 341–346.

Sedgewick, P. (1982) *Psychopolitics: the Politics of Health*. London: Pluto.

Seiderman, S. (1974) 'Ethnotherapy, a new hope for society.' *The International Journal of Group Psychotherapy*, April, No.2.

Shah, I. (1979) *World Tales*. Harmondsworth: Penguin Books.

Shedlock, M. (1951) *The Art of the Storyteller*. New York: Dover Publications.

Siegel, B.S. (1990) *Love, Medicine and Miracles*. New York: Harper and Row.

Singer, D.G. (1993) 'Fantasy and visualization.' In C.E. Schaefer *The Therapeutic Powers of Play*. Northvale, NJ: Jason Aronson.

Singer, J. (1973) *The Child's World of Make-believe*. New York: Academic Press.

Singer, J.L. (1981) *Daydreaming and Fantasy*. Oxford: Oxford University Press.

Slavson, S.R. (1950) *Analytic Group Psychotherapy*. New York: Columbia University Press.

Sloan, W. and Solano, C.H. (1984) 'The conversational styles of lonely males with strangers and roommates.' *Personality and Social Psychology Bulletin 10*, 293–301.

Smith, K. (1986) *I'm Not Complaining*. London: Shelter Housing Advice Centre.

Smith, P. (1980) *Group Processes and Social Change*. London: Harper and Row.

Smith, T.E., Yoshioka, M. and Winton, M. (1993) 'Qualitative understanding of reflecting teams.' *Journal of Systemic Therapies 12*, 3, 28–43.

Snortum, J.R. and Ellenhorn, L.J. (1974) 'Predicting and measuring the psychological impact of non verbal encounter techniques.' *The International Journal of Group Psychotherapy 2*, 217–229.

Solano, C.H. and Koester, N.H. (1989) 'Loneliness and communication problems: subjective anxiety and communication problems.' *Personality and Social Psychology Bulletin 15*, 126–133.

Spence, J. (1984) 'Perils and pitfalls of free-floating attention.' *Contemporary Psychoanalysis 20*, 37–76.

Stanislavski, K. cited in Bentley, E. (Repr. 1980) *The Theory of the Modern Stage*. Harmondsworth: Penguin.

Stenhouse, J. (1973) *The Evolution of Intelligence*. London: Allen and Unwin.

Stock, D. and Lieberman, M. (1962) 'Methodological issues in the assessment of total group phenomena in group therapy.' *This Journal 12*, 312–325.

Stockton, R., Moran, D.K. and Velkoff, P. (1987) 'Leadership of therapeutic small groups.' *Journal of Group Psychotherapy, Psychodrama and Sociometry 39*, 4, 157–165.

Storr, A. (1989) *Solitude*. London: Fontana Paperbacks.

Sutton-Smith, B. (ed) (1979) *Play and Learning*. New York: Gardner.

Szasz, T.S. (1956) 'Malingering: "Diagnosis" or social condemnation? Analysis of the meaning of "diagnosis in the light of some interrelations of social structure, value judgment, and the physician's role."' *American Medical Association, Archives of Neurology and Psychiatry 76*, 432.

Szasz, T. (1961) *The Myth of Mental Illness: Foundations of a Theory of Personal Conduct*. London: Secker.

Tambling, J. (1991) *Narrative and Ideology*. Stony Stratford: Open University Press.

Taudin Chabot, C. (ed) (1974) *Grimms Sprookjes*, Rotterdam, Lemniscaat, 387–388.

Teff, H. (1985) 'Consent to medical procedures: paternalism, self determination or therapeutic alliance.' *Law Quarterly Review 101*, 432–453.

Thompson, S. (repr. 1977) *The Folktale*. Berkeley: University of California Press.

Tillich, P. (1952) *The Courage to Be*. New Haven, CT: Yale University Press.

Timmer, D.A., Eitzen, D.S. and Talley, K.D. (1994) *Paths to Homelessness: Extreme Poverty and the Urban Housing Crisis*. Boulder: Westview Press.

Tinker, A. (1992) *Elderly People in Modern Society*. Harlow: Longman Group.

Townsend, P. (1986) 'Ageism and social policy.' In C. Philipson and A. Walter (eds) *Ageing and Social Policy*. London: Gower.

Turner, R.J. (1983) 'Direct, indirect and moderating effects of social support upon psychological distress and associated conditions.' In H.B. Kaplan (ed) *Psychological Stress: Trends in Theory and Research*. New York: Academic Press.

Turner, V. (1986) *The Anthropology of Performance*. New York: PAJ Publications.

Tyrrell, L. (1990) 'Storytelling and moral agency.' *The Journal of Aesthetics and Art Criticism 48*, 2, 115–126.

Ungerson, C. (1987) *Policy is Personal: Sex, Gender and Informal Care*. London: Tavistock.

Upton, D. and Thompson, P. (1992) 'Effectiveness of coping strategies employed by people with chronic epilepsy.' *Journal of Intellectual Disability Research 37*, 221–242.

Ussher, J. (1991) *Women's Madness: Mysogyny or Mental Illness?* London: Harvester Wheatsheaf.

Van der Post, L. (1971) *Patterns of Renewal*. Lebanon, Penns: Pendle Hill Pamphlet, No. 121.

VanderHart, O. (1989) *Rituals in Psychotherapy, Transition and Continuity*. New York: Irvington Publishers.

Vinogradov, S. and Yalom, I. (1989) *Group Psychotherapy*. Washington: American Psychiatric Press.

Von Franz, M.L. (1980) *Alchemy: An Introduction to the Symbolism and the Psychology*. Toronto: Inner City Books.

Von Franz, M.L. (1980) *The Psychological Meaning of Redemption Motifs in Fairy Tales.* Zurich: Inner City Books.

Waelder, G. (1965) *Psychoanalytic Avenues to Art.* New York: International University Press.

Watts, P. (1992) 'Therapy in drama.' In S. Jennings. *Drama Therapy, Theory and Practice 2.* London: Routledge.

Watzlawick, P. (1976) How Real is Real. New York: Random House.

Watzlawick, P., Weakland, J.H. and Fisch, R. (1974) *Het kan anders.* Deventer: Van Loghum Slaterus.

Watzlawick, P., Weakland, J. and Fisch, R. (1974) *Change: Principles of Problem Formation and Problem Resolution.* New York: W.W. Norton and Co.

Wells, G. (1987) *The Meaning Makers.* London: Hodder and Stoughton.

Wethered, A. (1993) *Movement and Drama in Therapy, a Holistic Approach.* London: Jessica Kingsley Publishers.

White, M. and Epston, D. (1990) *Narrative Means to Therapeutic Ends.* New York: W.W. Norton and Co.

White, R.T. (1982) 'Memory for personal events.' *Human Learning 1,* 171–183.

Whitehead, M. (1991) 'The concepts and principles of equity and principles of health.' *Health Promotion International 6,* 3.

Wiesel, E. (1966) *The Jews of Silence.* New York: Holt, Rinehart & Winston.

Wigren, J. (1994) 'Narrative completion in the treatment of trauma.' *Psychotherapy 31,* 3, 415–423.

Williams, J.R. (1995) 'Using story as metaphor, legacy, and therapy.' *Contemporary Family Therapy, An International Journal 17,* 1, 9–16.

Williams, M.D. and Hollan, J.D. (1981) 'The process of retrieval from very-long-term memory,' *Cognitive Science 5,* 87–119.

Wilson, W.J. (1996) *When Work Disappears; the World of the New Urban Poor.* New York: Alfred A Knopf.

Winnicott, D.W. (1969) *The Maturational Processes and the Facilitating Environment.* London: Karnac and the Institute of Psychoanalysis.

Winnicott, D.W. (Repr. 1980) *Playing and Reality.* Harmondsworth: Penguin Books.

Winston, A., McCulough, L. and Laikin, M. (1993) 'Clinical and research implications of patient–therapist interaction in brief psychotherapy.' *American Journal of Psychotherapy 47,* 4, 527–539.

Wohl, J. (1983) 'Integration of cultural awareness into psychotherapy.' *American Journal of Psychotherapy XLIII,* 3, 343–355.

Yalom, I. (1975) *The Theory and Practice of Group Psychotherapy.* New York: Basic Books.

Yalom, I.D. (1991) *Love's Executioner and Other Tales of Psychotherapy.* Harmondsworth: Penguin Books.

Yates, J.L. and Nasby, W. (1993) 'Dissociation, Affect, and Network Models of Memory: an integrative proposal.' *Journal of Traumatic Stress 6,* 3, 305–327.

Yolen, J. (ed) (1986) *Favorite Folktales from Around the World.* London: Pantheon.

Zeig, J. (1980) *A Teaching Seminar with Milton H. Erickson.* New York: Brunner/Mazel.

Zheleznova, I. (1969) *Folktales from Russian Lands.* New York: Dover Publications.

Zipes, J. (1979) *Breaking the Magic Spell, Radical Theories of Folk and Fairy Tales.* New York: Routledge.

Zipes, J. (1995) *Creative Storytelling.* New York: Routledge.

Subject Index

absent-minded listening
118–21, 173
acceptable conservation 35–7
active wisdom 3–4, 194–196
adolescents 11, 18, 62–64,
100–101
agency, concept of 96
alternatives 26, 224
analogies 18–19, 168, 226
animal tales 47–8
anticipation 85
apparent disengagement
117–18
articulation 61, 202
aspirations, mourning 92
assumptions 69, 220
astro-mythological school 48
audience responses 115–16
see also response tasks
authority
coercive 187
reliance on professional
99–101
auto-hypnosis 87
awareness
healing influence 223
through telling 217–19
through TSM 72

case descriptions 184–5
case-studies *see* practice
vignettes
chance 17
change
narrative flexibility 211–12
of perception 26
perspective 18
seeding 110–12
through inconsistency 57–8
through stories 1, 101–4
change-journeys 180
childlessness 15–16
co-operation, withholding 99
cognitive-behavioural
approach 199–200

coherency 209–12
comfort, desire to offer 59
communication 74
compassion, witnessed 181–3
concerns
shared 149
translated through stories
12–14
voiced 81–3
conflict 24–6, 192–194
confrontation, troublesome
situations 190
constructive imagination 87
containment 180, 181, 225
contemplation 96–8, 209–12
coping 199, 224–227
describing patterns 60–1
warm up exercise 62–3
creative mediums, expressions
83, 121–124
creative work
destruction of 124
developing appreciation
121–124, 125–6
sequence of relating to 125
creative-expressive tasks 42,
61, 67, 72, 74, 109, 224
curiosity 43, 80
cybernetic theory 58

day-dreaming 89
death 15–16, 56, 175, 198–9
defensiveness, listening 172
deficiencies, human needs
168–9
departure, themes of 154–5
depression 38, 81–83,
89–92, 164-168,
170–183, 2-3, 211, 221
see also fatalistic pessimism
developmental support 126–8
difference
exploration of 27–8, 113
negotiation of 24–7,
188–191
difficulties, facing 52–3,
218–219
dilemmas, sharing 166–9
disappointment 61
distinguishment 27
distress, unalleviated 215–16
dwelling places 163–6

economic circumstances,
narratives 186–8
see also poverty
elderly people 12, 22–24,
65–68, 75–77, 114–115
emotional growth 72–3
emotional unwellbeing
effects of 53–4
inability to tell 33–4
empowerment 74–112
engagement, attentive
listening 118–19
enquiries, stories 12–14
ergriffenheit 77
ethics, life stories 211–12
evolution theory 48–9
experiences
importance of telling 45
voicing 30–3
explanations, desire for 16,
209
exploratory thoughts 142
expression, creative mediums
83

facilitators, TSM 43,
100–103, 127, 135–138,
200–202, 223–224
fairy tales 47
fantasies
negative 89–92
self generated 184
fantasizing 87–9
fatalistic pessimism 89–92,
177
fears
listening 116–18
shared concerns 149
sharing stories 123–4
warm-up exercises 111
feedback, structured 74,
126–8
fictional stories 65–70, 102,
158, 225
folktales
motivational needs 168–9
study of 48–50
frozen images 213–16
fuzzy concepts, mental ill
health 4–6

good fortune 17
gossip 23–4

243

Author Index

Printed in Great Britain
by Amazon